The OFSTED Handbooks 20

(Combined)

Section A: The Education Inspection Handbook

Section B: Section 5 Inspections

Section C: Section 8 Inspections

Section D: Early Years Inspections

Section E: Further Education

Section F: Curriculum Guidance

Section G: Safeguarding Guidance

These booklets (!) are available on the DfE website for free download.
They are presented here as a single bound volume for your convenience.
Originally written by OFSTED (I have not changed content, only layout), they are
reproduced under the creative commons licence.

Abigail Hawkins

978-1077577350

Contents

SECTION F – Inspecting the curriculum **269**

SECTION G –Inspecting safeguarding in early years, education and skills settings **281**

SECTION A - The education inspection framework

Framework for inspections carried out, respectively, under section 5 of the Education Act 2005 (as amended), section 109 of the Education and Skills Act 2008, the Education and Inspections Act 2006 and the Childcare Act 2006

The education inspection framework sets out how Ofsted inspects maintained schools, academies, non-association independent schools, further education and skills provision and registered early years settings in England.

Introduction

1.   The education inspection framework has been devised by Her Majesty's Chief Inspector for use from September 2019. It sets out the principles that apply to inspection, and the main judgements that inspectors make when carrying out inspections of maintained schools, academies, non-association independent schools, further education and skills providers and registered early years settings in England.[1]

2.   The education inspection framework ('the framework') applies to the inspection of different education, skills and early years settings to ensure comparability when learners[2] move from one setting to another. It supports consistency across the inspection of different remits.

3.   The framework reflects relevant legislation for each type of setting.[3] It is accompanied by an inspection handbook for each of the four remits:

- early years
- maintained schools and academies
- non-association independent schools
- further education and skills.

4.   These handbooks set out how inspectors will make each of the inspection judgements. They reflect the needs and expectations of different phases and the differences between various age groups. Inspectors will inspect types of provision for which they have appropriate expertise and training.

Principles of inspection and regulation

5.   We are required to carry out our work in ways that encourage the services we inspect and regulate to improve, to be user-focused and to be efficient and effective in their use of resources.[4]

6.   Inspection provides independent, external evaluation and identifies what needs to improve in order for provision to be good or better. It is based on gathering a range of evidence that is evaluated against an inspection framework and takes full account of our policies and relevant legislation in areas such as safeguarding, equality and diversity.

7.   Inspection provides important information to parents, carers, learners and employers about the quality of education, training and care. These groups should be able to make informed choices based on the information published in inspection reports.

8.   The framework sets out the judgements that apply to all education, skills and early years provision. These are underpinned by consistent, researched criteria for reaching those judgements. Inspectors will take comparable approaches to gathering evidence in different settings, although there may be some variation, for example depending on the age of learners and the type of provision. Inspectors will comply with relevant guidance and codes of conduct,[5] but they will always try to be curious.

9.   Inspection provides assurance to the public and to government that minimum standards of education, skills and childcare are being met; that – where relevant – public

money is being spent well; and that arrangements for safeguarding are effective.

A force for improvement

10.   Ofsted exists to be a force for improvement through intelligent, responsible and focused inspection and regulation.[6] This is our guiding principle. The primary purpose of inspection under this framework is to bring about improvement in education provision. Through the use of evidence, research and inspector training, we ensure that our judgements are as valid and reliable as they can be. These judgements focus on key strengths, from which other providers can learn intelligently, and areas of weakness, from which the provider should seek to improve. Our inspections act as a trigger to others to take action.

Helping to protect learners

11.   Inspectors will always take into account how well learners are helped and protected so that they are kept safe. Although inspectors will not provide a separate numerical grade for this important aspect of a provider's work, they will always make a written judgement under 'leadership and management' about whether the arrangements for safeguarding learners are effective.

12.   'Inspecting safeguarding in early years, education and skills settings'[7] sets out the approach inspectors should take to inspecting safeguarding in all the settings covered by the framework. It should be read alongside the framework and handbooks.

13.   Inspectors are also required to be familiar with the statutory guidance about safeguarding. They should take this into account when inspecting:

- ■ 'Keeping children safe in education: statutory guidance for schools and colleges on safeguarding children and safer recruitment'[8]
- ■ 'Working together to safeguard children'.[9]

The Equality Act 2010

14.   The framework is intended to be a force for improvement for all learners. The framework and remit-specific criteria are clear that the expectation is that all learners will receive a high-quality, ambitious education.

15.   Inspectors will assess the extent to which the provider complies with the relevant legal duties as set out in the Equality Act 2010,[10] including, where relevant, the Public Sector Equality Duty and the Human Rights Act 1998.[11]

Expectations of inspectors

It is important that inspectors and providers establish and maintain a positive working relationship based on courteous and professional behaviour. We expect our inspectors to uphold the highest professional standards in their work, and to treat everyone they meet during inspections fairly and with respect and sensitivity.

16.   In meeting this expectation, inspectors will:

- ■ evaluate objectively, be impartial and inspect without fear or favour

- uphold and demonstrate Ofsted values at all times[12]
- evaluate provision in line with the framework, inspection handbooks, national standards or regulatory requirements
- base all evaluations on clear and strong evidence
- declare all actual and perceived conflicts of interest and have no real or perceived connection with the provider that could undermine the objectivity of the inspection
- report honestly and clearly, ensuring that judgements are fair and reliable
- carry out their work with integrity, treating all those they meet with courtesy, respect and sensitivity
- take all reasonable steps to prevent undue anxiety and to minimise stress
- act in the best interests and well-being of learners, prioritising the safeguarding of learners at all times
- maintain purposeful and productive communication with those being inspected and inform them of judgements sensitively, but clearly and frankly
- respect the confidentiality of information as far as possible, particularly when the information is about individuals and their work
- respond appropriately to reasonable requests
- take prompt and appropriate action on any safeguarding or health and safety issues
- use their title of Her Majesty's Inspector, Early Years Regulatory Inspector or Ofsted Inspector only in relation to their work for Ofsted.

Expectations of providers

17.   In order to establish and maintain a positive working relationship, we expect providers to:

- be courteous and professional, treating inspectors with respect and sensitivity
- enable inspectors to carry out their visit in an open and honest way
- enable inspectors to evaluate the provision objectively against the framework, handbooks and national standards or regulatory requirements
- provide evidence – or access to evidence – that will enable the inspector to report honestly, fairly and reliably about their provision. This includes the opportunity for inspectors to meet with learners
- work with inspectors to minimise disruption, stress and bureaucracy
- ensure the health and safety of inspectors while on their premises
- maintain purposeful and productive communication with the inspector or the inspection team
- bring any concerns about the inspection to the attention of inspectors promptly and in a suitable manner
- recognise that sometimes inspectors will need to observe practice and talk to staff and users without the presence of a manager or registered person.

Provision inspected under the education inspection framework

18.   The framework applies to inspections of:

- maintained schools and academies under section 513
- non-maintained special schools (as approved by the Secretary of State under section 342 of the Education Act 1996)
- pupil referral units
- non-association independent schools[14]
- further education colleges, sixth-form colleges and independent specialist colleges
- independent learning providers
- community learning and skills providers
- employers funded by the Education and Skills Funding Agency to train their own employees
- higher education institutions providing further education
- providers of learning in the judicial services
- National Careers Service – careers advice and guidance
- registered early years settings.

The grading scale used for inspection judgements

19.   We will use a four-point grading scale in all inspections to make the principal judgements:

- grade 1 – outstanding
- grade 2 – good
- grade 3 – requires improvement
- grade 4 – inadequate.

Judgements made by inspectors

20.   The framework ensures that inspectors make a coherent set of judgements across the different education, skills and early years settings. The remit handbooks set out the methods inspectors use to gather evidence and the main criteria they use to make judgements. In most instances, these methods and criteria are common across the different remits, but there will inevitably be some variation.

Overall effectiveness

21.   Inspectors will use all the available evidence to evaluate what it is like to be a learner in the provision. In making the judgements about a provider's overall effectiveness, inspectors will consider whether the standard of education, training or care is good or outstanding. If it is not at least good, inspectors will consider whether it requires improvement or is inadequate.

Key judgements

22.   Inspectors will also make graded judgements on the following areas using the four-

point scale:

- quality of education
- behaviour and attitudes
- personal development
- leadership and management.

What inspectors will consider when making judgements

23.   Inspectors will use the following criteria to make each of the graded judgements. These criteria are common for all the types of provision covered by the framework. Inspection remit handbooks explain how these criteria are applied in each context.

Quality of education

24.   Inspectors will make a judgement on the quality of education by evaluating the extent to which:

Intent

- leaders take on or construct a curriculum that is ambitious and designed to give all learners, particularly the most disadvantaged and those with special educational needs and/or disabilities (SEND) or high needs, the knowledge and cultural capital they need to succeed in life
- the provider's curriculum is coherently planned and sequenced towards cumulatively sufficient knowledge and skills for future learning and employment
- the provider has the same academic, technical or vocational ambitions for almost all learners. Where this is not practical – for example, for some learners with high levels of SEND – its curriculum is designed to be ambitious and to meet their needs
- learners study the full curriculum. Providers ensure this by teaching a full range of subjects for as long as possible, 'specialising' only when necessary

Implementation

- teachers[15] have good knowledge of the subject(s) and courses they teach. Leaders provide effective support for those teaching outside their main areas of expertise
- teachers present subject matter clearly, promoting appropriate discussion about the subject matter they are teaching. They check learners' understanding systematically, identify misconceptions accurately and provide clear, direct feedback. In doing so, they respond and adapt their teaching as necessary, without unnecessarily elaborate or differentiated approaches
- over the course of study, teaching is designed to help learners to remember in the long term the content they have been taught and to integrate new knowledge into larger concepts
- teachers and leaders use assessment well, for example to help learners embed and use knowledge fluently or to check understanding and inform teaching. Leaders understand the limitations of assessment and do not use it in a way that creates unnecessary burdens for staff or learners
- teachers create an environment that allows the learner to focus on learning. The resources and materials that teachers select – in a way that does not create unnecessary workload for staff – reflect the provider's ambitious

15

intentions for the course of study and clearly support the intent of a coherently planned curriculum, sequenced towards cumulatively sufficient knowledge and skills for future learning and employment

■ a rigorous approach to the teaching of reading develops learners' confidence and enjoyment in reading. At the early stages of learning to read, reading materials are closely matched to learners' phonics knowledge

Impact

■ learners develop detailed knowledge and skills across the curriculum and, as a result, achieve well. Where relevant, this is reflected in results from national tests and examinations that meet government expectations, or in the qualifications obtained

■ learners are ready for the next stage of education, employment or training. Where relevant, they gain qualifications that allow them to go on to destinations that meet their interests, aspirations and the intention of their course of study. They read widely and often, with fluency and comprehension.

Behaviour and attitudes

25.   Inspectors will make a judgement on behaviour and attitudes by evaluating the extent to which:

■ the provider has high expectations for learners' behaviour and conduct and applies these expectations consistently and fairly. This is reflected in learners' behaviour and conduct

■ learners' attitudes to their education or training are positive. They are committed to their learning, know how to study effectively and do so, are resilient to setbacks and take pride in their achievements

■ learners have high attendance and are punctual

■ relationships among learners and staff reflect a positive and respectful culture. Leaders, teachers and learners create an environment where bullying, peer-on-peer abuse or discrimination are not tolerated. If they do occur, staff deal with issues quickly and effectively, and do not allow them to spread.

Personal development

26.   Inspectors will make a judgement on the personal development of learners by evaluating the extent to which:

■ the curriculum extends beyond the academic, technical or vocational. It provides for learners' broader development, enabling them to develop and discover their interests and talents

■ the curriculum and the provider's wider work support learners to develop their character – including their resilience, confidence and independence – and help them know how to keep physically and mentally healthy

■ at each stage of education, the provider prepares learners for future success in

their next steps
- the provider prepares learners for life in modern Britain by:
  - equipping them to be responsible, respectful, active citizens who contribute positively to society
  - developing their understanding of fundamental British values
  - developing their understanding and appreciation of diversity
  - celebrating what we have in common and promoting respect for the different protected characteristics as defined in law.

Leadership and management

27.   Inspectors will make a judgement on the effectiveness of leadership and management by evaluating the extent to which:

- leaders have a clear and ambitious vision for providing high-quality, inclusive education and training to all. This is realised through strong, shared values, policies and practice
- leaders focus on improving staff's subject, pedagogical and pedagogical content knowledge to enhance the teaching of the curriculum and the appropriate use of assessment. The practice and subject knowledge of staff are built up and improve over time
- leaders aim to ensure that all learners complete their programmes of study. They provide the support for staff to make this possible and do not allow gaming or off-rolling[16]
- leaders engage effectively with learners and others in their community, including – where relevant – parents, carers, employers and local services
- leaders engage with their staff and are aware and take account of the main pressures on them. They are realistic and constructive in the way that they manage staff, including their workload
- leaders protect their staff from bullying and harrassment
- those responsible for governance understand their role and carry this out effectively. They ensure that the provider has a clear vision and strategy and that resources are managed well. They hold leaders to account for the quality of education or training
- those with responsibility for governance ensure that the provider fulfils its statutory duties, for example under the Equality Act 2010, and other duties, for example in relation to the 'Prevent' strategy and safeguarding, and promoting the welfare of learners
- the provider has a culture of safeguarding that supports effective arrangements to:
  - identify learners who may need early help or who are at risk of neglect, abuse, grooming or exploitation

- help learners reduce their risk of harm by securing the support they need, or referring in a timely way to those who have the expertise to help
- manage safe recruitment and allegations about adults who may be a risk to learners and vulnerable adults.

28. Inspectors will always report on whether arrangements for safeguarding learners are effective.

Arrangements for different types of provision

29.   In addition to the judgements set out in the framework, inspectors will need to make a variety of other judgements and carry out regulatory activity in different types of provision. This section sets out those additional judgements and activities.

Early years

30.   The framework sets out how we will inspect providers on the Early Years Register. In addition to inspection, we are also responsible for the registration and regulation of these providers. Details about the registration and regulation of settings on the Early Years Register can be found at:

www.gov.uk/government/publications/become-a-registered-early-years-or- childcare-provider-in-england

and www.gov.uk/government/publications/early-years-provider-non-compliance- action-by-ofsted.

Non-association independent schools

31.   Non-association independent schools are subject to the Independent School Standards: www.legislation.gov.uk/uksi/2014/3283/contents/made. Inspectors will check that schools meet these standards during inspection.

32.   We give maintained schools, academies and non-association independent schools that have early years foundation stage provision a separate grade for that provision as part of school inspections carried out under section 5 of the Education Act 2005 (as amended by the Education Act 2011) or section 109(1) and (2) of the Education and Skills Act 2008. We inspect provision for two- and three-year-olds in schools as part of a school inspection. This contributes to the judgement about the overall effectiveness of the school.

Schools with sixth forms

33.   We give maintained schools, academies and non-association independent schools a separate grade for sixth-form provision as part of school inspections carried out under section 5 of the Education Act 2005 (as amended by the Education Act 2011) or section 109(1) and (2) of the Education and Skills Act 2008. This contributes to the judgement about the overall effectiveness of the school.

Settings with residential and boarding provision

34.   The inspection of boarding and residential provision will be carried out under the Children Act 1989, as amended by the Care Standards Act 2000, regarding the national minimum standards for boarding or residential provision, as appropriate. Further details of how these boarding or residential inspections will be carried out can be found at: www.gov.uk/government/publications/the-framework-for-inspecting-boarding- and-residential-provision-in-schools

and

www.gov.uk/guidance/social-care-common-inspection-framework-sccif- residential-provision-of-further-education-colleges.

Further education and skills provision

35.   Further education and skills providers will also have the following types of provision graded where appropriate: education programmes for young people; adult learning programmes; apprenticeships; and provision for learners with high needs. These contribute to the judgement about the overall effectiveness of the provider.

SECTION 1 FOOTNOTES

[1] Paragraph 20 contains a full list of the settings covered by the education inspection framework.

[2] We use the term 'learners' for expediency throughout this framework to encompass in a single word those attending education, skills and registered early years settings. It should be read as including: 'children' in early years provision, 'pupils' in all schools, 'students' in sixth forms and colleges, and 'apprentices', 'trainees' and 'adult learners' in the range of further education and skills providers. Greater distinction is made in each of the inspection handbooks.

[3] These inspections are carried out under section 5 of the Education Act 2005 (as amended); www.legislation.gov.uk/ukpga/2005/18/contents; the Education and Inspections Act 2006; www.legislation.gov.uk/ukpga/2006/40/contents; section 109 of the Education and Skills Act 2008, The Education (Independent School Standards) Regulations 2014; www.legislation.gov.uk/uksi/2014/3283/contents/made; and the Childcare Act 2006; www.legislation.gov.uk/ukpga/2006/21/contents. All inspections carried out using the new common inspection framework will continue to meet relevant legislative requirements.

[4] As set out in the Education and Inspections Act 2006; www.legislation.gov.uk/ukpga/2006/40/contents.

[5] Such as the 'Powers of entry: code of practice', Home Office, March 2015; www.gov.uk/government/publications/powers-of-entry-code-of-practice.

[6] For more information see 'Ofsted strategy: 2017 to 2022', Ofsted, September 2017; www.gov.uk/government/publications/ofsted-strategy-2017-to-2022.

[7] 'Inspecting safeguarding in early years, education and skills settings', Ofsted, October 2018; www.gov.uk/government/publications/inspecting-safeguarding-in-early-years-education-and-skills- from-september-2015.

[8] 'Keeping children safe in education', Department for Education, March 2015; www.gov.uk/government/publications/keeping-children-safe-in-education--2.

[9] 'Working together to safeguard children', Department for Education, August 2018; www.gov.uk/government/publications/working-together-to-safeguard-children--2. [10] The Equality Act 2010www.legislation.gov.uk/ukpga/2010/15/contents.

[11] The Human Rights Act 1998 www.legislation.gov.uk/ukpga/1998/42/contents.

[12] For more information about our values, see 'Ofsted strategy: 2017 to 2022', Ofsted, September 2017; www.gov.uk/government/publications/ofsted-strategy-2017-to-2022.

[13] This includes all sponsor-led academies, academy converter schools, academy special schools, free schools, special free schools, maintained nursery schools and alternative provision academies.
University technical colleges and studio schools, 16 to 19 academies and 16 to 19 studio schools are also inspected under this framework.

[14] An independent school is defined in section 463 of the Education Act 1996, as amended as:
'any school at which full-time education is provided for—
a)   five or more pupils of compulsory school age, or
b)   at least one pupil of that age for whom a statement is maintained under section 324, or who is looked after by a local authority (within the meaning of section 22 of the Children Act 1989), and which is not a school maintained by a local education authority or a special school not so maintained.'
This definition brings into the scope of inspection a number of very small independent schools, many of which have dual registration as an independent children's home and provide exclusively for vulnerable looked after young people who may also be disabled or have a special educational need.

[15] Throughout the framework, the term 'teachers' should be read as including early years practitioners, lecturers, trainers and assessors.

[16] There is no legal definition of 'off-rolling'. However, we define 'off-rolling' as the practice of removing a learner from the provider's roll without a formal, permanent exclusion or by encouraging a parent to remove their child, when the removal is primarily in the interests of the provider rather than in the best interests of the learner. Off-rolling in these circumstances is a form of 'gaming'.

SECTION B –School inspection handbook

Handbook for inspecting schools in England under section 5 of the Education Act 2005

This handbook describes the main activities carried out during inspections of maintained schools and academies in England under section 5 of the Education Act 2005.

Introduction

1.   This handbook describes the main activities carried out during inspections of maintained schools and academies in England under section 5 of the Education Act 2005.[1] It sets out the evaluation criteria that inspectors use to make their judgements and on which they report.

2.   This handbook is primarily a guide for inspectors on how to carry out school inspections. However, it is made available to schools and other organisations to ensure that they are informed about the processes and procedures of inspection. It seeks to balance the need for consistency in inspections with the flexibility required to respond to the individual circumstances of each school. This handbook should not be regarded as a set of inflexible rules, but as an account of the procedures of inspection. Inspectors will use their professional judgement when they use this handbook. It applies to school inspections carried out from September 2019 under the education inspection framework (EIF).[2]

3.   The handbook has three parts:

■   Part 1. How schools will be inspected

This contains information about the processes before, during and after the inspection.

■   Part 2. The evaluation schedule

This contains the evaluation criteria inspectors use to make the graded judgements about schools and includes examples of the kinds of evidence and activities used by inspectors to make their judgements.

■   Part 3. Apply the EIF in different contexts

This contains guidance on how to apply the EIF in specific contexts and provisions.

Privacy notice

4. During inspection, inspectors will collect information about staff and children at the school by looking at school records, responses to the pupil survey and responses to the staff survey where appropriate, and by observing the everyday life of the school. Ofsted uses this information to prepare its report and for the purposes set out in its privacy policy.[3] In most cases, Ofsted will not record names. However, some of the information may make it possible to identify a particular individual. Ofsted will not publish any information that identifies an individual in the report, but we will usually name the headteacher and the proprietor.

5. Individuals and organisations have legal requirements to provide information to Ofsted. The Education Act 2005 gives Ofsted inspectors the power to inspect and take copies of any relevant records kept by schools. Regulations enable the Department for Education (DfE) to provide Ofsted with individual pupils' information that relates to school inspections.[4]

6. In the vast majority of settings, Ofsted will gather evidence electronically using a range of devices, including laptops, mobile phones and tablets. All evidence is securely transferred to Ofsted's systems. Inspectors may take photographs of pupils' work. These will be stored as evidence, but not retained by the inspector personally.

Part 1. How schools will be inspected

What are the legal requirements for the inspection of schools?
How schools are selected for inspection

7.   The EIF and this handbook set out the statutory basis for school inspections carried out under the Education Act 2005.

8.   The handbook applies to all schools in England that are to be inspected under section 5 of the Education Act 2005.[5] The schools subject to inspection under this section of the Act are:

- community, foundation and voluntary schools
- community and foundation special schools
- pupil referral units (PRUs)[6]
- maintained nursery schools
- academies[7]
- city technology colleges
- city technology colleges for the technology of the arts
- certain non-maintained special schools approved by the Secretary of State under section 342 of the Education Act 1996.

9.   An inspection of boarding or residential provision[8] in a boarding or residential special school will be integrated with the school inspection, where possible (for details, see part 3 of this document). Integrated inspections cannot be carried out when inspection cycles do not coincide. In these cases, we will only inspect the boarding or residential provision.

10.   All schools have a unique reference number (URN). Any institution with its own URN that we inspect will receive an inspection report.[9] We may try to coordinate the inspection of certain groups of schools, where this is possible.

11.   Ofsted is required to inspect at prescribed intervals all schools to which section 5 applies.[10] The regulations set the interval for section 5 inspections as 'within five school years from the end of the school year in which the last section 5 inspection took place'.[11] The exceptions to this requirement are schools that are, by regulations,[12] exempt from section 5 inspection (known as 'exempt schools').

Risk assessment

12.   We use risk assessment to ensure that our approach to inspection is proportionate, so that we can focus our efforts on where we can have the greatest impact. Risk assessment combines an assessment of each school, based on analysis of official national data, with a more in-depth desk-based review of a wider range of available information.

13.   We use a broad range of indicators to select schools for inspection. The risk assessment process normally takes place in time for the start of the third school year after the most recent inspection.[13]

14.   In a risk assessment, we analyse:

- progress and attainment data from the Department for Education
- school workforce census data
- the views of parents and carers,[14] including those shown by Ofsted Parent View,[15] our online questionnaire for parents
- qualifying complaints[16] about the school referred to us
- pupil mobility[17]
- time since last inspection, and inspection framework inspected under, for schools exempt from routine inspection.
- the outcomes of any inspections, such as survey inspections, that we have carried out since the last routine inspection
- statutory warning notices
- any other significant concerns that are brought to our attention.

15.   We may also carry out unannounced inspections and monitoring visits under section 8 of the Education Act 2005 at any time.

Outstanding/exempt schools

16.   Maintained primary and secondary schools and academies that were judged to be outstanding in their overall effectiveness at their most recent section 5 inspection are exempt from routine inspections under section 5. This exemption also applies to academy converter schools[18] when the overall effectiveness of the predecessor school was outstanding at its most recent section 5 inspection.

17.   This exemption does not apply to special schools (including maintained special schools, special free schools, alternative provision academies and non- maintained special schools), PRUs and maintained nursery schools, who will continue to be inspected under section 5.

18.   If Her Majesty's Chief Inspector (HMCI) or the Secretary of State has concerns about the performance of an exempt school (or any other school covered by section 5), HMCI has power to inspect it at any time under section 8(2) of the Act. Under section 8(1), the Secretary of State may require HMCI to carry out an inspection of an exempt school (or any other school covered by section 5). Under section 9(3) of the Act, the Secretary of State may also require HMCI to treat the section 8 inspection of an exempt school as if it were carried out under section 5.

19.   Exempt schools are subject to risk assessment. If the risk assessment process raises concerns about the performance of an exempt school, we may inspect it under section 8 of the Act at any time after the risk assessment. We will consider the length of time since the last inspection in the risk assessment. If no concerns arise from the risk assessment, the school will not be informed.

20.   If a risk assessment identifies sufficient concerns about a decline in the performance of pupils' academic/vocational/technical achievement and an overall decline in performance, these outstanding schools will receive a section 8 'no formal designation' inspection (see paragraph 23 for an explanation of this). If, during the course of the

inspection, the lead inspector finds that the school's overall effectiveness may be lower than outstanding, then the lead inspector may deem the section 8 inspection as a section 5 inspection.[19]

21.   If an exempt school makes structural changes, such as adding a new key stage or merging with another school, the school will receive a section 8 no formal designation inspection.

22.   In addition, exempt schools may be inspected between risk assessments if:

- safeguarding concerns, including a decline in the standards of pupils' behaviour and the ability of staff to maintain discipline, and/or welfare concerns suggest that we should inspect the school
- a subject or thematic survey inspection raises more general concerns
- we have received a qualifying complaint[20] that, taken alongside other available evidence, suggests that we should inspect the school
- concerns are raised about standards of leadership or governance
- concerns are identified about the curriculum (including if the statutory requirement to publish information to parents is not met)
- HMCI or the Secretary of State have concerns about a school's performance.

23.   If any of the concerns listed above are identified in exempt schools, we will usually inspect them under the section 8 no formal designation procedures, as set out in the section 8 handbook.[21]

Section 8 inspections of good and non-exempt outstanding schools

24.   The EIF supports proportionate inspections of schools' performance and circumstances. Consequently, good schools will normally receive a two-day section 8 inspection approximately every four years.

25.   Some good schools will be subject to a full section 5 inspection instead of a section 8 inspection. This will happen, for example, if a school has undergone significant change, such as in its age range, or if there are indications that the quality of provision may have deteriorated significantly. We will select these schools through our risk assessment process. The section 8 handbook explains how these inspections will be carried out.

26.   As is the case for all schools, a good school may still receive a 'no formal designation' inspection carried out under section 8 at any time in certain circumstances. For example, we may decide that we should inspect a school earlier than its next scheduled inspection if:

- there are safeguarding issues, including a decline in the standards of pupils' behaviour and the ability of staff to maintain discipline, and/or welfare concerns
- a subject or thematic survey inspection raises general concerns
- we have received a qualifying complaint about the school that, taken alongside other available evidence, suggests that it would be appropriate to do so

- concerns are raised about standards of leadership or governance
- concerns are identified about the breadth and balance of the curriculum (including if the statutory requirement to publish information to parents is not met)
- HMCI or the Secretary of State have concerns about the school's performance.

We may also inspect a school under section 8 if we select it as part of a sample to ensure that HMCI's Annual Report reflects evidence from a cross-section of schools of different types, phases and effectiveness.

27.   PRUs, special schools (including maintained special schools and non-maintained special schools) and maintained nursery schools that were judged good or outstanding at their previous section 5 inspection will normally receive an inspection under section 8 approximately every four years. This is to confirm that the quality of education remains good or outstanding.[22] These settings are not exempt from routine inspections if they are judged outstanding.

28   A section 8 inspection will not result in individual graded judgements. It cannot change the overall effectiveness grade of the school. If the inspection is converted to a section 5 inspection, then inspectors will make the full set of graded judgements, using the four-point grading scale required under section 5.[23]

29.   Usually, a section 8 inspection of a good school will be followed by a further section 8 inspection after approximately a four-year interval. However, if there is evidence that the school has improved towards outstanding or may no longer be good, inspectors will specify that the next inspection is a section 5 inspection, with the full range of graded judgements available.

30.   Our section 8 handbook sets out what is considered by inspectors on a section 8 inspection.[24]

Schools requesting an inspection

31.   Schools are able, via the appropriate authority (normally the school's governing body),[25] to request an inspection. We treat these inspections as an inspection under section 5. If we carry one out, HMCI may charge the appropriate authority for its cost.

Using evidence from section 5 and section 8 inspections

32   We may use the evidence that inspectors gather during section 5 and section 8 inspections to inform other work, such as national reporting.

Inspection of religious education and collective worship

33.   The Secretary of State designates certain schools as having a religious character.[26] In schools without a religious character, we inspect religious education (RE) and collective worship as part of inspections under section 5.

34.   This is different in schools with a religious character. In most of these schools, denominational education and collective worship are inspected by a body appointed by the maintained school's governing body under section 48 of the Education Act 2005 or as

provided in the academy's funding agreement.[27] In a voluntary controlled school designated as having a religious character, we inspect RE, but not collective worship.

35.   Inspectors may, however, gather evidence from anywhere relevant (including RE lessons and assemblies) to evaluate pupils' spiritual, moral, social and cultural education, personal development and/or behaviour and attitudes. The fact that the school has been designated as having a religious character must be referenced in the 'information about this school' section of the inspection report.

36.   Section 48 inspections (or the equivalent inspection of an academy) are carried out every three to five years[28] (and usually within two to three years of a new voluntary-aided school or academy/free school opening). The lead inspector on a section 5 inspection will check the section 48 arrangements. This includes when the next inspection is due and when the last inspection was. They will write about this in the 'leadership and management' section of the inspection report. They will ensure that the required consultation has taken place with the prescribed faith body when a school has a prescribed faith body and decides not to use that body's inspection service but to appoint its own inspector.

37.   Inspectors will familiarise themselves with any issues raised in any section 48 inspection (or equivalent) held since the last Ofsted inspection. Inspectors will not, however, use that evidence in an Ofsted inspection.[29] The lead inspector will report if the section 48 inspection (or equivalent inspection of an academy) is overdue and that, therefore, the school is failing in its statutory duty. They will do this in the 'leadership and management' section of the inspection report.

38.   If a section 48 inspection (or equivalent inspection of an academy) happens at the same time as an Ofsted section 5 inspection, inspectors will mention this in the 'information about this school' section.

New academies

39.   When a school becomes an academy, or when multiple schools come together to become an academy, the predecessor school(s) is/are closed. The new academy is legally a new school. Judgements made in any predecessor school's report are not judgements about the new academy. Inspectors may look at the performance of any predecessor school as part of pre-inspection planning. They can look at this data to consider whether the new academy has improved on, or declined from, its predecessor's performance and whether it has tackled any areas of weakness or built on strengths from the predecessor school. However, inspectors must take care not to give undue weight to any progress or attainment compared with those of the predecessor. Inspectors must not take account of the predecessor's key judgements or areas for improvement when reaching their judgements about the new academy. Inspectors will make clear to the new academy the extent to which they have taken account of the performance data from its predecessor school(s).

40.   Maintained schools that become academies are normally treated as new schools

for inspection purposes and are subject to a section 5 inspection as their first inspection. This will normally take place within three years of the new school opening. New converter academies whose predecessor schools were most recently judged good are eligible for an inspection under section 8 of the Education Act 2005,[30] as described in the section 8 handbook. New academies whose predecessor school was (or one of whose predecessor schools were) judged outstanding are not subject to routine section 5 inspection.

41.   The first section 5 report inspection of a new academy will state 'not previously inspected as an academy'.[31] The first section 5 inspection of a converter academy will include, in the context section, a statement that follows the example below:

'Piccadilly Gate Academy converted to become an academy school on 1 September 2019. When its predecessor school, Piccadilly Gate Secondary School, was last inspected by Ofsted, it was judged to be good overall.'

When can an inspection take place?

42.   Inspection can take place at any point from five school days after the first day pupils attend in Autumn term. For example, if pupils return to school on a Wednesday, inspection can take place as early as the following Wednesday.

Before the inspection

Clarification for schools

43.   The information below confirms our requirements. This is to dispel myths about inspection that can result in unnecessary workload in schools. It is intended to highlight specific practices that we do not require.

44.   Ofsted **will:**

- take a range of evidence, including that held in electronic form, into account when making judgements. This will include official national data, discussions with leaders, staff and pupils, questionnaire responses and work in pupils' books/folders/sketchbooks etc
- judge fairly schools that take radically different approaches to the curriculum. They will assess any school's curriculum favourably when leaders have built or adopted a curriculum with appropriate coverage, content, structure and sequencing and implemented it effectively
- report on any failure to comply with statutory arrangements when they form part of the inspection framework and evaluation schedule, including those relating to the workforce (see part 2 of this handbook)
- allow the school to invite as many governors or trustees as possible to meet inspectors during an inspection
- in academies, meet those directly responsible for management and governance, including the chief executive officer (CEO) or their delegate (or equivalent), the chair of the board of trustees and other trustees
- talk to the chair of governors/board of trustees by telephone if they are unable to attend a face-to-face meeting with the inspector in the school

- invite the headteacher (or equivalent) and, in academies, the CEO or their delegate, to observe the inspectors' final team meeting
- expect schools to maintain, as they are required to, the single central record detailing checks carried out. We expect multi-academy trusts (MATs) to maintain this in each of their academies and to ensure that the information is recorded in a way that allows for details of each individual academy to be provided separately and without delay.

45. Ofsted **will not**:
- grade individual lessons
- provide evidence from any lesson visit that could be used in capability/disciplinary proceedings or for the purposes of performance management
- create unnecessary workload for teachers through its recommendations
- routinely check personnel files, although it may look at a small sample
- advocate a particular method of planning (including lesson planning), teaching or assessment; it is up to schools to determine their practices and it is up to leadership teams to justify these on their own merits rather than by referring to this handbook.

46. Ofsted **does not** require schools to provide:
- evidence in any specific format, as long as it is easily accessible for inspectors
- curriculum planning in any specific format
- evidence for inspection beyond that set out in this handbook
- photographic evidence of pupils' work (although inspectors may request to take photographs themselves of pupils' work, which will be anonymised)
- any written record of teachers' oral feedback to pupils
- individual lesson plans
- previous lesson plans
- predictions of attainment and progress scores
- assessment or self-evaluation, other than that which is already part of the school's business processes
- performance and pupil-tracking information
- any specific document or plan in relation to the pupil premium other than its pupil premium strategy, and will not require any further school-generated data on the pupil premium, including information related to spending on individual students or to within-class or within-school gaps
- monitoring of teaching and learning and its link to teachers' professional development and the Teachers' standards,[32] other than that which is already part of the school's normal activity
- specific details of the pay grade of individual teachers who are observed

during inspection

- evidence about each teacher from each of the bulleted sub-headings in the teachers' standards
- anonymised lists of teachers meeting or not meeting performance thresholds for pay progression
- processes for the performance management arrangements for school leaders and staff.

47. Ofsted **does not** require schools to:

- do additional work or to ask pupils to do work specifically for the inspection
- carry out a specified amount of lesson observation
- use the Ofsted evaluation schedule to grade teaching or individual lessons
- ensure a particular frequency or quantity of work in pupils' books or folders
- include targets relating to the proportion of good or better teaching in headteacher objectives
- set teachers' performance targets based on commercially produced predictions of pupil achievement, or any other data set, from which it would then hold teachers to account
- retrospectively apply for DBS and other pre-employment checks for staff appointed before and continuously employed since the introduction of the Disclosure and Barring Service requirements
- take any specific steps with regard to site security; in particular, inspectors do not have a view about the need for perimeter fences
- take any specific steps to identify or track pupils or the work of individual pupils who would be included within the calculation of government pupil premium funding, other than that required for their pupil premium strategy
- carry out assessment or record pupils' achievements in any subject, including foundation subjects in primary schools, in a specific way, format or time
- use any particular format for policies relating to staff behaviour or have a separate code of conduct document
- be at similar stages of English Baccalaureate (EBacc) implementation as other schools, or provide additional information outside of their normal curriculum planning
- produce a self-evaluation document or summary in a particular format. Any assessment that is provided should be part of the school's business processes and not be generated solely for inspection purposes.

48. Ofsted **does not** specify:

- how planning (including curriculum and lesson planning) should be set out, the length of time it should take or the amount of detail it should contain
- that tutor groups/form time must include literacy, numeracy or other learning sessions

- the frequency, type or volume of marking and feedback
- the content of, or approach to, headteacher and staff performance management
- the format in which staff records should be maintained, beyond existing legal requirements.

Notification and introduction

49.   Ofsted will normally contact the school by telephone to announce the inspection between 10.30am and 2pm on the school day before the inspection.

50.   If the headteacher is unavailable when the notification call is made, we will ask to speak to the most senior member of staff available. Once we have informed the school by telephone that the inspection will take place, we will send confirmation to the school by email.

51.   During the initial notification phone call, the inspection support administrator will check the number of pupils on roll at the school, the governance arrangements for the school and whether the school has any SEND, nursery provision for two- and three-year-olds or additional resource provision.

52.   The inspection support administrator will then send the school a note setting out key information for leaders to be aware of before inspection. This will include:
- Ofsted's privacy notice
- informing the school that inspectors will use a range of technology to gather evidence electronically, including mobile devices, tablets and laptops
- informing the school that inspectors may request to take photographic evidence, for example of pupils' work and displays, but that inspectors will not take photographs of pupils.

Information that schools must provide by 8am on the day of inspection

53.   The inspection support administrator will also send the school a note requesting that the following information is available to inspectors by 8am the next day, at the formal start of the inspection:
- the school timetable, current staff list (indicating NQTs) and times for the school day
- any information about previously planned interruptions to normal school routines during the inspection
- records and analysis of exclusions, pupils taken off roll, incidents of poor behaviour and any use of internal isolation
- the single central record for the school
- records and analysis of sexual harassment or sexual violence
- records and analysis of bullying, discriminatory and prejudiced behaviour, either directly or indirectly, including racist, sexist, disability and homophobic/biphobic/transphobic bullying, use of derogatory language and racist incidents

- a list of referrals made to the designated person for safeguarding in the school and those who were subsequently referred to the local authority, along with brief details of the resolution
- a list of all pupils who have open cases with children's services/social care and for whom there is a multi-agency plan
- up-to-date attendance analysis for all groups of pupils
- documented evidence of the work of those responsible for governance and their priorities, including any written scheme of delegation for an academy in a MAT
- a summary of any school self-evaluation or equivalent
- the current school improvement plan or equivalent, including any planning that sets out the longer-term vision for the school, such as the school or the trust's strategy
- any reports from external evaluation of the school
- maps and other practical information
- access to Wi Fi, if it exists, so that inspectors can connect to the internet.

Preparation

54.	Once we have informed the school of the inspection, the lead inspector will contact the school by telephone and ask to speak to the headteacher. Inspectors' preparatory telephone conversations with headteachers will have two elements.

- A reflective, educationally focused conversation about the school's progress since the last inspection.
- A shorter inspection-planning conversation that focuses on practical and logistical issues.

55.	It may be that both these elements are discussed in a single telephone conversation. Alternatively, they may be carried out as two separate conversations with a break in between, as agreed between the lead inspector and the headteacher. In total, these conversations are likely to last around 90 minutes

Discussing the school's progress since the last inspection

56.	Inspectors will hold an introductory telephone conversation with school leaders on the day before the inspection begins. This should include giving school leaders the opportunity to explain their school's specific context and challenges. Inspection experience, including our pilots for this framework, shows that this helps both leaders and inspectors build stronger professional relationships.

57.	Inspectors will use this conversation to understand:

- the school's context, and the progress it has made since the previous inspection, including any specific progress made on areas for improvement identified at previous inspections that remain relevant under the current inspection framework
- the headteacher's assessment of the school's current strengths and weaknesses, particularly in relation to: the curriculum, the way teaching

supports pupils to learn the curriculum, the standards pupils achieve, pupils' behaviour and attitudes, and the personal development of pupils

- the specific areas of the school (for example, subjects, year groups, aspects of provision) that should be focused on during inspection.

58. This conversation will normally last up to 90 minutes. It will help inspectors and school leaders to establish a rapport before inspection and give them a shared understanding of the starting point of the inspection. It will also help inspectors to form an initial understanding of leaders' views of the school's progress and to shape the inspection plan. Our experience from piloting the new framework shows that this is the part of preparation that school leaders and inspectors often find to be the most helpful and constructive.

Inspection planning discussion

59. This discussion will be short and focused on practical issues. The lead inspector will:

- make the school aware of its statutory duty to inform parents of the inspection and that Ofsted's Parent View tool is the main method for gathering the views of parents at the point of inspection; inspectors will remind the school that our letter to parents containing the link to Ofsted Parent View may be sent electronically, or as a paper copy via pupils
- discuss the nature of the SEND resource base, if applicable
- discuss any nursery provision, before- and/or after-school care or holiday clubs led and managed directly by the school, particularly if these take two- to eight-year-olds[33]
- invite the headteacher, curriculum leaders and other leaders to take part in joint visits to lessons and to observe the main inspection team meetings
- make arrangements for meetings with relevant staff
- provide an opportunity for the school to ask any questions or to raise any concerns, such as perceived conflicts of interest.

60. The lead inspector will also use the discussion to establish whether the school has any pupils who attend off-site alternative provision, either full time or part time, run either by the school or in partnership with other schools. Where the school uses off-site alternative provision the lead inspector will request further details about this.

61. The lead inspector will also request that the school provides certain information as early as possible to aid preparation. This will include:

- a copy of the school timetable
- details of any relevant staff absence
- whether any teachers cannot be observed for any reason (for example, if they are subject to capability procedures)
- whether there is anyone working on site who is normally employed elsewhere in the MAT (if relevant)

62.   It is important that inspectors speak to those responsible leadership and governance during inspection. Since schools, and especially MATs, operate a wide variety of leadership and governance models, it is essential that inspectors establish who is responsible for leadership and governance.

63.   The lead inspector will therefore:

- establish what the governance structure of the school or academy is,[34] with reference to the range of functions delegated to local governing bodies or other committees
- confirm arrangements for meetings with the school and, if appropriate, MAT executive leaders, as well as representatives of those responsible for the governance of the school and anyone else they think relevant. The lead inspector should be guided by the school here as to who they need to meet in the structure of a MAT
- make arrangements for a meeting with the chair of the governing body or, if appropriate, the chair of the board of trustees and as many governors/trustees as possible. Inspectors will also ask the school to invite as many governors/trustees as possible to attend the final feedback meeting
- request either a face-to-face meeting or a telephone call with a representative from the local authority, diocese, sponsor or other relevant responsible body as appropriate
- request that a representative from the local authority, diocese, MAT, sponsor or other relevant responsible body is present at the final inspection feedback meeting as appropriate.

64.   If any issues arise, the lead inspector may also need further clarification from the school, for example when information is not available on the school's website or there are anomalies with the single central record that may be resolved.

Further inspection preparation carried out by the lead inspector

65.   In addition to the information requested from the school, inspectors will review and consider:

- all relevant information held by Ofsted, including:
    - data from our inspection data summary report (IDSR)[35]
    - inspection reports on the school
    - any surveys or monitoring letters
    - any complaints made about the school to Ofsted[36]
    - replies to questionnaires
    - information on our provider information portal[37], including any warning notices[38]
    - the most recent inspection report on the relevant local authority's children's services[39]
    - the main findings from the relevant local area's special educational needs

and disabilities (SEND) inspection[40]

- relevant publicly available information, such as the school's website[41]
- information published by local authorities, the DfE (including the Education and Skills Funding Agency and regional school commissioners) and the police.

Resource bases

66.   If the school has a SEND resource base delegated to it or the local authority maintains direct responsibility for the period when the pupils in the provision are in mainstream classes at the school being inspected, the resource base must be inspected. Inspectors must consider evidence about the resourced provision when making judgements about the school overall.

67.   During the lead inspector's planning conversation with the school, they will get specific information about any resource base, including:

- the number of pupils and the range of the needs of pupils placed in additionally resourced provision, together with pupils' timetables, including when they are taught in mainstream classes (with and without support) and when they receive specialist support in separate resourced provision
- the type(s) of language/communication systems used. If the specialist provision is for deaf pupils, it is important to establish, if British Sign Language is used, whether a British Sign Language interpreter will be provided by the school when inspectors are meeting with the pupils. The lead inspector will contact the inspection support administrator as soon as possible if this support is needed. Details will be available in the team room
- staffing arrangements and details of any outreach services provided by the resourced provision.

Requests for deferral or cancellation

68.   A school may request a deferral of its inspection. It may make a request to the inspection support administrator when it is notified of the inspection, or to the lead inspector on the day it is notified of the inspection. We will not normally consider deferrals if we receive them after 4.30pm on the day the school is notified. The inspection support administrator or lead inspector must immediately contact the regional duty desk. We will decide whether this should be granted in accordance with our deferral policy.[42]

69.   Normally, if pupils are receiving education in the school, an inspection will go ahead. In exceptional circumstances, however, an inspection might be cancelled or deferred after the school has been notified, following a request made by the school. We will aim to let the school know whether a request is granted on the same day it is made, but in some cases (particularly when the request for deferral comes later), this may happen by 8am the next morning.

70.   If a school is within six months of confirmed closure[43], but the school does not request a cancellation when the inspector makes contact, the inspection support

administrator will call the regional duty desk to highlight this and get advice about whether the inspection should still be carried out. Decisions will be made case by case.

71.   In the case of unannounced inspections, any requests for a deferral will be passed to Ofsted's relevant regional director, who will decide whether the request can be granted.

No-notice inspections

72.   We may carry out inspections without notice.[44] When this happens, the lead inspector will normally telephone the school about 15 minutes before arriving on site. In these cases, the inspector will make the initial call simply to inform the school that the inspection is about to begin and will leave all other arrangements until arriving at the school.

Seeking the views of registered parents and other stakeholders

73.   When a school is notified of a section 5 inspection, it is required to take such steps as are reasonably practicable to notify all registered parents of registered pupils[45] at the school, including those who have been excluded, attend alternative provision or are away from school. Schools are also required to notify relevant bodies, including providers of alternative provision.[46]

74.   Inspectors have a statutory duty to have regard of the views of parents and other relevant persons[47] at the point of a section 5 inspection. Our email confirming the inspection includes a letter that formally notifies parents. It also explains how to use Ofsted Parent View and how parents can contact inspectors. Schools will encourage parents to complete the Ofsted Parent View questionnaire by placing a link to it on their website.[48] In addition, inspectors will encourage the school to notify parents using its own electronic systems (such as text messages), if these are available.

75.   Inspectors will review the evidence from Ofsted Parent View throughout the inspection to ensure that all online responses received during the inspection are taken into account. If the response rate for Parent View is low, inspectors may take steps during the inspection to gather further evidence of parents' views.

76.   Inspectors will also take into account any other evidence from parents, including the results of any past surveys the school has carried out or commissioned. If individual parents raise serious issues, inspectors will follow these up with the school and record its response.

77.   During integrated inspections of boarding or residential special schools, social care regulatory inspectors will take account of the views that parents have given on Ofsted Parent View about the school's boarding or residential provision. Views of children and young people who are boarders or residential pupils and boarding staff will have been gathered through Ofsted's annual point-in-time surveys.[49]

Pupil and staff questionnaires

78.   The views of pupils and staff in schools are gathered through online questionnaires. The inspection support administrator sends online links to the school with

the formal notification of inspection. The school is asked to encourage staff and pupils to complete the online questionnaires, apart from those pupils in any boarding provision, whose views will have already been sought through the point-in-time survey. Pupils and staff should complete their questionnaires by 3pm on the first day of the inspection.

79.   As well as through online questionnaires, inspectors may gather evidence from parents or other stakeholders in person. This may include informal meetings at the start and/or end of the day. These meetings must take place without the presence of the headteacher or senior staff. In drawing on evidence from these meetings, every attempt must be made to protect the identity of individuals. There may be circumstances, however, in which it is not possible to guarantee the anonymity of the interviewee. Inspectors have a duty to pass on disclosures that raise child protection or safeguarding issues and/or when there are concerns about serious misconduct, bullying of staff or criminal activity.

The inspection

80.   Inspections do not normally last longer than two days. The size of the inspection team will vary according to the size and nature of the school.

Concurrent inspections

81.   We may schedule inspections at the same time for 'linked provision', which is when one or more schools have arrangements to share important aspects of their provision, such as sixth-form programmes or an inclusion unit. Inspectors will make sure that they communicate with each other before and during the inspections. They will also share evidence electronically. Inspectors will ensure that they give sufficient consideration to the emerging judgements of the linked provision.

82.   The inspection of boarding or residential provision in a school is carried out by one or more social care regulatory inspectors. Contact between the education and social care regulatory inspectors will take place before the inspection. Guidance on pre-inspection activity for integrated inspections is set out in the 'Social care common inspection framework (SCCIF): boarding schools and residential special schools'.[50]

Arrival time on the first full day of inspection

83.   On the first day of the inspection, inspectors will not arrive before 8am.

Gathering and recording evidence

84.   Although meetings with leaders are important, inspectors' first priority during inspections is to collect first-hand evidence.

85.   Inspectors will observe lessons; scrutinise pupils' work; talk to pupils about their work, gauging both their understanding and their engagement in learning; and gather pupils' perceptions of the typical quality of education and other aspects of life at the school in a range of subjects.

86.   Inspectors will evaluate evidence of the impact of the curriculum, including on the most disadvantaged pupils. This includes pupils with SEND. It also includes pupils who meet the criteria for the school to receive pupil premium funding: pupils claiming free school meals at any point in the last six years, looked after children (children in local authority care) and/or children who left care through adoption or another formal route.[51] In addition, it includes children in need of help and protection, receiving statutory local authority support from a social worker. Inspectors will give specific attention to the acquisition of knowledge and skills in lessons and on-site separate provision and evidence of learning in off-site alternative provision.

87.   Other evidence gathered by inspectors will include: discussions with pupils and staff; listening to pupils read; and looking at examples of pupils' work for evidence of progress in knowledge, understanding and skills towards defined endpoints. Inspectors will also scrutinise the school's records and documentation relating, for example, to the welfare and safety of pupils in alternative provision.

Evaluating different approaches to teaching

88. Ofsted does **not** advocate that any particular approach should be used exclusively in teaching. Different approaches to teaching can be effective. What is appropriate will depend on the aims of a particular lesson or activity, and its place in the sequence of teaching a particular topic. Nevertheless, any approach used has features that must be present to ensure that it is delivered effectively. Our research commentary sets out our understanding of those factors.[52]

Newly qualified teachers and trainees working in schools during section 5 inspections

89. When the lead inspector requests a copy of the current staff list, they must ask whether this includes:

- any newly qualified teachers (NQTs)
- any trainees on placement, including those on School Direct or School Direct (salaried) training routes.

90. Inspectors will meet NQTs where possible and may wish to observe lessons given by NQTs. In doing so, inspectors should give consideration to the fact that NQTs have less experience than other teachers, but must assess the effectiveness of the support and professional development put in place for NQTs and other teachers who are in the early stages of their careers, particularly in dealing with pupil behaviour. This must include the quality of mentoring and what the school has done to support their development in areas for improvement identified by initial teacher training providers. Inspectors should discuss how NQTs are supported by the school in managing pupil behaviour.

91. Inspectors will meet any trainees employed by the school on the School Direct (salaried) route to assess their support, mentoring and induction. Inspectors will **not** observe lessons given by trainees.

92. The teachers' standards state that providers will assess trainees against the standards in a way that is consistent with what could reasonably be expected of a trainee teacher before the awarding of qualified teacher status (QTS).[53] Inspectors will **not** take trainees' performance into account when assessing the quality of education.

Overarching approach to inspection

93. This EIF seeks to put a single, joined-up educational conversation at the heart of inspection. It is built around the connectedness of curriculum, teaching, assessment and standards within the 'quality of education' judgement. As a result, the inspection methodology for this judgement is structured to ensure that inspectors are able to gather evidence of how a school's activities to deliver a high-quality education for its pupils connect and work together to achieve the highest possible standards.

94. As set out in the 'preparation' section above (paragraphs 54–55), inspections under the EIF always begin with in-depth discussions with school leaders and curriculum leaders about the school's curriculum. Inspectors ask about what leaders intend pupils to learn. What are the end points they wish them to reach, what are the key concepts that they need to understand, and in what order will they learn them? They will also ask about pupils' behaviour and attitudes and personal development.

95. During inspection, inspectors will probe leaders' understanding further but, most importantly, they will focus on gathering first-hand evidence. Inspectors will visit lessons, talk to individual teachers and pupils, and look at pupils' work (in its widest sense) together with curriculum leaders to see whether it matches leaders' intentions. Inspectors will then draw all this evidence together from different pupils, classes and year groups.

96. The crucial element here is the **connection** between different pieces of evidence. Inspectors will not emphasise one specific type of evidence above all others. Instead, inspectors will focus on gathering evidence that is balanced and connected. Our research on work scrutiny and lesson visits has shown that having a variety of types of connected evidence strengthens the conclusions that inspectors are able to reach.

97. This evidence will always lead inspectors back to the overall quality of education on offer. The focus will not be on one particular lesson, book or pupil. Rather, the focus will be on the interconnection of all of these pieces of evidence and what they tell inspectors and leaders about whether pupils are learning the curriculum and making progress in the sense of knowing more, remembering more and being able to do more. The evidence from our substantial piloting of the EIF is that this approach enables inspectors and leaders to build up a clear picture of whether the school is meeting the criteria set out in the 'quality of education' judgement.

Joint visits to lessons

98. One element of the inspection approach will be visits to lessons. The lead inspector will invite the headteacher, curriculum leaders and other leaders to take part in joint visits to lessons.

99. Inspectors will **not** take a random sample of lessons to visit. Instead, they will connect lesson visits to other evidence: discussions with curriculum leaders, teachers and pupils, and work scrutiny. Inspectors will visit several lessons in which the same subject is being taught, including lessons to different year groups. Lesson visits are **not** about evaluating individual teachers or their teaching; there will be no grading of the teaching observed by inspectors. Instead, inspectors will view lessons across a faculty, department, subject, key stage or year group and then aggregate insights as to how what is going on in lessons contributes to the school's curriculum intentions. This will then provide part of the evidence for an overall view of quality of education or behaviour and attitudes.

100. In summary, lesson visits are primarily useful for gathering evidence about how lessons contribute to the quality of education. Inspectors can use these visits to gather evidence about how well the curriculum is implemented. They do this by looking at what is going on in lessons for one or more subjects or themes, triangulating this with evidence collected through discussions with the staff and pupils involved, and scrutinising the pupils' work, wherever possible derived from the lessons visited and the relevant sequence of lessons (see below).

101. Lesson visits are also useful for gathering evidence that contributes to the 'behaviour and attitudes' judgement by providing direct evidence about how behaviour is

managed within individual classrooms and how pupils respond. This evidence will complement the other evidence that inspectors gather about behaviour during inspection.

Work scrutiny

102. Another element of the inspection approach will be scrutinising pupils' work. The lead inspector will invite curriculum leaders and teachers to take part in joint scrutiny of pupils' work.

103. Inspectors will **not** take a random sample of exercise books/folders/sketchbooks/electronic files and so on (which we refer to as 'pupils' books and other work'). Instead, they will scrutinise pupils' books and other work across a faculty, department, subject, key stage or year group and aggregate insights to provide part of the evidence for an overall view of the quality of education. Inspectors will **not** evaluate individual workbooks or teachers. Inspectors will **not** use work scrutiny to evaluate teachers' marking. Inspectors will connect work scrutiny to lesson visits and, where at all possible, conversations with pupils and staff.

104. Inspectors can use work scrutiny to contribute to an evaluation of whether the work that pupils do over time reflects the intended curriculum. Work scrutiny will help inspectors to form a view of whether pupils know more and can do more, and whether the knowledge and skills they have learned are well sequenced and have developed incrementally. Inspectors will synthesise what they find in order to contribute to their overall assessment of the quality of education across a faculty, department, subject, key stage or year group.

Talking to and observing pupils outside lessons

105. Inspectors will ensure that they talk to and observe pupils in a range of situations outside normal lessons to evaluate other aspects of personal development, behaviour and attitudes, for example:

- at the start and finish of the school day
- during lunchtime, including in the dining hall, and breaktimes or playtimes
- during assemblies and tutor periods
- when moving between lessons
- during enrichment activities (including clubs and activities outside of the normal timetabled curriculum).

106. Inspectors will take advantage of opportunities to gather evidence from a wide range of pupils, both formally and informally. During informal conversations with pupils, inspectors must ask them about their experiences of teaching, learning and behaviour in the school, including the prevention of bullying and how the school deals with any form of harassment and violence, discrimination and prejudiced behaviour, if they happen. Inspectors will ensure that all questions are appropriate. They would not expect any school staff to be present.

Meeting those responsible for governance

107. Inspectors will always seek to meet those responsible for governance during the

inspection.

108. In a maintained school or standalone academy, this will usually include maintained school governors or academy trustees and sponsors (including sponsor representatives, where they exist).[54]

109. In a school that is part of a MAT, the board of trustees is the governance body. Often, local governing bodies can appear responsible for governance, when in reality it is trustees who are accountable for the academy trust. Local governing bodies are committees to which trustees have often chosen to delegate some specific responsibilities, but in some cases they may act purely as advisory bodies and engage with the community. Their responsibilities will normally be set out in the trust's scheme of delegation. Sometimes, their powers are delegated from the managers of the MAT; in this case, they are part of the school's management, not its governance. Inspectors will therefore need to be careful to establish who has overall responsibility for governance. Inspectors will also ensure that meetings are with those who are directly responsible for exercising governance of the school and for overseeing its performance.

110. The role that governors and trustees play in the school's performance is evaluated as part of the judgement on the effectiveness of leadership and management, and each report will contain a separate paragraph that addresses the governance of the school.

111. As with the meetings between inspectors and pupils, parents and staff, meetings or telephone discussions with those responsible for governance should take place without the headteacher or other senior staff being present.

Meeting leaders

112. The lead inspector will meet the headteacher regularly throughout the inspection to:

- provide updates on emerging issues, including initial general findings about the quality of education and to enable further evidence to be provided
- allow the headteacher to raise concerns, including those related to the conduct of the inspection or of individual inspectors
- alert the headteacher to any serious concerns.

113. The inspection team will meet at different points during the course of the inspection. In particular, the team should:

- meet briefly in the middle of day 1
- meet at the end of day 1 to discuss and record emerging findings; the headteacher should be invited
- meet at the end of day 2 to finalise judgements and identify areas for improvement
- draw together the key inspection findings and write up the evaluation for team meetings.

114. The lead inspector will invite the headteacher to the final team meeting at the end

of day 2. It is important that the lead inspector makes it clear that observers who are invited to attend the final team meeting are there to listen to the scrutiny of evidence and agreed judgements made by the inspection team. As appropriate, the lead inspector may request that observers clarify key points during the meeting.

115.   In a MAT, the headteacher (or equivalent) may report to a CEO (or equivalent) who is, in turn, accountable to the board of trustees. The CEO is part of the executive staff (and may be a trustee). They should be invited to the final meeting or be allowed to send a delegate.

116.   If, by the end of day 2 or during day 2, there is evidence that the school might be judged as inadequate or requires improvement, the lead inspector will alert the headteacher to this possibility. It must be emphasised that final judgements are not made until the final team meeting at the end of day 2.

Reaching final judgements

117.   Inspection activity, including lesson observations, will continue during day 2. The team will also ensure that time is set aside to complete any feedback to staff and to prepare for the final team meeting and the final feedback. During the final team meeting, an electronic summary evaluation form will be completed. The main points for feedback to the school will be recorded as the meeting progresses.

Providing feedback

118.   The on-site inspection ends with a final feedback meeting with the school. Those connected with the school who may attend include:

- the headteacher and other senior leaders, agreed by the lead inspector and headteacher
- for maintained schools, the chair of the school's governing body and as many governors as possible
- for academies, including academies that are part of a MAT, the chair of the board of trustees and as many trustees as possible
- in an academy that is part of a MAT, the CEO or their delegate or equivalent
- a representative from the local authority (for maintained schools) sponsor and/or the designated responsible body
- in an aligned or integrated inspection, social care regulatory inspectors and education inspectors will feed back together to both education and residential staff.

Due to the diverse nature of school governance, in some schools a single individual may have more than one of the above roles.

119.   During this meeting, the lead inspector will ensure that the headteacher, those responsible for governance and all attendees are clear:

- about the provisional grades awarded for each key judgement. The lead inspector must give sufficient detail to enable all attendees to understand how judgements have been reached and for those responsible for the governance of the school to play a part in beginning to plan how to tackle any areas for improvement

- that the grades are provisional and so may be subject to change as a result of quality assurance procedures or moderation and must, therefore, be treated as restricted and confidential to the relevant senior personnel (as determined by the school). They may be shared with school staff and all those responsible for the governance of the school, irrespective of whether they attended the meeting, so long as they are clearly marked as provisional and subject to quality assurance. Information about the inspection outcomes should be shared more widely only when the school receives a copy of the final inspection report
- that the main findings of the inspection and the main points provided orally in the feedback, subject to any change, will be referred to in the text of the report, although the text of the report may differ slightly from the oral feedback
- about any recommendations for improvement
- that, on receipt of the draft report, they must ensure that the report is not shared with any third party outside those with specific responsibility for the governance of the school, or published under any circumstances
- that the headteacher is invited and encouraged to complete the post-inspection survey
- about the implications of the school being placed in a category of concern if the school is judged to be inadequate
- when a school requires special measures, whether it may appoint NQTs[55]
- about the procedure for making a complaint about the inspection
- if the school is being placed in a category of concern, that they may make comments on the judgements in the draft report during quality assurance. That is, they are not limited to factual accuracy comments.

120.   Regulations state that a maintained school that has been judged to require special measures may not appoint NQTs unless HMCI has given permission in writing.[56] When the lead inspector has informed a maintained school that it may not appoint NQTs, the school must seek approval if it later wishes to appoint NQTs, by writing to the relevant Ofsted regional director, giving supporting reasons. The restriction on appointing NQTs does not extend to trainee teachers who joined employment-based training programmes[57] at the school prior to the notice.

Schools that are judged as requires improvement

121.   A school that is judged as requires improvement (overall effectiveness grade 3) is a school that is not good but overall provides an acceptable standard of education. The judgement of requires improvement is not a formal category of concern, but the school may be subject to monitoring by Ofsted. This will not normally apply to a school that has been judged as requires improvement for the first time. We will inspect the school again under

section 5, usually within 30 months of the publication of the previous section 5 report.

122.   When the school is judged as requires improvement, inspectors will direct the school to Ofsted's section 8 handbook.

123.   If, at the next section 5 inspection, the school has not demonstrated that it has improved to good, the lead inspector will need to consider whether the school continues to require improvement or may be inadequate. If the school has demonstrated improvement in some areas and there is a general upward trend, but key aspects of performance remain less than good, the school may be judged as requires improvement again. In that case, there will normally be monitoring before another section 5 inspection takes place within 30 months of the publication of the previous section 5 report. These considerations will be made at each section 5 re-inspection of a school that was previously judged as requires improvement.

Schools causing concern

124.   Schools whose overall effectiveness is judged to be inadequate (grade 4) will be deemed to be in a formal category of concern.

Procedures for judging a school as inadequate

125.   If, by the end of the first day of the inspection or during day 2, the lead inspector thinks it is possible that the school's overall effectiveness is inadequate and that it might be judged to have serious weaknesses[58] or to require special measures, they **must** ring Ofsted's regional duty desk.

126.   The lead inspector will be asked for their name and the name and URN of the school. They will then be put through to one of Her Majesty's Inspectors (HMI) on duty. In this call, the lead inspector **must** talk through the evidence used by inspector(s) in reaching an emerging provisional judgement of inadequate. The overall effectiveness judgement is not confirmed at this point. The lead inspector **must** record the main points of the conversation on an evidence form.

127.   During the second day of the inspection, the lead inspector may contact the regional duty desk again to discuss emerging findings. If the inspection team has made the provisional judgement that the school is inadequate and has serious weaknesses or requires special measures, the lead inspector **must** telephone the regional duty desk before the final oral feedback meeting with the school. The lead inspector will be prepared to explain briefly the reasons and underpinning evidence for the inadequate judgement.

Special measures

128.   A school requires **special measures** if:

- it is failing to give its pupils an acceptable standard of education and
- the persons responsible for leading, managing or governing are not demonstrating the capacity to secure the necessary improvement in the school.[59]

129.   If inspectors consider that the evidence shows that the overall effectiveness of the school is inadequate, they **must** conclude that the school is failing to give an acceptable

standard of education. Inspectors **must** then consider whether leaders, managers and governors are failing to demonstrate the capacity to improve the school. If so, then the school requires special measures.

Serious weaknesses

130.   If inspectors consider that the evidence shows that the overall effectiveness of the school is inadequate, but consider that leaders, managers and governors demonstrate the capacity to improve the school, they will instead judge the school to have serious weaknesses. A school with serious weaknesses will have one or more of the key judgements graded inadequate (grade 4) and/or have important weaknesses in the provision for pupils' spiritual, moral, social and cultural development.

Informing a school that it is deemed to be causing concern

131.   If a school is provisionally judged to require special measures or to have serious weaknesses, inspectors **must** use the following words **during the final feedback to the school,** indicating that the overall effectiveness judgement is subject to moderation by HMIs and, in the case of special measures, agreement by HMCI.

When the school has serious weaknesses:

'In accordance with section 44 of the Education Act 2005, Her Majesty's Chief Inspector is likely to be of the opinion that this school has serious weaknesses[60] because it is performing significantly less well than it might in all the circumstances reasonably be expected to perform.'

When the school requires special measures:

'In accordance with section 44 of the Education Act 2005, Her Majesty's Chief Inspector is likely to be of the opinion that this school requires special measures because it is failing to give its pupils an acceptable standard of education and the persons responsible for leading, managing or governing the school are not demonstrating the capacity to secure the necessary improvement in the school.'

Implications for a school causing concern

132.   If a school is judged to be causing concern, the timescale for publishing the report is extended so that the school can make comments on the inspection judgements. Judgements can be moderated in light of those comments and, in the case of schools judged to require special measures, confirmed either by HMCI or a regional director on HMCI's behalf.

133.   Maintained schools and PRUs that are judged to be causing concern will be subject to an academy order. The Secretary of State has a duty to make an academy order for all maintained schools judged to have serious weaknesses ('requiring significant improvement') and those that require special measures. This includes maintained special schools, but excludes maintained nursery schools and non-maintained special schools. For academies that are causing concern, the Secretary of State has a power to terminate the funding agreement, and the academy may become part of a trust or be 'rebrokered'[61] to another trust.

134.   Maintained schools or PRUs that have been issued with an academy order and academies that are being brokered or rebrokered to new sponsors following termination of their funding agreements will normally receive monitoring inspections if they have not been brokered or rebrokered after nine months.

135.   There is still a requirement for the local authority, proprietor or trust to prepare a statement of action, even though these schools will become new sponsored academies once the new funding agreements are in place. However, with the exception of any safeguarding concerns, which the statement of action must address, the purpose of the statement will be to set out how the relevant authority and the school will support the transition to the new academy or trust.

136.   Whether becoming a new academy or being brokered or rebrokered, these schools will become new sponsored academies. We will then inspect them as new schools within three years of operation and normally in the third year. However, in exceptional circumstances, schools that are becoming new academies or being rebrokered may receive a section 8 inspection before their next section 5 inspection.

137.   Academies judged to have serious weaknesses, and which are not brokered or rebrokered, will be subject to monitoring by Ofsted.[62] They will normally be re-inspected within 30 months of the publication of the inspection report in which they were judged to have serious weaknesses.

138.   Academies judged to require special measures, and which are not rebrokered, will be subject to monitoring by Ofsted. The timing of the next section 5 inspection will be determined by the academy's rate of improvement. However, it will normally take place within 30 months of the publication of the inspection report that judged it to require special measures.

139.   Maintained nursery schools and non-maintained special schools judged inadequate are not subject to academy orders. We will monitor them as set out in the section 8 handbook.

Taking a school out of a category of concern

140.   When an inspection team judges that a school that has been subject to special measures no longer requires special measures, inspectors **must** use the following words during the final feedback to the school:

'In accordance with section 13 (4) of the Education Act 2005, Her Majesty's Chief Inspector is of the opinion that the school no longer requires special measures.'

141.   When an inspection team judges that a school previously judged to have serious weaknesses no longer has serious weaknesses, inspectors **must** use the following words during the final feedback to the school:

'In accordance with section 13 (5) of the Education Act 2005, Her Majesty's Chief Inspector is of the opinion that the school no longer requires significant improvement.'

After the inspection

Arrangements for publishing the report[63]

142. The lead inspector is responsible for writing the inspection report and submitting the evidence to Ofsted shortly after the inspection ends. The text of the report will explain the judgements and reflect the evidence. The findings in the report should be consistent with the feedback given to the school at the end of the inspection.

143. Inspection reports will be quality assured before we send a draft copy to the school. The draft report is restricted and confidential to the relevant personnel (as determined by the school), including those responsible for governance, and should not be shared more widely or published.

144. The school will be invited to comment on the draft report and informed of the timescales in which to do so. This is normally one working day, except if the school is registered with us as a children's home and an 'aligned' inspection of the school and the children's home provision has taken place. Except in the case of schools causing concern, comments must be limited to the factual accuracy of the report. We will notify the school of the lead inspector's response.

145. We may share a draft of the inspection report with the DfE, funding bodies or regional schools commissioners if HMCI considers it necessary to do so. This will only take place following moderation and/or quality assurance.

146. Typically, schools will receive an electronic version of the final report within 25 working days of the end of the inspection. In most circumstances, the final report will be published on Ofsted's website within 30 working days.

147. Once a school has received its final report, it is required to take such steps as are reasonably practicable to ensure that every parent of a registered pupil at the school receives a copy of the report within five working days.[64] After that time, the report will normally be published on Ofsted's website. However, we may publish the report any time after the school has received it.

148. We will notify the DfE and/or the relevant funding body before final publication. In all cases, the inspection process should not be treated as complete until all inspection activity has been carried out and the final version of the inspection report has been sent to the school.

The inspection evidence base

149. The evidence base for the inspection will be retained in line with Ofsted's retention and disposal policy. This is normally for six years from when the report is published. We may decide that retaining it for longer is warranted for research purposes.

Quality assurance and complaints

Quality assurance

150. All inspectors are responsible for the quality of their work. The lead inspector must ensure that inspections are carried out in accordance with the principles of inspection and the Ofsted code of conduct.

151. We monitor the quality of inspections through a range of formal processes. HMI/Senior HMI visit some schools, or monitor remotely to quality assure inspections. We may also evaluate the quality of an inspection evidence base.

The lead inspector will be responsible for feeding back to team inspectors about the quality of their work and their conduct.

152. All schools are invited to take part in a post-inspection evaluation in order to contribute to inspection development.

Handling concerns and complaints

153. The great majority of Ofsted's work is carried out smoothly and without incident. If concerns do arise during an inspection, they should be raised with the lead inspector as soon as possible, in order to resolve issues before the inspection is completed. The lead inspector will seek advice where necessary. Any concerns raised and actions taken will be recorded in the inspection evidence.

154. If it is not possible to resolve concerns during the inspection, the school may wish to lodge a formal complaint. The lead inspector will ensure that the school is informed that it is able to make a formal complaint and that information about how to complain is available on Ofsted's website.[65]

Part 2. The evaluation schedule – how we will judge schools

155. The evaluation schedule is not exhaustive. It does not replace the professional judgement of inspectors. Inspectors must interpret the way that grades are described according to pupils' age, stage and phase of education.

156. Inspectors will make judgements on the following:

- overall effectiveness

and the four key judgements:

- the quality of education
- behaviour and attitudes
- personal development
- leadership and management

and, where relevant, judgements on the quality of provision in:

- early years education
- the sixth form.

157. Inspectors use the following four-point scale to make all judgements:

- grade 1: outstanding
- grade 2: good
- grade 3: requires improvement
- grade 4: inadequate.

Reaching a judgement of outstanding

158. This handbook introduces a new method of evaluating whether a school is outstanding in one or more judgement areas. Outstanding is a challenging and exacting judgement. In order to reach this standard, inspectors will determine whether the school meets **all** the criteria for good under that judgement, and does so securely and consistently. In other words, it is not enough that the school is strong against some aspects of the judgement and not against others, but it must meet each and every good criterion. In addition, there are further criteria set out under the outstanding judgement, which the school will also need to meet. Our aim in making this change is that schools should only be judged outstanding in a particular area if they are performing exceptionally, and this exceptional performance in that area is consistent and secure across the whole school.

Reaching a judgement of good, requires improvement or inadequate

159. A judgement of good or requires improvement will continue to follow the best- fit approach. Inspectors will consider whether the overall quality of the school is most closely aligned to the descriptors set out. Again, as in the past, a school will be inadequate under a particular judgement if one or more of the inadequate criteria applies in the case of that school.

Overall effectiveness

160. Inspectors must use all their evidence to evaluate what it is like attend the school. In making their judgements about a school's overall effectiveness, inspectors will consider

whether the standard of education is good or whether it exceeds good and is outstanding. If it is not good, then inspectors will consider whether it requires improvement or is inadequate.

161.　In judging the overall effectiveness, inspectors will take account of the four key judgements.

162.　In coming to each of these key judgements, inspectors will also draw on evidence from the inspection of any early years provision or sixth-form provision and consider its impact in the wider context of the school.

163.　Inspectors will judge the effectiveness of any early years provision or sixth-form provision. For either case or both, inspectors must give a grade, summarise the key findings and explain the effectiveness grading in the inspection report. However, inspectors may decide not to give a grade and a written section in the report on the provision in early years or in sixth-form provision if there is the risk that it is possible to identify individual pupils because numbers are so small. Typically, this will be when there are fewer than five pupils.

164.　The grade for early years and/or the grade for the sixth-form provision may be the same as, or higher or lower than, the overall effectiveness grade. Inspectors will take into account the size of the early years and sixth-form provision in relation to the size of the school when considering the impact of these judgements on the overall effectiveness grade. Inspectors will explain any difference between the early years and/or sixth-form provision grade(s) and the overall effectiveness grade in the report.

165.　Inspectors will always make a written judgement about the effectiveness of the arrangements for safeguarding pupils.

166.　Before making the final judgement on overall effectiveness, inspectors will always consider the spiritual, moral, social and cultural development of pupils at the school, and evaluate the extent to which the school's education provision meets different pupils' needs, including pupils with SEND.

Grade descriptors for overall effectiveness

Outstanding (1)

- **The quality of education is outstanding.**

- **All other key judgements are likely to be outstanding. In exceptional circumstances, one of the key judgements may be good, as long as there is convincing evidence that the school is improving this area sustainably and securely towards outstanding. Typically this will mean meeting each and every one of the good criteria but falling short on the outstanding for that key judgement.**

- **Safeguarding is effective.**

Good (2)

- The quality of education is at least good.

- All other key judgements are likely to be good or outstanding. In exceptional circumstances, one of the key judgement areas may require improvement, as long as there is convincing evidence that the school is improving this area sustainably and securely towards good.

- Safeguarding is effective.

Requires improvement (3)

- Other than in exceptional circumstances, it is likely that, when the school is judged as requires improvement in any of the key judgements, the school's overall effectiveness will also be requires improvement.

- Safeguarding is effective. If there are any weaknesses in safeguarding, they are easily rectified and there are no serious failings that leave pupils either being harmed or at risk of harm.

Inadequate (4)

- The judgement on the overall effectiveness will be inadequate when any one of the key judgements is inadequate and/or safeguarding is ineffective.

The quality of education

167.   Inspectors will take a rounded view of the quality of education that a school provides to all its pupils, including the most disadvantaged pupils (see definition in paragraph 86) , the most able pupils and pupils with SEND. Inspectors will consider the school's curriculum, which is the substance of what is taught with a specific plan of what pupils need to know in total and in each subject.

168.   Inspectors will consider the extent to which the school's curriculum sets out the knowledge and skills that pupils will gain at each stage (we call this '**intent**'). They will also consider the way that the curriculum developed or adopted by the school is taught and assessed in order to support pupils to build their knowledge and to apply that knowledge as skills (we call this '**implementation**'). Finally, inspectors will consider the outcomes that pupils achieve as a result of the education they have received (we call this the '**impact**').

Intent

169.   In evaluating the school's educational intent, inspectors will primarily consider the curriculum leadership provided by school, subject and curriculum leaders.

170.   The judgement focuses on factors that both research and inspection evidence indicate contribute most strongly to an effective education where pupils achieve highly. These factors are listed below.

- The school's curriculum is rooted in the solid consensus of the school's leaders about the knowledge and skills that pupils need in order to take advantage of opportunities, responsibilities and experiences of later life. In this way, it can powerfully address social disadvantage.

- It is clear what end points the curriculum is building towards and what pupils need to know and be able to do to reach those end points.
- The school's curriculum is planned and sequenced so that new knowledge and skills build on what has been taught before and towards its clearly defined end points.
- The curriculum reflects the school's local context by addressing typical gaps in pupils' knowledge and skills.
- The curriculum remains as broad as possible for as long as possible. Pupils are able to study a strong academic core of subjects, such as those offered by the EBacc.
- There is high academic/vocational/technical ambition for all pupils, and the school does not offer disadvantaged pupils or pupils with SEND a reduced curriculum.

Curriculum flexibility

171.   The curriculum sets out the aims of a programme of education. It also sets out the structure for those aims to be implemented, including the knowledge and skills to be gained at each stage. It enables the evaluation of pupils' knowledge and skills against those expectations.

172.   All pupils in maintained schools are expected to study the basic curriculum, which includes national curriculum[66], religious education and age-appropriate relationship and sex education[67]. Academies are expected to offer all pupils a broad curriculum[68] that should be similar in breadth and ambition.

173.   We will judge schools taking radically different approaches to the curriculum fairly. We recognise the importance of schools' autonomy to choose their own curriculum approaches. If leaders are able to show that they have thought carefully, that they have built a curriculum with appropriate coverage, content, structure and sequencing, and that it has been implemented effectively, then inspectors will assess a school's curriculum favourably.

Curriculum narrowing

174.   Our research has shown that some schools narrow the curriculum available to pupils, particularly in key stages 2 and 3. Our research also shows that this has a disproportionately negative effect on the most disadvantaged pupils.[69] In key stage 1, inspectors need to check that pupils are able to read,[70] write and use mathematical knowledge, ideas and operations so they are able to access a broad and balanced curriculum at key stage 2. In secondary education, inspectors will expect to see a broad, rich curriculum. Inspectors will be particularly alert to signs of narrowing in the key stage 2 and 3 curriculums. If a school has shortened key stage 3, inspectors will look to see that the school has made provision to ensure that pupils still have the opportunity to study a broad range of subjects, commensurate with the national curriculum, in Years 7 to 9.

175.   At the heart of an effective key stage 4 curriculum is a strong academic core: the

EBacc. The government's response to its EBacc consultation, published in July 2017, confirmed that the large majority of pupils should be expected to study the EBacc. It is therefore the government's national ambition that 75% of Year 10 pupils in state-funded mainstream schools should be starting to study EBacc GCSE courses nationally by 2022 (taking their examinations in 2024), rising to 90% by 2025 (taking their examinations in 2027). This is an ambition, and not a target for any individual school. Inspectors will not make a judgement about the quality of education based solely or primarily on its progress towards the EBacc ambition. Nevertheless, it is an important factor in understanding a school's level of ambition for its pupils. It is, therefore, important that inspectors understand what schools are doing to prepare for this to be achieved, and they should take those preparations into consideration when evaluating the intent of the school's curriculum.

Cultural capital

176. As part of making the judgement about the quality of education, inspectors will consider the extent to which schools are equipping pupils with the knowledge and cultural capital they need to succeed in life. Our understanding of 'knowledge and cultural capital' is derived from the following wording in the national curriculum:[71]

'It is the essential knowledge that pupils need to be educated citizens, introducing them to the best that has been thought and said and helping to engender an appreciation of human creativity and achievement.'

Sources of evidence specific to curriculum intent

177. Inspectors will draw evidence about leaders' curriculum intent principally from discussion with senior and subject leaders. Inspectors will explore:

- whether leaders are following the national curriculum and basic curriculum or, in academies, a curriculum of similar breadth and ambition
- how carefully leaders have thought about what end points the curriculum is building towards, what pupils will be able to know and do at those end points, and how leaders have planned the curriculum accordingly. This includes considering how the intended curriculum will address social disadvantage by addressing gaps in pupils' knowledge and skills
- how leaders have sequenced the curriculum to enable pupils to build their knowledge and skills towards the agreed end points
- how leaders have ensured that the subject curriculum contains content that has been identified as most useful, and ensured that this content is taught in a logical progression, systematically and explicitly enough for all pupils to acquire the intended knowledge and skills
- how the curriculum has been designed and taught so that pupils read at an age-appropriate level.

178. Inspectors will bear in mind that developing and embedding an effective curriculum takes time, and that leaders may only be partway through the process of adopting or redeveloping a curriculum. If leaders have an accurate evaluative

understanding of current curriculum practice in their school and have identified appropriate next steps to improve curriculum quality and develop curriculum expertise across the school, inspectors will evaluate 'intent' favourably when reaching the holistic quality of education judgement. They will recognise that the criteria for a judgement of good are the best fit.

179. Inspectors will also consider any documents that leaders normally use in their curriculum planning, but will not request materials to be produced or provided in any specific format for inspection.

Implementation

180. In evaluating the implementation of the curriculum, inspectors will primarily evaluate how the curriculum is taught at subject and classroom level.

181. Research and inspection evidence suggest that the most important factors in how, and how effectively, the curriculum is taught and assessed are that:

- Teachers have expert knowledge of the subjects that they teach. If they do not, they are supported to address gaps in their knowledge so that pupils are not disadvantaged by ineffective teaching.
- Teachers enable pupils to understand key concepts, presenting information clearly and encourage appropriate discussion.
- Teachers check pupils' understanding effectively, and identify and correct misunderstandings.
- Teachers ensure that pupils embed key concepts in their long-term memory and apply them fluently.
- The subject curriculum is designed and delivered in a way that allows pupils to transfer key knowledge to long-term memory. It is sequenced so that new knowledge and skills build on what has been taught before and pupils can work towards clearly defined end points.
- Teachers use assessment to check pupils' understanding in order to inform teaching, and to help pupils embed and use knowledge fluently and develop their understanding, and not simply memorise disconnected facts.

Developing understanding, not memorising disconnected facts

182. Learning can be defined as an alteration in long-term memory. If nothing has altered in long-term memory, nothing has been learned. However, transfer to long-term memory depends on the rich processes described above. In order to develop understanding, pupils connect new knowledge with existing knowledge. Pupils also need to develop fluency and unconsciously apply their knowledge as skills. This must not be reduced to, or confused with, simply memorising facts. Inspectors will be alert to unnecessary or excessive attempts to simply prompt pupils to learn glossaries or long lists of disconnected facts.

The school's use of assessment

183.   When used effectively, assessment helps pupils to embed knowledge and use it fluently, and assists teachers in producing clear next steps for pupils. However, assessment is too often carried out in a way that creates unnecessary burdens for staff and pupils. It is therefore important that leaders and teachers understand its limitations and avoid misuse and overuse.

184.   Inspectors will therefore evaluate how assessment is used in the school to support the teaching of the curriculum, but not substantially increase teachers' workloads by necessitating too much one-to-one teaching or overly demanding programmes that are almost impossible to deliver without lowering expectations of some pupils.

185.   The collection of data can also create an additional workload for leaders and staff. Inspectors will look at whether schools' collections of attainment or progress data are proportionate, represent an efficient use of school resources, and are sustainable for staff. The Teacher Workload Advisory Group's report, 'Making data work',[72] recommends that school leaders should not have more than two or three data collection points a year, and that these should be used to inform clear actions.

186.   Schools choosing to use more than two or three data collection points a year should have clear reasoning for what interpretations and actions are informed by the frequency of collection; the time taken to set assessments, collate, analyse and interpret the data; and the time taken to then act on the findings. If a school's system for data collection is disproportionate, inefficient or unsustainable for staff, inspectors will reflect this in their reporting on the school.

Sources of evidence specific to curriculum implementation

187.   The following activities will provide inspectors with evidence about the school's implementation of its intended curriculum:

- discussions with curriculum and subject leaders and teachers about the programme of study that classes are following for particular subjects or topics, the intended end points towards which those pupils are working, and their view of how those pupils are progressing through the curriculum
- discussions with subject specialists and leaders about the content and pedagogical content knowledge of teachers, and what is done to support them
- discussions with classroom teachers about how often they are expected to record, upload and review data
- observations of and interviews with pupils or classes who are following this curriculum in lessons, including scrutinising the pupils' work[73]
- reviews of schemes of work or other long-term planning (in whatever form subject leaders normally use them), usually in discussion with curriculum leaders.

188.   Inspectors should refer to the 'Lesson observation and work scrutiny' section in Part 1 of this handbook for guidance about what constitutes an appropriate sample of

pupils.

189.   In order to triangulate evidence effectively, inspectors will ensure that they gather a variety of these types of evidence in relation to the same sample of pupils. Inspectors will also ensure that the samples of pupils they choose are sufficient to allow them to reach a valid and reliable judgement on the quality of education offered by the school overall. Guidance on how to ensure that this evidence is both sufficiently valid and reliable is set out under 'Overarching approach to inspection' in Part 1 of this handbook.

Impact

190.   When inspectors evaluate the impact of the education provided by the school, their focus will primarily be on what pupils have learned.

191.   Inspection experience and research show that the most important factors to consider are that:

- A well-constructed, well-taught curriculum will lead to good results because those results will reflect what pupils have learned. There need be no conflict between teaching a broad, rich curriculum and achieving success in examinations and tests.
- Disadvantaged pupils and pupils with SEND acquire the knowledge and cultural capital they need to succeed in life.
- National assessments and examinations are useful indicators of pupils' outcomes, but they only represent a sample of what pupils have learned. Inspectors will balance outcomes with their first-hand assessment of pupils' work.
- All learning builds towards an end point. Learners are being prepared for their next stage of education, training or employment at each stage of their learning. Inspectors will consider whether pupils are ready for the next stage by the point they leave the school or provision that they attend.
- Pupils in sixth form are ready for the next stage and are going on to appropriate, high-quality destinations. Inspectors will also consider this.
- If pupils are not able to read to an age-appropriate level and fluency, they will be incapable of accessing the rest of the curriculum, and they will rapidly fall behind their peers. (See paragraphs 280–282).

Inspectors will not use schools' internal assessment data as evidence

192.   Inspectors will not look at non-statutory internal progress and attainment data[74] on section 5 and section 8 inspections of schools.[75] That does not mean that schools cannot use data if they consider it appropriate. Inspectors will, however, put more focus on the curriculum and less on schools' generation, analysis and interpretation of data. Teachers have told us they believe this will help us play our part in reducing unnecessary workload. Inspectors will be interested in the conclusions drawn and actions taken from any internal assessment information, but they will not examine or verify that information first hand. Inspectors will still use published national performance data as a starting point on

inspection.

193. Inspectors will use the official IDSR as a starting point and get to see first hand the quality of education as experienced by pupils and understand how well leaders know what it is like to be a pupil at the school.

194. Inspectors will ask schools to explain why they have decided to collect whatever assessment data they collect, what they are drawing from their data and how that informs their curriculum and teaching.

Sources of evidence specific to curriculum impact

195. Inspectors will gather evidence of the impact of the quality of education offered by the school from the following sources:

- the progress that pupils are making in terms of knowing more, remembering more and being able to do more
- nationally generated performance information about pupils' progress and attainment. This information is available in the IDSR, which is available to schools and inspectors, and will be analysed for its statistical significance in advance by Ofsted's data and insight team
- first-hand evidence of how pupils are doing, drawing together evidence from the interviews, observations, work scrutinies and documentary review described above (see 'Implementation – sources of evidence')
- nationally published information about the destinations to which its pupils progress when they leave the school[76]
- in primary schools, listening to a range of pupils read
- discussions with pupils about what they have remembered about the content they have studied
- how well pupils with SEND are prepared for the next stage of education and their adult lives.[77]

196. Inspectors will recognise that some schools are in turn-around, including when they have been brokered into a MAT or rebrokered from one to another. In these schools, the quality of education may have been poor and may now be showing significant and sustained improvement. In these situations, nationally generated performance data may lag behind the current quality of education in the school and so inspectors will view the national data in this context.

Reaching a single quality of education judgement, drawing together intent, implementation and impact

197. Inspectors will **not** grade intent, implementation and impact separately. Instead, inspectors will reach a single graded judgement for the quality of education, drawing on all the evidence they have gathered and using their professional judgement.

Grade descriptors for the quality of education

Note: Some sections of the criteria appear in [square brackets] below. This is to mark that they are transitional only, because we recognise that not all schools will have had the opportunity to complete the process of adopting or constructing their curriculum fully by

September 2019. We will review these bracketed sections before September 2020 to decide whether they should be deleted.

Outstanding (1)

- The school meets all the criteria for a good quality of education securely and consistently.
- The quality of education provided is exceptional.
- In addition, the following apply.
- The school's curriculum intent and implementation are embedded securely and consistently across the school. It is evident from what teachers do that they have a firm and common understanding of the school's curriculum intent and what it means for their practice. Across all parts of the school, series of lessons contribute well to delivering the curriculum intent.
- The work given to pupils, over time and across the school, consistently matches the aims of the curriculum. It is coherently planned and sequenced towards cumulatively sufficient knowledge and skills for future learning and employment.
- Pupils' work across the curriculum is consistently of a high quality.
- Pupils consistently achieve highly, particularly the most disadvantaged. Pupils with SEND achieve exceptionally well

In order to judge whether a school is **good** or **requires improvement**, inspectors will use a 'best fit' approach, relying on the professional judgement of the inspection team.

Good (2)

Intent

- Leaders adopt or construct a curriculum that is ambitious and designed to give all pupils, particularly disadvantaged pupils and including pupils with SEND, the knowledge and cultural capital they need to succeed in life. This is either the national curriculum or a curriculum of comparable breadth and ambition. [If this is not yet fully the case, it is clear from leaders' actions that they are in the process of bringing this about.]
- The school's curriculum is coherently planned and sequenced towards cumulatively sufficient knowledge and skills for future learning and employment. [If this is not yet fully the case, it is clear from leaders' actions that they are in the process of bringing this about.]
- The curriculum is successfully adapted, designed or developed to be ambitious and meet the needs of pupils with SEND, developing their knowledge, skills and abilities to apply what they know and can do with increasing fluency and independence. [If this is not yet fully the

case, it is clear from leaders' actions that they are in the process of bringing this about.]

- Pupils study the full curriculum; it is not narrowed. In primary schools, a broad range of subjects (exemplified by the national curriculum) is taught in key stage 2 throughout each and all of Years 3 to 6. In secondary schools, the school teaches a broad range of subjects (exemplified by the national curriculum) throughout Years 7 to 9. [If this is not yet fully the case, it is clear from leaders' actions that they are in the process of bringing this about.] The school's aim is to have the EBacc at the heart of its curriculum, in line with the DfE's ambition,[78] and good progress has been made towards this ambition.

Implementation

- Teachers have good knowledge of the subject(s) and courses they teach. Leaders provide effective support for those teaching outside their main areas of expertise.

- Teachers present subject matter clearly, promoting appropriate discussion about the subject matter being taught. They check pupils' understanding systematically, identify misconceptions accurately and provide clear, direct feedback. In so doing, they respond and adapt their teaching as necessary without unnecessarily elaborate or individualised approaches.

- Over the course of study, teaching is designed to help pupils to remember long term the content they have been taught and to integrate new knowledge into larger ideas.

- Teachers and leaders use assessment well, for example to help pupils embed and use knowledge fluently, or to check understanding and inform teaching. Leaders understand the limitations of assessment and do not use it in a way that creates unnecessary burdens on staff or pupils.

- Teachers create an environment that focuses on pupils. The textbooks and other teaching materials that teachers select – in a way that does not create unnecessary workload for staff – reflect the school's ambitious intentions for the course of study. These materials clearly support the intent of a coherently planned curriculum, sequenced towards cumulatively sufficient knowledge and skills for future learning and employment.

- The work given to pupils is demanding and matches the aims of the curriculum in being coherently planned and sequenced towards cumulatively sufficient knowledge.

- Reading is prioritised to allow pupils to access the full curriculum offer.

- A rigorous and sequential approach to the reading curriculum develops pupils' fluency, confidence and enjoyment in reading. At all stages, reading attainment is assessed and gaps are addressed quickly and effectively for all pupils. Reading books connect closely to the phonics knowledge pupils are taught when they are learning to read.
- The sharp focus on ensuring that younger children gain phonics knowledge and language comprehension necessary to read, and the skills to communicate, gives them the foundations for future learning.
- Teachers ensure that their own speaking, listening, writing and reading of English support pupils in developing their language and vocabulary well.

Impact

- Pupils develop detailed knowledge and skills across the curriculum and, as a result, achieve well. This is reflected in results from national tests and examinations that meet government expectations, or in the qualifications obtained.
- Pupils are ready for the next stage of education, employment or training. They have the knowledge and skills they need and, where relevant, they gain qualifications that allow them to go on to destinations that meet their interests and aspirations and the intention of their course of study. Pupils with SEND achieve the best possible outcomes.
- Pupils' work across the curriculum is of good quality.
- Pupils read widely and often, with fluency and comprehension appropriate to their age. They are able to apply mathematical knowledge, concepts and procedures appropriately for their age.

Requires improvement (3)

- The quality of education provided by the school is not good.

Inadequate (4)

The quality of education is likely to be inadequate if any one of the following applies.

- The school's curriculum has little or no structure or coherence, and leaders have not appropriately considered sequencing. Pupils experience a jumbled, disconnected series of lessons that do not build their knowledge, skills or understanding.

- The pupils' experiences in lessons contribute weakly to their learning of the intended curriculum.

- The range of subjects is narrow and does not prepare pupils for the opportunities, responsibilities and experiences of life in modern Britain.

- Pupils cannot communicate, read, write or apply mathematics sufficiently well for their age and are therefore unable to succeed in the next year or stage of education, or in training or employment. (This does not apply for some pupils with SEND.)

- The progress that disadvantaged pupils make is consistently well below that of other pupils nationally and shows little or no improvement.

- Pupils with SEND do not benefit from a good-quality education. Expectations of them are low, and their needs are not accurately identified, assessed or met.

- Pupils have not attained the qualifications appropriate for them to progress to their next stages of education, training or employment.

Behaviour and attitudes

198.　The behaviour and attitudes judgement considers how leaders and staff create a safe, calm, orderly and positive environment in the school and the impact this has on the behaviour and attitudes of pupils.

199.　The judgement focuses on the factors that research and inspection evidence[79] indicate contribute most strongly to pupils' positive behaviour and attitudes, thereby giving them the greatest possible opportunity to achieve positive outcomes. These factors are:

- A calm and orderly environment in the school and the classroom, as this is essential for pupils to be able to learn.
- The setting of clear routines and expectations for the behaviour of pupils across all aspects of school life, not just in the classroom.
- A strong focus on attendance and punctuality so that disruption is minimised.
- Clear and effective behaviour and attendance policies with clearly defined consequences that are applied consistently and fairly by all staff. Children, and particularly adolescents, often have particularly strong concepts of fairness that may be challenged by different treatment by different teachers or of different pupils.
- Pupils' motivation and positive attitudes to learning as important predictors of attainment. The development of positive attitudes can also have a longer-term impact on how pupils approach learning tasks in later stages of education.
- A positive and respectful school culture in which staff know and care about pupils.
- An environment in which pupils feel safe, and in which bullying, discrimination and peer-on-peer abuse – online or offline– are not accepted and are dealt with quickly, consistently and effectively whenever they occur.

200.　Our evidence for the importance of each of these factors comes from our inspection experience, areas of agreement in academic research and our own research. A full note of how the criteria relate to the available research can be found in our research commentary.[80]

Pupils who have particular needs

201.　The school may be working with pupils with particular needs in order to improve their behaviour or their attendance. When this is the case, 'behaviour and conduct that reflects the school's high expectations and their consistent, fair implementation' are likely to include demonstrable improvement in the attendance and behaviour of these pupils, taking account of the individual circumstances of the school.

Pupils who are not in the school during the inspection

202.　Inspectors will gather evidence about the typical behaviour of all the pupils who attend the school, including those who are not present on the day of inspection. If there is evidence that a school has deliberately removed pupils from the school site on the day of inspection or has arranged for them to be absent, and inspectors reasonably believe that this was done in order to have an impact on the inspection, then inspectors are likely to judge both behaviour and attitudes and leadership and management to be inadequate.

Exclusions

203. Headteachers have the right to exclude pupils when there are legitimate reasons for them to do so. Used correctly, exclusion is a vital measure for headteachers to use. Exclusions must be legal and justified. Permanent exclusions should only be used as a last resort, in response to a serious breach or persistent breaches of the school's behaviour policy, and when allowing the pupil to remain in school would seriously harm the education or welfare of the pupil or others in the school.

204. If a school uses fixed-term and internal exclusions, inspectors will evaluate their effectiveness, including the rates, patterns and reasons for exclusion and whether any pupils are repeatedly excluded. Schools should have a strategy for reintegrating a pupil who returns to school following a fixed-term exclusion and for managing their future behaviour. Inspectors will consider how well the school is recognising and acting to address any patterns that exist, because disruptive behaviour or sudden changes in behaviour can be an indication of unmet needs or a change in another aspect of a young person's life.

205. Inspectors will consider whether the school is developing the use of alternative strategies to exclusion and taking account of any safeguarding risks to pupils who may be excluded. Inspectors will recognise when schools are doing all that they can to support pupils at risk of exclusion, including through tenacious attempts to engage local support services.

Sources of evidence specific to behaviour and attitudes

206. Inspectors will hold discussions with pupils and staff to gather evidence about school culture and practice in relation to pupils' behaviour, support for staff and other systems. In setting up discussions, inspectors will select a sample of staff who research suggests are most affected by pupils' challenging behaviour. These are trainees, supply staff, NQTs, administrative support staff and catering staff, as well as other members of staff. The discussions will provide inspectors with valuable information that includes the views of those who most urgently require the school's support in managing pupils' behaviour. Where practically possible, inspectors should carry out discussions with individuals, not groups, to allow members of staff to give clear evidence without being influenced by the views or expectations of others in the group when talking about a sensitive issue.

207. Inspectors will speak to pupils from a range of different backgrounds and who have different experiences of the school's approach to behaviour. This should include pupils who have experienced sanctions under the school's behaviour policy. Inspectors will take into account the views of these pupils, their experiences of others' behaviour and attitudes towards them, and their understanding of the importance of positive behaviour in

school and beyond school.

208.   Inspectors will evaluate the experience of particular individuals and groups, such as pupils for whom referrals have been made to the local authority (and check, for a small sample of these pupils, how the referral was made and the thoroughness of the follow-up), pupils with SEND, children looked after, those with medical needs and those with mental health needs. In order to do this, inspectors will look at the experience of a small sample of these pupils and consider the way the school is working with the multi-agency group to ensure that the child receives the support they need. For pupils with SEND, this will include ensuring that appropriate reasonable adjustments are made in accordance with the Equality Act 2010 and the SEND code of practice.

209.   The pupil and staff surveys used in inspection contain questions about safeguarding, behaviour and discipline, bullying, how respondents feel about the school and how well supported and respected they feel they are in the school. Inspectors will meet school leaders to account for the results of the pupil and staff interviews and surveys.

210.   Over the course of inspection, inspectors will carry out evidence-gathering activities. In some cases, inspectors will be able to gather this evidence as part of other activities they are carrying out. The activities are:

- observing pupils' behaviour in a range of different classes at different times of the day
- observing pupils at breaktimes, lunchtimes, between lessons and, if they are led and managed by the school, before- and after-school clubs
- observing pupils' punctuality in arriving at school and at lessons
- observing pupils' respect for, and courtesy and good manners towards, each other and adults, and their pride in themselves and their school
- evaluating the school's analysis of, and response to, pupils' behaviour over time, in whatever format the school already has
- analysing absence and persistent absence rates for all pupils, and for different groups compared with national averages for all pupils; this includes the extent to which low attenders are improving their attendance over time and whether attendance is consistently low
- evaluating the prevalence of permanent exclusion, the procedures surrounding this and the reasons for it, and the support given to make sure that it is a last resort
- evaluating the effectiveness of fixed-term and internal exclusions, including the rates and reasons for exclusion
- assessing the school's work to follow up and support fixed-term excluded pupils
- gathering the views of parents, staff, those with responsibility for governance and other stakeholders
- gathering evidence about the typical behaviour of pupils who are not in school

during the inspection, for example whether they have had fixed-term or internal exclusions in the two years before inspection

■ balancing evidence seen during the inspection and evidence of trends over time

■ visiting any off-site unit that the school runs (on its own or in partnership with other schools) for pupils whose behaviour is poor or who have low attendance. Inspectors will assess safeguarding procedures, the quality of education and how effectively the unit helps to improve pupils' behaviour, learning and attendance. For more information, see 'Off-site provision' (paragraphs 226–229).

Grade descriptors for behaviour and attitudes

In order for behaviour and attitudes to be judged outstanding, it must meet all of the good criteria securely and consistently and it must also meet the additional outstanding criteria.

Outstanding (1)

- **The school meets all the criteria for good in behaviour and attitudes securely and consistently.**

- **Behaviour and attitudes are exceptional.**

In addition, the following apply:

- **Pupils behave with consistently high levels of respect for others. They play a highly positive role in creating a school environment in which commonalities are identified and celebrated, difference is valued and nurtured, and bullying, harassment and violence are never tolerated.**

- **Pupils consistently have highly positive attitudes and commitment to their education. They are highly motivated and persistent in the face of difficulties. Pupils make a highly positive, tangible contribution to the life of the school and/or the wider community. Pupils actively support the well-being of other pupils.**

Pupils behave consistently well, demonstrating high levels of self-control and consistently positive attitudes to their education. If pupils struggle with this, the school takes intelligent, fair and highly effective action to support them to succeed in their education.

211.   In order to judge whether a school is good or requires improvement, inspectors will use a 'best fit' approach, relying on the professional judgement of the inspection team.

Good (2)

- **The school has high expectations for pupils' behaviour and conduct. These expectations are commonly understood and applied consistently and fairly. This is reflected in pupils' positive behaviour and conduct. Low-level disruption is not tolerated and pupils' behaviour does not disrupt lessons or the day-to-day life of the school. Leaders support all staff well in managing pupil behaviour. Staff make sure that pupils follow appropriate routines.**

- **Leaders, staff and pupils create a positive environment in which bullying is not tolerated. If bullying, aggression, discrimination and derogatory language occur, they are dealt with quickly and effectively and are not allowed to spread.**

- **There is demonstrable improvement in the behaviour and attendance of pupils who have particular needs.**

- **Pupils' attitudes to their education are positive. They are committed to their** learning, know how to study effectively and do so, are resilient to setbacks and take pride in their achievements.

- Pupils have high attendance, come to school on time and are punctual to lessons. When this is not the case, the school takes appropriate, swift and effective action.

- Fixed-term and internal exclusions are used appropriately. The school reintegrates excluded pupils on their return and manages their behaviour effectively. Permanent exclusions are used appropriately[81] as a lastresort.

- Relationships among pupils and staff reflect a positive and respectful culture; pupils are safe and they feel safe.

Requires improvement (3)

- Behaviour and attitudes in the school are not good.

- Pupils are safe and they feel safe.

Inadequate (4)

Behaviour and attitudes are likely to be inadequate if any one of the following applies.

- Leaders are not taking effective steps to secure good behaviour from pupils and a consistent approach to discipline. They do not support staff adequately in managing behaviour.

- Pupils' lack of engagement and persistent low-level and/or high-level wilful disruption contribute to reduced learning and/or disorderly classrooms.

- A significant minority of pupils show a lack of respect for each other and/or staff and a lack of self-discipline. Pupils frequently ignore or rebut requests from teachers to moderate their conduct. This results in poor behaviour around the school.

- Pupils show negative attitudes towards the value of good manners and behaviour as important factors in school life, adult life and work.

- Attendance is consistently low for all pupils or groups of pupils and shows little sign of sustained improvement.

- Incidents of bullying or prejudiced and discriminatory behaviour, both direct and indirect, are frequent.

- Pupils have little confidence in the school's ability to tackle harassment, bullying, violence and/or discriminatory behaviour successfully.

- Pupils or particular groups of pupils are not safe or do not feel safe at school and/or at alternative placements.

Personal development

212. The curriculum provided by schools should extend beyond the academic, technical or vocational. Schools support pupils to develop in many diverse aspects of life. The personal development judgement evaluates the school's intent to provide for the personal development of all pupils, and the quality with which the school implements this work. It recognises that the impact of the school's provision for personal development will often not be assessable during pupils' time at school.

213. At the same time as the school is working with pupils, those pupils are also being influenced by other factors in their home environment, their community and elsewhere. Schools can teach pupils how to build their confidence and resilience, for example, but they cannot always determine how well young people draw on this. Schools are crucial in preparing pupils for their adult lives, teaching them to understand how to engage with society and providing them with plentiful opportunities to do so. In this judgement, therefore, inspectors will seek to evaluate the quality and intent of what a school provides (either directly or by drawing on high-quality agencies and providers, for example the Duke of Edinburgh award scheme, Cadet Forces and the National Citizenship Service), but will not attempt to measure the impact of the school's work on the lives of individual pupils.

214. This judgement focuses on the dimensions of the personal development of pupils that our education system has agreed, either by consensus or statute, are the most significant. These are:

- developing responsible, respectful and active citizens who are able to play their part and become actively involved in public life as adults
- developing and deepening pupils' understanding of the fundamental British values of democracy, individual liberty, the rule of law and mutual respect and tolerance
- promoting equality of opportunity so that all pupils can thrive together, understanding that difference is a positive, not a negative, and that individual characteristics make people unique
- promoting an inclusive environment that meets the needs of all pupils, irrespective of age, disability, gender reassignment, race, religion or belief, sex or sexual orientation
- developing pupils' character, which we define as a set of positive personal traits, dispositions and virtues that informs their motivation and guides their conduct so that they reflect wisely, learn eagerly, behave with integrity and cooperate consistently well with others. This gives pupils the qualities they need to flourish in our society
- developing pupils' confidence, resilience and knowledge so that they can keep themselves mentally healthy
- enabling pupils to recognise online and offline risks to their well-being – for example, risks from criminal and sexual exploitation, domestic abuse, female

genital mutilation, forced marriage, substance misuse, gang activity, radicalisation and extremism – and making them aware of the support available to them

■ enabling pupils to recognise the dangers of inappropriate use of mobile technology and social media

■ developing pupils' understanding of how to keep physically healthy, eat healthily and maintain an active lifestyle, including giving ample opportunities for pupils to be active during the school day and through extra-curricular activities

■ developing pupils' age-appropriate understanding of healthy relationships through appropriate relationship and sex education

■ providing an effective careers programme in line with the government's statutory guidance on careers advice that offers pupils:

 – unbiased careers advice

 – experience of work, and

 – contact with employers to encourage pupils to aspire, make good choices and understand what they need to do to reach and succeed in the careers to which they aspire[82]

■ supporting readiness for the next phase of education, training or employment so that pupils are equipped to make the transition successfully.

Spiritual, moral, social and cultural development

215. Inspectors will evaluate the effectiveness of the school's provision for pupils' spiritual, moral, social and cultural education.[83] This is a broad concept that can be seen across the school's activities, but draws together many of the areas covered by the personal development judgement.

216. Provision for the spiritual development of pupils includes developing their:

■ ability to be reflective about their own beliefs (religious or otherwise) and perspective on life

■ knowledge of, and respect for, different people's faiths, feelings and values

■ sense of enjoyment and fascination in learning about themselves, others and the world around them

■ use of imagination and creativity in their learning

■ willingness to reflect on their experiences.

217. Provision for the moral development of pupils includes developing their:

■ ability to recognise the difference between right and wrong and to readily apply this understanding in their own lives, and to recognise legal boundaries and, in doing so, respect the civil and criminal law of England

■ understanding of the consequences of their behaviour and actions

■ interest in investigating and offering reasoned views about moral and ethical issues and ability to understand and appreciate the viewpoints of others on these issues.

218. Provision for the social development of pupils includes developing their:

■ use of a range of social skills in different contexts, for example working and socialising with other pupils, including those from different religious, ethnic and socio-economic backgrounds

■ willingness to participate in a variety of communities and social settings, including by volunteering, cooperating well with others and being able to resolve conflicts effectively

■ acceptance of and engagement with the fundamental British values of democracy, the rule of law, individual liberty and mutual respect and tolerance of those with different faiths and beliefs. They will develop and demonstrate skills and attitudes that will allow them to participate fully in and contribute positively to life in modern Britain.

219. Provision for the cultural development of pupils includes developing their:

■ understanding and appreciation of the wide range of cultural influences that have shaped their own heritage and that of others

■ understanding and appreciation of the range of different cultures in the school and further afield as an essential element of their preparation for life in modern Britain

■ ability to recognise, and value, the things we share in common across cultural, religious, ethnic and socio-economic communities

■ knowledge of Britain's democratic parliamentary system and its central role in shaping our history and values, and in continuing to develop Britain

■ willingness to participate in and respond positively to artistic, musical, sporting and cultural opportunities

■ interest in exploring, improving understanding of and showing respect for different faiths and cultural diversity and the extent to which they understand, accept, respect and celebrate diversity. This is shown by their respect and attitudes towards different religious, ethnic and socio-economic groups in the local, national and global communities.

Relationships and Sex Education

220. From September 2019, schools are able to follow a new relationships and sex education and health education curriculum. From September 2020, they will be required by law to follow it. Primary-age children must be taught about positive relationships and respect for others, and how these are linked to promoting good mental health and well-being. In addition, sex education will become mandatory at secondary level.

221. If a school is failing to meet its obligations, inspectors will consider this when reaching the personal development judgement.

Sources of evidence specific to personal development

222. Inspectors will use a range of evidence to evaluate personal development,

including:

- the range, quality and take-up of extra-curricular activities offered by the school[84]
- how curriculum subjects such as citizenship, RE, and other areas such as personal, social, health and economic education, and relationship and sex education, contribute to pupils' personal development
- how well leaders promote British values through the curriculum, assemblies, wider opportunities, visits, discussions and literature
- how well leaders develop pupils' character through the education that they provide
- where appropriate, the quality of debate and discussions that pupils have
- pupils' understanding of the protected characteristics[85] and how equality and diversity are promoted
- the quality of careers information, education, advice and guidance, and how well it benefits pupils in choosing and deciding on their next steps.

Grade descriptors for personal development

223.   In order for personal development to be judged outstanding, it must meet all of the good criteria securely and consistently, and it must also meet the additional outstanding criteria.

Outstanding (1)

- **The school meets all the criteria for good in personal development securely and consistently.**
- **Personal development is exceptional.**

In addition, the following apply:

- **The school consistently promotes the extensive personal development of pupils. The school goes beyond the expected, so that pupils have access to a wide, rich set of experiences. Opportunities for pupils to develop their talents and interests are of exceptional quality.**
- **There is strong take-up by pupils of the opportunities provided by the school. The most disadvantaged pupils consistently benefit from this excellent work.**
- **The school provides these rich experiences in a coherently planned way, in the curriculum and through extra-curricular activities, and they considerably strengthen the school's offer.**
- **The way the school goes about developing pupils' character is exemplary and is worthy of being shared with others.**

In order to judge whether a school is good or requires improvement, inspectors will use a 'best fit' approach, relying on the professional judgement of the inspection team.

Good (2)

- The curriculum extends beyond the academic, vocational or technical and provides for pupils' broader development. The school's work to enhance pupils' spiritual, moral, social and cultural development is of a high quality.

- The curriculum and the school's effective wider work support pupils to be confident, resilient and independent, and to develop strength of character.

- The school provides high-quality pastoral support. Pupils know how to eat healthily, maintain an active lifestyle and keep physically and mentally healthy. They have an age-appropriate understanding of healthy relationships.

- The school provides a wide range of opportunities to nurture, develop and stretch pupils' talents and interests. Pupils appreciate these and make good use of them.

- The school prepares pupils for life in modern Britain effectively, developing their understanding of the fundamental British values of democracy, the rule of law, individual liberty, tolerance and respect.

- The school promotes equality of opportunity and diversity effectively. As a result, pupils understand, appreciate and respect difference in the world and its people, celebrating the things we share in common across cultural, religious, ethnic and socio-economic communities.

- Pupils engage with views, beliefs and opinions that are different from their own in considered ways. They show respect for the different protected characteristics as defined in law and no forms of discrimination are tolerated.

- The school provides pupils with meaningful opportunities to understand how to be responsible, respectful, active citizens who contribute positively to society. Pupils know how to discuss and debate issues and ideas in a considered way.

- Secondary schools prepare pupils for future success in education, employment or training. They use the Gatsby Benchmarks[86] to develop and improve their careers provision and enable a range of education and training providers to speak to pupils in Years 8 to 13. All pupils receive unbiased information about potential next steps and high-quality careers guidance. The school provides good quality, meaningful opportunities for pupils to encounter the world of work.

Requires improvement (3)

- Personal development in the school is not good.

Inadequate (4)

Personal development is likely to be inadequate if any one of the following applies.

- **A significant minority of pupils do not receive a wide, rich set of experiences.**

- **Leaders and those responsible for governance, through their words, actions or influence, directly and/or indirectly, undermine or fail to promote equality of opportunity in the school.**

- **Leaders and those responsible for governance are not protecting pupils from radicalisation and extremist views. Policy and practice are poor, which means that pupils are at risk.**

- **Leaders and those responsible for governance are actively undermining fundamental British values and are not protecting pupils from radicalisation and extremist views.**

- **Pupils or groups of pupils are discriminated against, and the school is not taking effective action to address this.**

- **Pupils are unprepared for life in modern Britain.**

- **The school does not ensure that pupils get access to unbiased information about potential next steps, high-quality careers guidance and opportunities for encounters with the world of work.**

Leadership and management

224. The leadership and management judgement is about how leaders, managers and those responsible for governance ensure that the education that the school provides has a positive impact on all its pupils. It focuses on the areas where inspection and research indicate that leaders and managers can have the strongest effect on the quality of the education provided by the school. Important factors include:

- leaders' high expectations of all pupils in the school, and the extent to which these are embodied in leaders' and staff's day-to-day interactions with pupils

- the extent to which leaders focus their attention on the education provided by the school. There are many demands on leaders, but a greater focus on this area is associated with better outcomes for pupils

- whether continuing professional development for teachers and staff is aligned with the curriculum, and the extent to which this develops teachers' content knowledge and teaching content knowledge over time, so that they are able to deliver better teaching for pupils

- the extent to which leaders create coherence and consistency across the school so that pupils benefit from effective teaching and consistent expectations, wherever they are in the school

- whether leaders seek to engage parents and their community thoughtfully and positively in a way that supports pupils' education. Also, whether leaders are thoughtful in drawing boundaries and resisting inappropriate attempts to influence what is taught and the day-to-day life of the school

■ the extent to which leaders take into account the workload and well-being of their staff, while also developing and strengthening the quality of the workforce

■ the extent to which leaders' and managers' high ambitions are for all pupils, including those who are harder to reach. This includes ensuring that practices such as 'off-rolling' do not take place and that the way the school uses the pupil premium is founded on good evidence.

■ whether leaders and those responsible for governance all understand their respective roles and perform these in a way that enhances the effectiveness of the school.

225.   Our evidence for the importance of each of these factors comes from our inspection experience, areas of consensus in academic research and our own research. A full note of how the criteria relate to the available research can be found in our research commentary.[87]

226.   Paragraphs 271–280 set out the importance and place of safeguarding.

Leadership and management in school

227.   Research suggests that leadership and management can be highly effective when they are shared by different individuals and distributed across different levels in a school. Inspectors will look at the work of headteachers, senior leaders, subject leaders and others with leadership and management roles when reaching this judgement.

Leadership and management in multi-academy trusts[88]

228.   When a school is part of a MAT, it is important for inspectors to remember that the trust is one entity, and that leaders and managers of the MAT are responsible for the quality of education provided in all the schools that make up the MAT.

229.   It is highly likely that parts of some of the leadership functions described in the grade criteria are performed by MAT leaders (for example, the CEO or an education director) and not solely by individual leaders of the school. School leaders are responsible for giving inspectors accurate and appropriate information about those roles and responsibilities. If leadership functions are performed by MAT leaders, then inspectors will consider whether they need to meet MAT leaders to gather evidence.

230.   MAT leaders may request to meet inspectors as a part of the inspection. They may also request to attend key inspection team meetings at the end of each inspection day. These are appropriate requests and should be accommodated. These individuals, however, should abide by the same code of conduct as all others involved in the inspection.[89]

Governance

231.   Inspectors will seek evidence of the impact of those responsible for governance.

232.   In a maintained school, those responsible for governance are the school governors. In a stand-alone academy, it is the trustees.

233. In a MAT, the trustees are responsible for governance. Inspectors will ask to speak to one or more of the trustees. It may be that, on occasion, the trustees have chosen to delegate some of their powers to the members of the 'academy committee' or 'local governing board' at school level.[90] If inspectors are informed that a local governing body has delegated responsibilities, they should establish clearly which powers are with the trustees, which are with the leaders of the MAT and which are with the local governing board. They should then ensure that both their inspection activities and the inspection report reflect this.

234. Inspectors will need to bear in mind, when inspecting academies that are part of a MAT, that governance functions can be quite different from those in a maintained school. Some functions that a governing body in a maintained school would carry out may be done by management or executive staff in a trust. If this is the case, it will still be important for inspectors to ascertain the trust board's role in that process and how it ensures that these functions are carried out properly.

235. The governance handbook[91] sets out the purpose of governance, which is to provide confident, strategic leadership, and to create robust accountability, oversight and assurance for educational and financial performance.

236. The governance handbook also sets out the statutory functions of all boards, no matter what type of school or how many schools they govern. There are three core functions:

- ensuring clarity of vision, ethos and strategic direction
- holding executive leaders to account for the educational performance of the school and its pupils, and the performance management of staff
- overseeing the financial performance of the school and making sure that its money is well spent, including the pupil premium.

237. Inspectors will explore how governors carry out each of these functions. For example, the clarity of the school's vision, ethos and strategic direction will have a significant impact on the decisions that leaders make about the curriculum. Inspectors will consider whether the work of governors in this respect is supporting the school to provide a high-quality education for its pupils.

238. In addition, those with governance/oversight are responsible for ensuring that the school fulfils its statutory duties, for example under the Equality Act 2010, and other duties, for example in relation to the 'Prevent' duty and safeguarding. Please note that, when inspectors consider whether governors are fulfilling this responsibility, they are not expected to construct or review a list of duties.

239. Inspectors will report clearly on governance in the inspection report.

Use of the pupil premium

240. Inspectors will gather evidence about the use of the pupil premium, particularly regarding:

- the level of pupil premium funding received by the school in the current academic year and levels of funding received in previous academic years

- how leaders and governors have spent the pupil premium, their rationale for this spending and its intended impact
- the learning and progress of disadvantaged pupils, as shown by published outcomes data.

Evaluating the impact of external support

241.   If the school has received support, for example from the local authority, inspectors will not evaluate and report on the quality and the impact of the support and challenge on improvement in the school. Instead, they will comment on the action that the school has taken and the impact that this has had on the quality of the school's work.

242.   If a school is part of a MAT and is receiving support from within the MAT, inspectors will be clear that this is internal, not external, support.

Inspecting off-site provision

243.   Inspectors must evaluate how well a school continues to take responsibility for its pupils who attend alternative or off-site provision. Inspectors need to be assured that leaders have ensured that the alternative provision is a suitable and safe placement that will meet pupils' academic/vocational/technical needs, pastoral needs and, if appropriate, SEND needs. Inspectors will speak to a selection of pupils who attend off-site provision, where possible.

244.   Inspectors must ask the school about the registration status of any alternative providers that they use. Any provider of alternative provision must be registered as an independent school if it caters full time for five or more pupils of compulsory school age, or one pupil who is looked after or has an education, health and care (EHC) plan. If a school uses alternative provision that should be registered but is not, inspectors will carefully consider whether this affects the likelihood that pupils are safeguarded effectively.

245.   Inspectors will normally visit a sample of any part-time unregistered alternative providers during the inspection, as directed by the relevant Ofsted region. This is to assess the adequacy of the school's quality assurance process. Inspectors should visit any registered alternative provision site that Ofsted has not yet inspected to assess the adequacy of the school's quality assurance process.

246.   Inspectors will consider the quality of registered alternative provision using Ofsted's latest inspection report and assess its impact on the overall quality of education for pupils in a proportionate way.

247.   Inspectors will consider:

- the reasons why leaders considered off-site provision to be the best option for the pupils concerned
- whether leaders have made the appropriate checks on the registration status of the provision
- what safeguarding checks leaders have made and continue to make to ensure that the provision is a safe place for their pupils to attend

- the extent to which leaders ensure that their pupils will benefit from a well-taught, broad and balanced curriculum
- the extent of pupils' progress and attainment
- the attendance and behaviour of the pupils who attend the provision
- how well the provision promotes the pupils' personal development.

248. If a school uses a provider that is not registered, the inspector must contact the duty desk so that staff can notify Ofsted's unregistered schools team. Following the inspection, the team will determine if we need to take further action because there is reasonable cause to believe that the setting is operating as an unregistered school.

249. A school is likely to be judged inadequate for leadership and management if:
- it is making ineffective or inappropriate use of alternative provision
- it is using inappropriate alternative provision
- leaders have not taken the necessary steps to assure themselves of the suitability of a provision
- leaders are not aware of how many of their pupils attend alternative provision
- leaders are not taking responsibility for their pupils who attend alternative provision.

Gaming

250. Inspectors will challenge leaders and managers about unusual patterns of examination entry that appear to 'game the system', for example if they are entering pupils for courses that are not in their educational best interest. The IDSR will provide inspectors with areas to investigate when nationally available data suggests that gaming may be taking place. If inspectors uncover evidence that deliberate and substantial gaming is taking place, the leadership and management judgement is likely to be inadequate.

251. Inspectors will also challenge leaders and managers about unusual patterns in the way that the school records attendance, including the use of inaccurate register codes or changes to when the register is taken. For example, if inspectors reasonably believe that a school is inaccurately recording attendance, has changed the timing of session registration to game attendance rates or is using part-time timetables inappropriately, then inspectors are likely to judge leadership and management to be inadequate.

Inclusion and off-rolling

252. Schools should have an inclusive culture that supports arrangements to:
- identify early those pupils who may be disadvantaged or have additional needs or barriers to learning
- meet the needs of those pupils, drawing, when necessary, on more specialist support, and help those pupils to engage positively with the curriculum
- ensure pupils have a positive experience of learning and achieve positive outcomes.

253. There is no legal definition of 'off-rolling'. However, we define 'off-rolling' as:
The practice of removing a pupil from the school roll without a formal, permanent exclusion

or by encouraging a parent to remove their child from the school roll, when the removal is primarily in the interests of the school rather than in the best interests of the pupil. Off-rolling in these circumstances is a form of 'gaming'.

254.   When an inspection finds evidence of off-rolling taking place by our definition, inspectors should always address this in the inspection report. They may, depending on the scale and impact, need to consider it when reaching the judgement. If the off-rolling is lawful, inspectors must be careful to consider the context of the off-rolling and be clear about what impact the off-rolling has had on pupils involved and on the school. There are many different activities that can constitute off-rolling, so there can be no hard and fast rules as to how it should be addressed. However, if inspectors determine the school to be off- rolling according to our definition, then the leadership and management of the school are likely to be judged inadequate.

255.   There are other reasons why a school might remove a pupil from the school roll, such as when a pupil moves house or a parent decides, without encouragement or coercion by the school, to home educate their child. This is not off-rolling. If the pupil transfers to the roll of their alternative provision, and this is genuinely in the best interest of the pupil, this is not off-rolling. If a school appropriately removes a pupil from the roll due to a formal permanent exclusion and follows the proper processes, this is not off-rolling. Headteachers have the right to exclude pupils when there are legitimate reasons for them to do so. Used correctly, exclusion is a vital measure for headteachers to use.

256.   Dual-registering or dual-coding a pupil in two schools or providers, or using alternative provision while they remain registered at the school, is not off-rolling because the pupil has not left the roll of their school. However, this may still be a form of gaming if it is not in the best interests of the pupil. Managed moves can be a effective tool in breaking a cycle of poor pupil behaviour, but they can also be a form of off-rolling. Managed moves are not off-rolling only when they are genuinely used in a pupil's best interests, within the statutory guidance. If a school uses managed moves, inspectors may ask to see evidence of the ways in which these have been carried out.

257.   Inspectors will be interested in high numbers of pupils moving on and off roll, but this may not in itself mean that off-rolling is taking place.

Safeguarding

258.   All schools should have a culture of safeguarding. This means they should have effective arrangements to:
- always act in the best interests of children, pupils and students to protect them online and offline
- **identify** children, pupils and students who may need early help, and who are at risk of harm or have been harmed. This can include, but is not limited to, neglect, abuse (including by their peers), grooming or exploitation
- secure the **help** that children, pupils and students need, and if required, referring in a timely way to those who have the expertise to help

- **manage** safe recruitment and allegations about adults who may be a risk to children, pupils, students and vulnerable adults.

259.   Inspectors will not grade this aspect of a school's work. However, inspectors will always make a written judgement under 'leadership and management' in the report about whether the arrangements for safeguarding children and pupils are effective.

260.   Inspectors must go beyond ensuring that schools meet statutory requirements, and beyond simply reviewing documents, to evaluate the safeguarding culture that has been established in the school.

261.   As well as understanding Ofsted's inspecting safeguarding policies, inspectors should be familiar with relevant, including statutory, guidance on safeguarding:

- 'Keeping children safe in education: statutory guidance for schools and colleges'[92]
- 'Working together to safeguard children'[93]
- 'Positive environments where children can flourish'.[94]

262.   On all inspections, inspectors need to determine whether there have been any safeguarding incidents or allegations since the last inspection, and whether the school has taken appropriate action to safeguard the children affected and/or to deal with allegations.[95]

263.   On a very small number of occasions, inspectors may come across, during an inspection, evidence or allegations of child abuse. Inspectors must not attempt to investigate any incident of child abuse but will satisfy themselves that concerns about a child's safety are referred, as appropriate, to the relevant local authority's children's services department. The referral will normally be made by the safeguarding lead for the school.[96]

264.   If a child discloses to an inspector on site that they are suffering or at risk of abuse, the inspector will stop all other activity and focus on ensuring that the child receives the help they need. Specific guidance on what to do in this situation can be found in 'Safeguarding concerns: guidance for inspectors'.[97]

265.   The guidance 'Inspecting safeguarding in early years, education and skills settings' explains how incidents will be covered in the inspection report.[98]

266.   Safeguarding is ineffective when there are serious or widespread failures in the school's/setting's safeguarding arrangements that give cause for concern because children are not protected and statutory requirements are not being met, or because insufficient action is being taken to remedy weaknesses following a serious failure of safeguarding arrangements.

267.   The following are examples of what ineffective safeguarding might include.

- Safeguarding allegations about staff members are not being handled appropriately.
- Children, pupils and students or particular groups of children, pupils and students do not feel safe in school/the setting.

- Children, pupils and students have little confidence that the school/setting will address concerns about their safety, including risk of abuse.
- For schools: pupils are frequently missing from school (including for part of the school day), but this is not addressed appropriately by staff.
- Incidents of bullying or prejudiced and discriminatory behaviour are common.

The impact of safeguarding on the leadership and management judgement

268.   When safeguarding is ineffective, this is likely to lead to an inadequate leadership and management judgement. However, there may be circumstances when it is appropriate to judge a setting as requires improvement, rather than inadequate, if there are minor weaknesses in safeguarding arrangements that are easy to put right and do not leave children either being harmed or at risk of harm.

Segregation

269.   It is unlawful for schools to segregate pupils on the basis of any protected characteristics such as sex, race or faith, while at school, unless permitted by the Equality Act 2010 for:

- positive action to alleviate a disadvantage associated with a certain characteristic. This could, for example, include pupils of one race or sex getting additional work experience in a sector in which they are under- represented, or separating the pupils by gender for teaching in subjects if the school has evidence that this improves their academic outcomes (section 158)
- competitive sport, games or other competitive activities in which physical strength, stamina or physique are significant factors in determining success or failure. A school is allowed to organise separate events for boys and girls (section 195).

270.   If an inspector believes that a school may be segregating pupils, they will contact the duty desk. If segregation is taking place, inspectors will write about this clearly in the inspection report.

- A school is unlikely to be judged as good or outstanding in leadership and management if it is segregating pupils unlawfully.
- If the school has genuine and imminent plans to reintegrate pupils, a judgement of requires improvement will normally be appropriate.
- In other cases, the grade will likely be inadequate for leadership and management.

Sources of evidence specific to leadership and management

271.   Evidence used to evaluate the impact of leaders' work, both currently and over time, includes, but is not limited to:

- meetings with leaders, including MAT senior staff if appropriate, to discuss how well they know the school and the quality of education that it provides for pupils
- meetings with those responsible for governance, as appropriate, to evaluate

how well they fulfil their statutory duties, including their duties under the Equality Act and in relation to safeguarding

- documentary evidence provided by the school that demonstrates the effectiveness of the school's provision
- interviews with staff and pupils to evidence how well leaders have created a positive culture
- first-hand evidence gathered during the course of inspection
- responses to the staff and pupil questionnaires and Ofsted Parent View; these will be particularly useful for judging the culture that has been established in the school by leaders and managers
- any evidence the school has from regularly surveying its staff and the way in which leaders and managers have responded to concerns raised by staff or parents, for example about how senior leaders support teachers to tackle low-level disruptive behaviour
- if there are unusual patterns of pupil movement, discussions with school leaders, the local authority and (where appropriate) the MAT about those movements.

272. Inspectors will always report on the school's activity to gather the views of staff, whether through the school's internal procedures or through it using the Ofsted questionnaire. They will do this in the 'Information about this inspection' section.

Grade descriptors for leadership and management

273. In order for the leadership and management of a school to be judged outstanding, it must meet all of the good criteria securely and consistently, and it must also meet the additional outstanding criteria.

Outstanding (1)

- **The school meets all the criteria for good in leadership and management securely and consistently.**

- **Leadership and management are exceptional.**

In addition, the following apply:

- **Leaders ensure that teachers receive focused and highly effective professional development. Teachers' subject, pedagogical and pedagogical content knowledge consistently build and develop over time. This consistently translates into improvements in the teaching of the curriculum.**

- **Leaders ensure that highly effective and meaningful engagement takes place with staff at all levels and that issues are identified. When issues are identified, in particular about workload, they are consistently dealt with appropriately and quickly.**

- **Staff consistently report high levels of support for well-being issues.**

274.   In order to judge whether a school is good or requires improvement, inspectors will use a 'best fit' approach, relying on the professional judgement of the inspection team.

Good (2)

- Leaders have a clear and ambitious vision for providing high-quality education to all pupils. This is realised through strong, shared values, policies and practice.

- Leaders focus on improving teachers' subject, pedagogical and pedagogical content knowledge in order to enhance the teaching of the curriculum and the appropriate use of assessment. The practice and subject knowledge of staff, including newly qualified teachers, build and improve over time.

- Leaders aim to ensure that all pupils successfully complete their programmes of study. They provide the support for staff to make this possible. They create an inclusive culture and do not allow gaming or off- rolling.

- Leaders engage effectively with pupils and others in their community, including, when relevant, parents, employers and local services. Engagement opportunities are focused and purposive.

- Leaders engage with their staff and are aware and take account of the main pressures on them. They are realistic and constructive in the way they manage staff, including their workload.

- Leaders protect staff from bullying and harassment.

- Those responsible for governance understand their role and carry this out effectively. Governors/trustees ensure that the school has a clear vision and strategy, that resources are managed well and that leaders are held to account for the quality of education.

- Those with responsibility for governance ensure that the school fulfils its statutory duties, for example under the Equality Act 2010, and other duties, for example in relation to the 'Prevent' duty and safeguarding.

- The school has a culture of safeguarding that supports effective arrangements to: identify pupils who may need early help or who are at risk of neglect, abuse, grooming or exploitation; help pupils reduce their risk of harm by securing the support they need, or referring them in a timely way to those who have the expertise to help; and manage safe recruitment and allegations about adults who may be a risk to pupils.

Requires improvement (3)

- Leadership and management are not good.

- Safeguarding is effective, or there are minor weaknesses in safeguarding arrangements that are easy to put right and do not leave children either being harmed or at risk of harm.

Inadequate (4)

Leadership and management are likely to be inadequate if one or more of the following applies.

- The capacity for improving the quality of education provided by the school, or for improving the personal development and behaviour and attitudes of pupils, is poor or leaders are overly dependent on external support.[99]

- Leaders are not doing enough to tackle weaknesses in the school.

- The improvements that leaders and those responsible for governance have made are unsustainable or have been implemented too slowly.

- The school is systematically gaming its results, entering pupils for courses that are not in their educational best interest.

- There is evidence that pupils have been removed from the school roll without a formal, permanent exclusion or by the school encouraging a parent to remove their child from the school roll, and leaders have taken insufficient action to address this.

- Leaders are not aware of, or are not taking effective action to stem, the decline in the attainment or progress of disadvantaged pupils.

- There is a clear breach of one or more of the legal responsibilities of those responsible for governance, and that breach is serious because of the extent of its actual or potential negative impact on pupils. The proprietor/governing body either is unaware of the breach, or has taken insufficient action to correct it and/or to remedy the negative or potential negative impact on pupils and/or to ensure that a suitable system is in place to prevent a similar breach in the future.

- Safeguarding is ineffective. The school's arrangements for safeguarding pupils do not meet statutory requirements, or they give serious cause for concern, or the school has taken insufficient action to remedy weaknesses following a serious incident.

Evaluating the quality of early years education in schools

275.   Inspectors are required to grade the standards of education and care in any early years provision in schools and to write a section in the inspection report that summarises its effectiveness.

276.   Inspectors must use all their evidence to evaluate what it is like to be a child in the early years provision, taking account of the ages of the children and whether they attend part time or full time.

277.   The effectiveness of the arrangements for safeguarding children is reflected in the main judgement for the school.

278.   Inspectors should take account of all the judgements made across the evaluation schedule. In particular, they should consider:

- the extent to which leaders and staff plan, design and implement the curriculum
- the extent to which the curriculum and care practices meet the needs of the range of children who attend, particularly any children with SEND
- the progress all children make in their learning and development relative to their starting points and their readiness for the next stage of their education
- children's personal, social and emotional development, including whether they feel safe and are secure, stimulated and happy.

279.   Inspectors will particularly consider the intent, implementation and impact of the school's early years curriculum. They will evaluate the impact that the quality of education has on children, particularly the most disadvantaged and those with SEND.

280.   Inspectors will look at the children's achievements at the end of Reception over time, by the proportions reaching a good level of development. However, inspectors need to get beyond the data as quickly as possible to ascertain how well the curriculum is meeting children's needs. This will be evident in how well children know and remember more. Inspectors need to make careful inferences about children's current progress by drawing together evidence from a range of sources.

281.   Schools that take two- and three-year-olds as part of their early years provision do not need to register that provision with Ofsted. We will inspect provision for two- and three-year olds under section 5. Inspectors should ensure that the judgement on the effectiveness of early years provision includes evaluation of the provision for two- and three-year-olds. Inspectors should also note if any children receive additional funding.

282.   Any care that a school provides for children in the early years age range, before and/or after the school day or during school holidays, is considered as part of the evaluation of early years provision.

283.   Inspectors will consider how well:[100]

- leaders assure themselves that the aims of the early years foundation stage (EYFS) are met and that it is sufficiently challenging for the children it serves. Staff ensure that the content, sequencing and progression in the seven areas of learning are secured as appropriate

- the content of the EYFS curriculum is taught in a logical progression, systematically and in a way that is explained effectively, so that it gives children the necessary foundations for the rest of their schooling
- children develop, consolidate and deepen their knowledge, understanding and skills across all the areas of learning in the EYFS. In Reception, staff teach children to read systematically by using synthetic phonics[101] and books that match the children's phonic knowledge
- staff develop children's communication and language through singing songs, nursery rhymes and playing games
- staff develop children's love of reading through reading aloud and telling stories and rhymes
- children demonstrate their attitudes and behaviours through the key characteristics of effective learning:
  - playing and exploring
  - active learning
  - creative thinking and thinking critically.

284. In addition, when observing provision for two- and three-year-olds, inspectors will consider the extent to which leaders and staff are:

- knowledgeable about the typical development and characteristics of learning for two- and three-year-olds, including their emotional and physical dependence on adults
- aware of the large difference in development between children who are just two and those approaching their fourth birthday
- responsive when children need comforting, and provide support appropriate to the individual needs of the child
- attentive to children's care needs and use times caring for them as an opportunity to help children's learning
- giving children time to be in familiar, small groups and opportunities to be in smaller, quieter areas for play
- patient and attentive when allowing two- and three-year-olds to express their ideas
- listening to children and responding to their verbal and non-verbal communication, rather than interrupting them.

Grade descriptors
Intent
Outstanding (1)

- **The school meets all the criteria for good in the effectiveness of early years**
  securely and consistently.

- The quality of early years education provided is exceptional.

In addition, the following apply:

- The EYFS curriculum provides no limits or barriers to the children's achievements, regardless of their backgrounds, circumstances or needs. The high ambition it embodies is shared by all staff.

- The impact of the curriculum on what children know, can remember and do is strong. Children demonstrate this through being deeply engaged and sustaining high levels of concentration. Children, including those from disadvantaged backgrounds, do well. Children with SEND achieve the best possible outcomes.

- Children are highly motivated and are eager to join in. They share and cooperate well, demonstrating high levels of self-control and respect for others. Children consistently keep on trying hard, particularly if they encounter difficulties.

Good (2)

- Leaders adopt or construct a curriculum that is ambitious and designed to give children, particularly the most disadvantaged, the knowledge, self-belief and cultural capital they need to succeed in life.

- The curriculum is coherently planned and sequenced. It builds on what children know and can do, towards cumulatively sufficient knowledge and skills for their future learning.
- There is a sharp focus on ensuring that children acquire a wide vocabulary, communicate effectively and, in Reception, secure a knowledge of phonics, which gives them the foundations for future learning, especially in preparation for them to become confident and fluent readers.
- The school's approach to teaching early reading and synthetic phonics is systematic and ensures that all children learn to read words and simple sentences accurately by the end of Reception.
- The school has the same academic ambitions for almost all children. For children with particular needs, such as those with SEND, their curriculum is designed to be ambitious and to meet their needs.

Implementation[102]

- Children benefit from meaningful learning across the curriculum.
- Staff are knowledgeable about the areas of learning they teach. They manage the EYFS curriculum and pedagogy in relation to the learning needs of their children. Staff are expert in teaching systematic, synthetic phonics and ensure that children practise their reading from books that match their phonics knowledge.

- Staff present information clearly to children, promoting appropriate discussion about the subject matter being taught. They communicate well to check children's understanding, identify misconceptions and provide clear explanations to improve their learning. In so doing, they respond and adapt their teaching as necessary.
- Staff read to children in a way that excites and engages them, introducing new ideas, concepts and vocabulary.
- Staff are knowledgeable about the teaching of early mathematics. They ensure that children have sufficient practice to be confident in using and understanding numbers. The mathematics curriculum provides a strong basis for more complex learning later on. Over the EYFS, teaching is designed to help children remember long term what they have been taught and to integrate new knowledge into larger concepts. This is checked well by staff and leaders. Leaders understand the limitations of assessment and avoid unnecessary burdens on staff or children.
- Staff create an environment that supports the intent of an ambitious, coherently planned and sequenced curriculum. The resources are chosen to meet the children's needs and promote learning.
- The curriculum and care practices promote and support children's emotional security and development of their character. Leaders and staff are particularly attentive to the youngest children's needs.
- Staff give clear messages to children about why it is important to eat, drink, rest, exercise and be kind to each other. They teach children to take managed risks and challenges as they play and learn, supporting them to be active and develop physically.
- Staff provide information for parents about their children progress, in line with the requirements of the EYFS. They provide information to parents about supporting their child's learning at home, including detail about the school's method of teaching reading and how to help their children learn to read.

Impact

- Children develop detailed knowledge and skills across the seven areas of learning in an age-appropriate way. Children develop their vocabulary and use it across the EYFS curriculum. By the end of Reception, children use their knowledge of phonics to read accurately and with increasing speed and fluency.
- Children are ready for the next stage of education, especially Year 1 in school, if applicable. They have the knowledge and skills they need to benefit from what school has to offer when it is time to move on. By the

end of Reception, children achieve well, particularly those children with lower starting points.

- By the end of Reception, children have the personal, physical and social skills they need to succeed in the next stage of their education. Most children achieve the early learning goals, particularly in mathematics and literacy.

- Children enjoy, listen attentively and respond with comprehension to familiar stories, rhymes and songs that are appropriate to their age and stage of development. Children develop their vocabulary and understanding of language across the seven areas of learning.

- Children demonstrate their positive attitudes to learning through high levels of curiosity, concentration and enjoyment. They listen intently and respond positively to adults and each other. Children are developing their resilience to setbacks and take pride in their achievements.

- Children are beginning to manage their own feelings and behaviour, understanding how these have an impact on others. They are developing a sense of right from wrong.

Requires improvement (3)

- The effectiveness of the early years is not yet good.

Inadequate (4)

The effectiveness of the early years is likely to be inadequate if one or more of the following applies.

- A poorly designed and implemented curriculum does not meet children's needs or provide the necessary foundations for the rest of their schooling.

- Leaders and/or staff have a poor understanding of the areas of learning they teach and the way in which young children learn.

- Assessment is overly burdensome. It is unhelpful in determining what children know, understand and can do.

- By the end of Reception, children cannot communicate, read or spell phonically decodable words as well as they should. They do not have basic fluency in number and shape, space and measure.

- Children are not well prepared for the next stage of their learning, particularly those who receive additional funding or have SEND. Strategies for engaging parents are weak and parents do not know what their child is learning or how to help them improve.

- The attainment and progress of children, particularly those who are disadvantaged, are consistently low and show little or no

92

improvement, indicating that children are underachieving considerably.

Evaluating sixth-form provision in schools

285.   Inspectors are required to grade the quality of education in any sixth-form provision in schools and to write a section in the inspection report that summarises its effectiveness. Inspectors must use all their evidence to evaluate what it is like to be a student in the sixth form.

286.   The effectiveness of the arrangements for safeguarding students is reflected in the main judgement for the school.

287.   Inspectors should take account of the key judgement areas in the evaluation schedule. They should consider:

- the extent to which leaders and teachers have high expectations for achievement and progress and the effectiveness of the systems they use to monitor and develop the quality of sixth-form programmes for all students, including the most disadvantaged and those with high needs
- how leaders and teachers develop a curriculum that provides progression, stretch, mathematics and English for those young people without GCSE grades 9 to 4 (or legacy grades A* to C), as well as work experience or industry placements and non-qualification activities[103]
- the effectiveness of high-quality impartial careers guidance in enabling all students to make progress and move on to a higher level of qualification, employment or further training when they are ready to do so.

288.   Through observing teaching and training activities and by holding discussions with students, teachers and support staff, inspectors will consider how well:

- students develop personal, social and independent learning skills
- students achieve high levels of punctuality and attendance
- students' conduct and attitudes, including in non-qualification or enrichment activities and/or work experience, prepare them for employment or progress to higher levels of study.

289.   Inspection of apprenticeships training is **not** in the scope of section 5 or section 8 inspections of schools.

Grade descriptors Outstanding (1)

- **The school meets all the criteria for good in the effectiveness of sixth form provision securely and consistently.**
- **The quality of sixth form provision provided is exceptional.**

In addition, the following apply:

- **The work that sixth-form students do over time embodies consistently demanding curriculum goals. It matches the aims of the curriculum in being coherently planned and sequenced towards** building sufficient knowledge and skills for future learning and destinations.

- The impact of the taught curriculum is strong. Students acquire and develop high-quality skills and produce work of a consistently high standard.

- Sixth-form students demonstrate consistently highly positive attitudes and commitment to their education. They have consistently high levels of respect for others.

- The sixth form consistently and extensively promotes learners' personal development. The sixth form goes beyond the expected, so that learners have access to a wide, rich set of experiences that teach learners why it is important to contribute actively to society. This is achieved through activities that strengthen considerably the sixth form's offer.

Good (2)

- Leaders adopt or construct study programmes that are ambitious, appropriately relevant to local and regional employment and training priorities and designed to give sixth-form students, particularly those with high needs and the most disadvantaged, the knowledge and skills they need to succeed in life. [If this is not yet fully the case, it is clear from leaders' actions that they are in the process of bringing this about.]

- The curriculum is coherently planned and sequenced towards cumulatively sufficient knowledge and skills for future learning and employment. [If this is not yet fully the case, it is clear from leaders' actions that they are in the process of bringing this about.]

- The school is ambitious for all its sixth-form students, including those with SEND and those who have high needs. This is reflected in the curriculum. The curriculum remains ambitious and is tailored, where necessary, to meet individual needs. [If this is not yet fully the case, it is clear from leaders' actions that they are in the process of bringing this about.]

- Sixth-form students study the intended curriculum. The school ensures this by teaching all components of the full programmes of study.

- Teachers have expert knowledge of the subject(s) and courses they teach. Leaders provide effective support for those teaching outside their main areas of expertise. When relevant, teachers have extensive and up-to-date vocational expertise.

- Teachers present information and/or demonstrate skills clearly, promoting appropriate consideration of the subject matter being taught. They check students' understanding systematically, identify misconceptions and provide clear, direct feedback. In doing this, they

95

respond and adapt their teaching as necessary without recourse to unnecessary, time-consuming, individualised approaches to subject matter.

- The work that teachers give to sixth-form students is demanding. It ensures that students build knowledge and acquire skills, improving and extending what they already know and can do.

- Teachers encourage students to use subject-specific, professional and technical vocabulary well.

- Over the course of study, teachers design and use activities to help students to remember long term the content they have been taught, to integrate new knowledge into larger concepts and to apply skills fluently and independently.

- Teachers and leaders use assessment well. For example, they use it to help students embed and use knowledge fluently and flexibly, to evaluate the application of skills, or to check understanding and inform teaching. Leaders understand the limitations of assessment and do not use it in a way that creates unnecessary burdens on staff or students.

- Teachers create an environment that allows sixth-form students to focus on learning. The resources and materials that teachers select and produce – in a way that does not create unnecessary workload for staff – reflect the school's ambitious intentions for the course of study. These materials clearly support the intent of a coherently planned curriculum, sequenced towards cumulatively sufficient knowledge and skills for future learning, independent living and employment.

- Students develop detailed knowledge across the curriculum and, as a result, achieve well in their study programmes. Students make substantial and sustained progress from their identified and recorded starting points in their study programmes. Where appropriate, this is reflected in results in national examinations that meet government expectations, or in the qualifications obtained.

- Students are ready for the next stage of education, employment or training. They have gained qualifications or met the standards that allow them to go on to destinations that meet their interests, aspirations and intended course of study. Students with high needs have greater independence in making decisions about their lives.

- Students have high attendance and are punctual. Their attitudes to their education are positive. Where relevant, attitudes improve over time.

- The sixth form prepares its students for future success in education, employment or training. It does this through providing: unbiased information to all about potential next steps; high-quality, up-to-date and locally relevant careers guidance, and opportunities for good quality, meaningful encounters with the world of work.

Requires improvement (3)

- The quality of education in the sixth form is not yet good.

Inadequate (4)

The quality of education is likely to be inadequate if any one of the following applies.

- The design, coverage or teaching of the curriculum does not provide adequately for all students.
- The curriculum does not prepare students for the opportunities, responsibilities and experiences of life in modern Britain.
- Weak assessment practice means that teaching fails to meet students' needs.
- The attainment and progress of students are consistently low and show little or no improvement over time, indicating that students are underachieving considerably.
- Students do not develop or improve the English and mathematical skills they need to succeed in the next year or stage of education, or in training or employment.
- Students have not attained the qualifications, skills or behaviours appropriate for them to progress to their next stage of education, training or employment.
- Students' attendance is consistently low and shows little sign of sustained improvement. Their lack of engagement, motivation or enthusiasm inhibits their progress and development.

The school does not ensure that sixth-form students get access to unbiased information about potential next steps, high-quality careers guidance, or opportunities for encounters with the world of work.

Part 3. Applying the EIF in different contexts

Applying the EIF to the teaching of early reading in infant, junior, primary and lower-middle schools

290.   During all inspections of infant, junior, primary and lower-middle schools, inspectors must focus on how well pupils are taught to read as a main inspection activity. They will pay particular attention to pupils who are reading below age-related expectations (the lowest 20%) to assess how well the school is teaching phonics and supporting all children to become confident, fluent readers.

291.   Inspectors will listen to several low-attaining pupils in Years 1 to 3 read[104] from unseen books appropriate to their stage of progress. They should also draw on information from the school's policy for teaching reading, phonics assessments, phonics screening check results and lesson observations.

292.   In reaching an evaluation against the 'quality of education' judgement, inspectors will consider whether:

- the school is determined that every pupil will learn to read, regardless of their background, needs or abilities. All pupils, including the weakest readers, make sufficient progress to meet or exceed age-related expectations
- stories, poems, rhymes and non-fiction are chosen for reading to develop pupils' vocabulary, language comprehension and love of reading. Pupils are familiar with and enjoy listening to a wide range of stories, poems, rhymes and non-fiction
- the school's phonics programme matches or exceeds the expectations of the national curriculum and the early learning goals. The school has clear expectations of pupils' phonics progress term-by-term, from Reception to Year 2
- the sequence of reading books shows a cumulative progression in phonics knowledge that is matched closely to the school's phonics programme. Teachers give pupils sufficient practice in reading and re-reading books that match the grapheme-phoneme correspondences they know, both at school and at home
- reading, including the teaching of systematic, synthetic phonics, is taught from the beginning of Reception
- the ongoing assessment of pupils' phonics progress is sufficiently frequent and detailed to identify any pupil who is falling behind the programme's pace. If they do fall behind, targeted support is given immediately
- the school has developed sufficient expertise in the teaching of phonics and reading.

Applying the EIF to the teaching of mathematics

293.   Inspectors will evaluate the quality of a school's mathematics education through

lesson observations, discussions with pupils and scrutiny of their work, reviewing curriculum plans, discussions with curriculum leaders, and examining any published data.

294.   Inspectors will consider what steps the school has taken to ensure that:

- pupils understand and remember the mathematical knowledge, concepts and procedures appropriate for their starting points, including knowledge of efficient algorithms. This should also ensure that pupils are ready for the next stage, whether that is the next lesson, unit of work, year or key stage, including post-16 mathematics

- the school's curriculum planning for mathematics carefully sequences knowledge, concepts and procedures to build mathematical knowledge and skills systematically and, over time, the curriculum draws connections across different ways of looking at mathematical ideas

- the curriculum divides new material into manageable steps lesson by lesson

- the school's curriculum identifies opportunities when mathematical reasoning and solving problems will allow pupils to make useful connections between identified mathematical ideas or to anticipate practical problems they are likely to encounter in adult life. Pupils have sufficient understanding of, and unconscious competence in, prerequisite mathematical knowledge, concepts and procedures that are necessary to succeed in the specific tasks set

- within the curriculum, there are sufficient opportunities planned to revisit previously learned knowledge, concepts and procedures; this is to ensure that, once learned, mathematical knowledge becomes deeply embedded in pupils' memories. This then allows rapid and accurate recall and frees pupils' attention so they can work with increasing independence, apply their mathematical knowledge to more complex concepts and procedures, and gain enjoyment through a growing self-confidence in their ability

- there is flexibility in curriculum planning so that the school can address identified gaps in pupils' mathematical knowledge that hinder their capacity to learn and apply new content. Those pupils behind age-related expectations are provided with the opportunities to learn the mathematical knowledge and skills necessary to catch up with their peers

- there are objective assessments that can identify when all pupils have gained the intended understanding and unconscious competence in knowledge, concepts and procedures necessary before they move on to new or more complex content

- teaching models new procedures and uses resources and approaches that enable pupils to understand the mathematics they are learning

- all teachers of mathematics, including non-specialist teachers of mathematics, have sufficient mathematical and teaching content knowledge to deliver topics effectively

- pupils' mathematical knowledge is developed and used, where appropriate, across the curriculum.

Applying the EIF in maintained nursery schools

295.   Maintained nursery schools are early education providers that are legally constituted as schools. This is why we inspect them using the school inspection handbook. Like maintained schools, they normally have a headteacher, governing body, delegated budget and at least one teacher with qualified teacher status (QTS).

296.   Maintained nursery schools tend to have more disadvantaged children on roll than other early education providers. These schools are also likely to have a higher proportion of children already identified as having SEND.[105]

297.   All parts of the EIF apply to maintained nursery schools and to early years provision in mainstream schools. However, as with all provision, maintained nursery schools have some specific factors that should be taken into account. Inspectors will gather and evaluate evidence about:

- How well leaders identify children's early starting points, particularly those children with SEND.
- How well leaders develop and adapt the early years foundation stage (EYFS) curriculum so that it is coherently sequenced to meet all children's needs and starting points.
- How successfully leaders involve parents, carers and, as necessary, other professionals/specialist services in deciding how best to support children.
- Whether leaders are ambitious for all children and consider their cultural capital when preparing them for the next stage in their education
- How well leaders include disadvantaged pupils and those with SEND in all aspects of school life.
- How well children's learning and development are shared with parents as required by the EYFS, and the extent to which parents are supported to help their child to learn.
- The extent to which staff use the seven areas of learning to introduce children to new ideas, vocabulary and syntax, and to develop children's love of stories, poems, songs and rhymes.
- Relevant findings from any inspection of the local area's arrangements for identifying, assessing and meeting the needs of young children with SEND (LA SEND inspection).[106]

298.   Inspectors will use all their evidence to evaluate what it is like to be a child in the provision.

299.   Inspectors will spend most of the inspection time gathering first-hand evidence by observing the quality of the daily routines and activities of children and staff. Inspectors will also discuss children's development with staff. Much of this will be through incidental conversations prompted by observing the children at play and the interactions between

them and adults.

300.	The choice of teaching methods is a decision for providers. The inspector will judge the quality of the provision in relation to the impact it has on children's learning, development and well-being.

Applying the EIF in junior, middle and studio schools, and university technical colleges

301.	There are some schools that start and stop at non-standard ages for pupils, so we take into account national expectations differently.

302.	Pupils at junior schools, on average, have higher attainment scores at the end of key stage 2 than pupils at all other primary schools. However, on average, they also have lower progress scores. This may be for a variety of reasons, and inspectors will take this into account when comparing their results with those of pupils in schools that start education from the beginning of key stage 1.

303.	Pupils at middle schools, on average, have lower progress scores at the end of key stage 2 than pupils at primary schools. Due to the age range of pupils at middle schools, pupils will have only attended a middle school for a short time before they take their key stage 2 tests and will still have a number of years left at the school. Inspectors will taken this into account when comparing pupils' results to those of schools that start educating their pupils from the beginning of key stage 1.

304.	The government's ambition for all mainstream secondary schools is for 75% of pupils nationally to be entered for the EBacc by 2021. However, this ambition specifically does not apply to university technical colleges (UTCs) and studio schools because they provide a specialist technical and professional education.

305.	The progress 8 accountability measure is not the most appropriate performance indicator for UTCs and studio schools. These establishments typically start educating pupils at age 14 and have a focus on preparing pupils for their future careers. Inspectors will pay attention to other measures, particularly pupils' destinations when they leave the UTC or studio school.

306.	In common with all inspections covered by this handbook, when inspectors are evaluating these types of school on either a section 5 or a section 8 inspection, they will not look at non-statutory internal progress and attainment data. Inspectors will be interested in the conclusions drawn and actions taken from any internal assessment information, but they will not examine or verify that information first hand. Inspectors will still use published national performance data as a starting point on inspection. Inspectors will be particularly aware of, and sensitive to, the issues and caveats relating to using nationally published progress data in these types of schools.

Applying the EIF in special schools and in mainstream schools' provision for pupils with SEND

307.	Pupils with SEND have a range of different needs and starting points. Some pupils have severe, complex or profound needs that have a significant impact on their cognitive development, especially the way that they are able to make alterations to their long-term memory. Other pupils have starting points at least as high as other pupils of their age, for instance some pupils with sensory impairments.

308. All parts of the EIF apply to state-funded and non-maintained special schools provision and to mainstream schools' provision for pupils with SEND in. However, as with all provision, SEND provision has some specific factors that should be taken into account. Inspectors will gather and evaluate evidence about:

- Whether leaders are ambitious for all pupils with SEND.
- How well leaders identify, assess and meet the needs of pupils with SEND.
- How well leaders develop and adapt the curriculum so that it is coherently sequenced to all pupils' needs, starting points and aspirations for the future.
- How successfully leaders involve parents, carers and, as necessary, other professionals/specialist services in deciding how best to support pupils with SEND.
- How well leaders include pupils with SEND in all aspects of school life.
- How well the school assesses learning and development of pupils with SEND, and whether pupils' outcomes are improving as a result of the different or additional provision being made for them, including outcomes in:
  - communication and interaction
  - cognition and learning
  - physical health and development
  - social, emotional and mental health.
- How well pupils with SEND are prepared for their next steps in education, employment and training, and their adult lives, including: further/higher education and employment, independent living, participating in society and being as healthy as possible in adult life.[107]

309. Because of the often vastly different types of pupils' needs, inspectors will not compare the outcomes achieved by pupils with SEND with those achieved by other pupils with SEND in the school, locally or nationally.

310. Pupils with SEND often have significant and complex vulnerabilities and can face additional safeguarding challenges. Inspectors will evaluate the ways in which leaders have made appropriate and effective safeguarding arrangements that reflect these additional vulnerabilities.

311. The government's ambition for all secondary schools is for 75% of pupils to be entered for the EBacc by 2021. This ambition does not apply to special schools with secondary-age pupils. In addition, the progress 8 accountability measure may not always be the most appropriate performance indicator for these schools.

Applying the EIF in pupil referral units and alternative provision in free schools and academies

312 All parts of the EIF apply to PRUs and other alternative provision in free schools

and academies. However, in the same way that all school contexts are different, so are PRU and other alternative providers. Inspectors will gather and evaluate evidence about:

- how well leaders identify, assess and meet the needs of pupils when they first begin to attend the PRU or other alternative provider, including pupils with SEND
- how well leaders develop and adapt the curriculum so it is coherently sequenced and meets all pupils' needs, starting points and aspirations for the future
- how successfully leaders involve parents, carers and, as necessary, other professionals/specialist services in deciding how best to support pupils
- whether leaders are ambitious for all pupils, and the extent to which those responsible for governance understand the particular context of the provision
- how well leaders include pupils in all aspects of school life, giving particular emphasis to how well they are prepared for their next steps in education, employment and training, and adult lives
- how well schools assess pupils' learning and development, and whether

pupils' outcomes are improving as a result of the different or additional provision being made for them, including outcomes for pupils with SEND.

313.   Pupils in PRUs and other alternative providers often have significant, complex vulnerabilities. In the same way as with other schools, inspectors will evaluate the ways in which leaders have made appropriate and effective safeguarding arrangements for pupils in the light of their higher vulnerability to safeguarding risks.

314.   If pupils in PRUs and other alternative providers attend off-site alternative provision, inspectors will evaluate the extent to which these placements are safe and effective in promoting pupils' progress. Inspectors must visit a sample of the alternative providers used.

315.   PRUs and other alternative providers may have different objectives in their work related to the reasons why a pupil is placed in alternative provision, the needs of the pupil, the duration of placements and the proportion of time that pupils stay with the provider each week. For instance, in a PRU that provides short- term placements for excluded pupils or those at risk of exclusion, the core work may emphasise specific improvements in pupils' attitudes, behaviour and/or attendance alongside their academic/vocational/technical achievement or be aiming to reintegrate pupils into mainstream schools. Alternative providers may also offer services to schools and other educational settings to help them support children with additional needs in their settings. An alternative provision setting may be the permanent destination for some pupils. Inspectors will evaluate schools' success in these areas, while bearing in mind that we expect high academic/vocational/technical aspirations for all pupils.

316.   Inspectors will take the school's official records as a starting point for discussions about attendance. They must evaluate pupils' attendance as a percentage of a full-time

timetable, even when temporary part-time arrangements are in place. Leaders may have a range of ways of evaluating pupils' attendance, given that pupils often join and leave the school roll at various times of the year. Inspectors will take into account pupil turnover in the provision when considering evidence for attitudes and behaviour.

317.	Often, pupils attending PRUs and other alternative providers have had poor attendance in the past. Inspectors will evaluate the improvement in pupils' attendance from their starting points when this is relevant. Inspectors will also evaluate the ways in which leaders take account of pupils' weak attendance in their safeguarding systems and the clarity of their attendance recording. If schools use part-time timetables, and pupils are not attending other provision or placements in addition, inspectors will evaluate the extent to which they are well monitored, aspirational and effective in getting pupils into the education full time, quickly and in line with DfE guidance. These timetables should not be open-ended and should result in swift full-time education for the pupils.

318.	Transitions into PRU and alternative providers are often complex, involving dual registration, periods of non-attendance and meetings with a range of services and families. When evaluating pupils' attainment and progress, inspectors will consider the ways in which leaders have identified, assessed and met the needs of pupils. They will evaluate the progress that pupils have made since they began to attend the alternative provision. For pupils have left the PRU or other alternative provider, inspectors will consider how well the progress they made there enabled them to move on to suitable destinations and, post-16, to take courses at an appropriately demanding level. They will also look closely at how effective liaison is with other schools to ensure that there are appropriately high expectations, and as far as reasonably possible, continuity in pupils' education programmes. Inspectors will also look at whether the provider works closely with families, schools and other agencies to ensure a smooth transition to and from alternative provision. They will look at whether it sets expectations that reintegration back into mainstream education is a key component of a placement.

Applying the EIF when evaluating the quality of boarding and residential provision in schools

319.	When the full inspection of a school's education provision and the full residential inspection are both due at the same time, we usually combine them into one inspection of the whole school. These are integrated inspections and are carried out by one team, leading to one published report.

320.	Integrated inspections take place:

- in a boarding or residential special school when both inspections are due during the same year
- when we carry out an emergency or monitoring inspection of both the boarding/residential and education provision
- when we are inspecting the education provision at a boarding/residential school under section 5.

321.   In integrated inspections, lead inspectors will consider the timing of team meetings so that the social care regulatory inspector is available to join them. It is important that the findings of the social care regulatory inspector contribute to judgements about the school.

322.   Inspectors must work closely together to plan sufficient time to discuss their findings throughout the inspection. The lead education inspector will join the social care regulatory inspector on some inspection activities so that they can gain a full picture of provision at the school. This is particularly important in assessing personal development, behaviour and attitudes and the strength of the links between the day school and boarding provision.

323.   The inspection of education in a school that is also registered as a children's home may take place as a stand-alone inspection of the education provision or be aligned with the full inspection of the children's home.[108] When possible, we will attempt to align both inspections so that inspectors may work together and share evidence.

324.   When the education inspection takes place as a stand-alone event, inspectors must read the most recent education and children's home reports on the preparation day. They must make themselves aware of any current issues concerning children's welfare that may affect aspects of the school inspection and ensure that they take these into consideration during the inspection.

325.   When the education and children's homes inspections are aligned, the education and social care regulatory inspectors will work together to share evidence.

326.   If the school provides boarding or residential provision, inspectors will make the three key judgements on that provision. These judgements are made in accordance with the guidance and grade descriptors in the 'Social care common inspection framework (SCCIF): boarding schools and residential special schools'.[109]

327.   If the provision does not meet one or more of the national minimum standards, this will be set out in the inspection report.

328.   Inspectors must consider the impact of the judgements on the boarding/residential provision on the judgements for the whole school. In order to do this, they will need to take account of the proportion of boarders/residential pupils in the school and the seriousness of the issues found.

329.   For the effectiveness of leadership and management, the grades for the school and boarding should either be the same as, or within one grade of, each other. The report will clearly state the reasons for any differences.

FOOTNOTES

[1] In this handbook, any reference to the Education Act 2005 includes any amendments made by the Education and Inspections Act 2006, the Education and Skills Act 2008, the Academies Act 2010 and the Education Act 2011.

[2] 'Education inspection framework: draft for consultation', Ofsted, 2019; www.gov.uk/government/publications/education-inspection-framework-draft-for-consultation.

[3] Schools: Ofsted privacy notice, Ofsted, June 2018; www.gov.uk/government/publications/ofsted-privacy-notices/schools-ofsted-privacy-notice.

[4] Section 3(5)(b) of the Education (Individual Pupil Information) (Prescribed Persons) (England) Regulations 2009 (Amended); www.legislation.gov.uk/uksi/2009/1563/made.

[5] There is a separate handbook for inspections carried out under section 8 of the Education Act 2005: 'School inspection handbook: Section 8', Ofsted, September 2019; www.gov.uk/government/publications/handbook-for-short-monitoring-and-unannounced-behaviour- school-inspections.

[6] Paragraph 21 of Schedule 1, Part 1, to the Education (Pupil Referral Units) (Application of Enactments) (England) Regulations 2007 (SI 2007/2979) makes Part 1 of the Education Act 2005 (School inspections and other inspections by school inspectors) apply in relation to units as if they were schools.

[7] This includes all academy family schools: sponsor-led academies, academy converter schools, academy special schools, free schools, special free schools, alternative provision free schools, university technical colleges and studio schools. The further education and skills inspection handbook applies to 16 to 19 academies; www.gov.uk/government/publications/further-education-and-skills- inspection-handbook.

[8] We inspect boarding/residential provision under the Children Act 1989, as amended by the Care Standards Act 2000, having regard to the national minimum standards for boarding schools or residential special schools, as appropriate. These inspection follow the 'Social care common inspection framework (SCCIF): boarding schools and residential special schools', Ofsted, March 2018; www.gov.uk/government/publications/the-framework-for-inspecting-boarding-and-residential- provision-in-schools.

[9] Schools that work in partnership with other schools, through federations, managed groups, chains or other collaborative activities, but that have a separate URN will be inspected as individual schools and separate inspection reports will be published.

[10] Under section 5(1) of the Education Act 2005.

[11] Education (School Inspection) (England) Regulations 2005 as amended by Regulation 2(3) of the Education (School Inspection) (England) (Amendment) Regulations 2015 (SI 2015/170).

[12] The Education (Exemption from School Inspection) (England) Regulations 2012; www.legislation.gov.uk/uksi/2012/1293/made.

[13] 'Methodology note: the risk assessment of good and outstanding providers', Ofsted, April 2018; www.gov.uk/government/publications/ofsted-standards-for-official-statistics.

[14] From now on in this handbook, 'parents' will refer to mothers, fathers and/or carers.

[15] https://parentview.ofsted.gov.uk.

[16] We have specific powers (under section 11A–C of the Education Act 2005) to investigate certain complaints about schools, known as qualifying complaints. Further guidance is available in 'Complain about a school or childminder'; www.gov.uk/complain-about-school.

[17] This measures the amount of pupils leaving the school before the normal leaving age, or joining after the normal joining age, for that school.

[18] Academy converter schools are schools that have been approved by the Secretary of State to convert to become an academy.

[19] Section 9 of the Education Act 2005 states that these section 8 inspections can be treated as section 5 inspections.

[20] https://www.gov.uk/government/organisations/ofsted/about/complaints-procedure

[21] Handbook for short, monitoring and unannounced behaviour school inspections, Ofsted, September 2019; www.gov.uk/government/publications/handbook-for-short-monitoring-and-unannounced- behaviour-school-inspections.

[22] Some of these good schools will automatically receive a section 5 inspection instead of a section 8 inspection when evidence indicates that the quality of provision may have deteriorated significantly.

[23] Immediate conversion happens in only a very small percentage of cases, where inspectors believe a section 5 inspection may find the school to be inadequate in one or more of the graded judgements or where there are serious concerns about safeguarding, pupils' behaviour or the quality of education.

[24] Handbook for short, monitoring and unannounced behaviour school inspections, Ofsted, September 2019; www.gov.uk/government/publications/handbook-for-short-monitoring-and-unannounced- behaviour-school-inspections.

[25] The term 'governing body' is used to define the accountable authority for the school. In the case of an academy, including schools within a MAT, this will be the board of trustees.

[26] A school with religious character – often called a faith school – is designated under section 69(3) of the School Standards and Framework Act 1998; www.legislation.gov.uk/ukpga/1998/31/contents. In a faith school, pupils are educated in the context of the principle of a religion. It is normal for there to be a formal link with a religious organisation.

[27] Regulation 9 of The Education (School Inspection) (England) Regulations 2005: www.legislation.gov.uk/uksi/2005/2038/regulation/9/made.

[28] Regulation 4 of The Education (School Inspection) (England) (Amendment) Regulations 2009: www.legislation.gov.uk/uksi/2009/1564/made.

[29] Protocol between Ofsted and signatory faith group inspectorates.

[30] This also applies to outstanding special schools and PRUs that convert to academy status, because these schools are not exempt from routine inspection.

[31] This will not apply if an existing academy is re-brokered and receives a new URN.

[32] 'Teachers' standards', Department for Education, 2011; www.gov.uk/government/publications/teachers-standards.

[33] 'Registering school-based childcare provision, Ofsted, August 2012; www.gov.uk/government/publications/factsheet-childcare-registering-school-based-provision.

[34] This must be checked with the headteacher as part of the call. If MATs have delegated responsibility to local governing bodies, this should be set out in a scheme of delegation. Academies should also set out their governance structure in their annual financial statements, which can generally be found through the DfE performance tables site. Inspectors should clarify where responsibility lies and who they should talk to during the inspection, especially where a school is part of a MAT.

[35] Inspection data summary report, Ofsted, January 2017; www.gov.uk/government/collections/using- ofsteds-inspection-dashboard.

[36] Further internal guidance is available to inspectors about getting information on complaints in preparation for inspections.

[37] The provider information portal (PIP) provides a high-level view for Ofsted inspectors of information about providers that Ofsted inspects and regulates.

[38] Warning notices for academies are listed at www.gov.uk/government/publications/list-of-letters-to-academy-trusts-about-poor-performance. Inspectors should also note that they can locate individual warning notices on GOV.UK by putting the name of the academy followed by the words 'warning notice' into the search box.

[39] 'Framework, evaluation criteria and inspector guidance for the inspections of local authority children's services', Ofsted, November 2017; www.gov.uk/government/publications/inspecting-local- authority-childrens-services-from-2018.

[40] The handbook for the inspection of local areas' effectiveness in identifying and meeting the needs of

children and young people who have special educational needs and/or disabilities, Ofsted, April 2016; www.gov.uk/government/publications/local-area-send-inspection-guidance-for-inspectors.

[41] Guidance for schools about information required on a maintained school's website is available at www.gov.uk/guidance/what-maintained-schools-must-publish-online. Non-statutory guidance for academies and free schools about information on their websites is available at www.gov.uk/guidance/what-academies-free-schools-and-colleges-should-publish-online.

[42] 'Deferring Ofsted inspections', Ofsted, June 2016; www.gov.uk/government/publications/deferring- ofsted-inspections.

[43] As set out, for example, in a funding agreement.

[44] We will consider inspection without notice when there are serious concerns about one or more of the following: the breadth and balance of the curriculum; rapidly declining standards; safeguarding; a decline in standards of pupils' behaviour and the ability of staff to maintain discipline; and standards of leadership or governance.

[45] Under section 6(1) of the Education Act 2005.

[46] Under regulation 4 of the Education (School Inspection) (England) Regulations 2005.

[47] Prescribed under section 7 of the Education Act 2005.

[48] https://parentview.ofsted.gov.uk.

[49] 'Point-in-time survey for boarders or residential pupils about a school's boarding houses or residential provision', Ofsted, October 2018; www.gov.uk/government/publications/social-care-online- questionnaires-guidance-for-providers.

[50] 'Social care common inspection framework (SCCIF): boarding schools and residential special schools', Ofsted, March 2018; www.gov.uk/government/publications/the-framework-for-inspecting- boarding-and-residential-provision-in-schools.

[51] 'Pupil premium: funding and accountability for schools', Department for Education and Education and Skills Funding Agency, March 2014; www.gov.uk/pupil-premium-information-for-schools-and- alternative-provision-settings.

[52] 'Education inspection framework: overview of research', Ofsted, January 2019; www.gov.uk/government/publications/education-inspection-framework-overview-of-research.

[53] Teachers' standards, Department for Education, July 2011; www.gov.uk/government/publications/teachers-standards.

[54] Inspectors should take account of the specific context of the school in deciding who to include in the invitation. For example, this may include inviting diocesan representatives for a multi-academy company.

[55] In the case of an academy made subject to special measures, the lead inspector will make a recommendation on whether the academy may appoint NQTs.

[56] www.legislation.gov.uk/uksi/2012/1115/regulation/6/made.

[57] A scheme established, or having effect as if established, by the Secretary of State for the purposes of paragraph 10 of Schedule 2 to the Qualifications Regulations 2003.

[58] In law, this is referred to as 'requiring significant improvement'.

[59] As set out under section 44 of the Education Act 2005.

[60] Described in the section as 'requires significant improvement'.

[61] Rebrokerage takes place when the Secretary of State terminates academy arrangements using the powers in sections 2A to 2D of the Academies Act 2010 and enters into new academy arrangements for the same school or schools under section 1 of the Academies Act.

[62] As set out in the school inspection handbook: Section 8, Ofsted, September 2019; www.gov.uk/government/publications/handbook-for-short-monitoring-and-unannounced-behaviour- school-inspections.

[63] The term 'report' is used to describe the formal written outcome from the inspection.

[64] Under section 14(4)(c) of the Education Act 2005.

[65] 'Complaints about Ofsted', Ofsted, 2018; www.gov.uk/government/publications/complaints-about- ofsted.

[66] The national curriculum sets out requirements for English, mathematics, science, physical education and computing in key stages 1–4; for art and design, design and technology, geography, history and music in key stages 1–3; for languages in key stages 2–3; and for citizenship in key stages 3–4.

[67] Schools will be required to teach relationships education (key stages 1 and 2), relationships and sex education (key stage 3 and 4) and health education (all key stages 1-4) from September 2020.

[68] The Education Act 2002 for state-funded schools and section 1A of the Academies Act 2010 for academies. State-funded schools are also required to: teach basic curriculum; promote the spiritual, moral, social, cultural, mental and physical development of pupils at the school and of society; and prepare pupils at the school for the opportunities, responsibilities and experiences of later life.
Maintained schools must teach the national curriculum. Academies must include English, mathematics, science and religious education in their curriculum.

[69] See our curriculum commentary phase 1: www.gov.uk/government/speeches/hmcis-commentary- october-2017.

[70] Some schools are exempt from the learning and development requirements of the EYFS, where this is the case, the expectation would be that pupils are able to read and write fluently by Years 5 to 6 .

[71] Sections 3.1 and 3.2, 'National curriculum in England: framework for key stages 1 to 4', Department for Education, 2014; www.gov.uk/government/publications/national-curriculum-in-england- framework-for-key-stages-1-to-4/the-national-curriculum-in-england-framework-for-key-stages-1-to-4.

[72] 'Teacher workload advisory group report and government response', Department for Education, 2018; www.gov.uk/government/publications/teacher-workload-advisory-group-report-and- government-response.

[73] Work for some pupils, such as those who have profound or multiple learning difficulties, includes relevant assessment information such as photographs, video and records of observations made by teachers and teaching assistants.

[74] This does not include relevant assessment information (such as photographs, video and records of observations) made by teachers and teaching assistants for pupils who have profound or multiple learning difficulties.

[75] Although they will consider the school's use of assessment.

[76] Destinations of KS4 and KS5 pupils: 2017, Department for Education, 2018; www.gov.uk/government/statistics/destinations-of-ks4-and-ks5-pupils-2017.

[77] Special educational needs and disability code of practice: 0 to 25 years, Department for Education and Department of Health, January 2015, section 8, preparing for adulthood from the earliest years; www.gov.uk/government/publications/send-code-of-practice-0-to-25.

[78] This ambition applies to secondary schools only, and does not apply to university technical colleges, studio schools, alternate provision or special schools.

[79] 'HMCI commentary: curriculum and the new education inspection framework', Ofsted, September 2018; www.gov.uk/government/speeches/hmci-commentary-curriculum-and-the-new-education- inspection-framework.

[80] 'Education inspection framework: overview of research', Ofsted, January 2019; www.gov.uk/government/publications/education-inspection-framework-overview-of-research.

[81] www.gov.uk/government/publications/school-exclusion.

[82] See the government's statutory careers guidance: 'Careers guidance and access for education and training providers', Department for Education, March 2015; www.gov.uk/government/publications/careers-guidance-provision-for-young-people-in-schools.

[83] As per section 5 of the Education Act 2005.

[84] Inspectors will consider how successfully the curriculum is enriched and extended for pupils in special schools, taking into account specific factors such as the local area's arrangements for providing home to school transport for children and young people with SEND.

[85] Under the Equality Act 2010; www.legislation.gov.uk/ukpga/2010/15/section/4.

[86] The Gatsby Benchmarks are a framework of eight guidelines that define the best careers provision in schools and colleges; www.gatsby.org.uk/education/focus-areas/good-career-guidance.

[87] 'Education inspection framework: overview of research', Ofsted, January 2019; www.gov.uk/government/publications/education-inspection-framework-overview-of-research.

[88] In this handbook, a reference to a MAT includes multi-academy companies.

[89] 'Conduct of inspectors during Ofsted inspections', Ofsted, February 2016; www.gov.uk/government/publications/conduct-of-inspectors-during-ofsted-inspections.

[90] All MATs should have, and publish, a scheme of delegation clearly setting out everything that has been delegated by the board of trustees to the local governing board or any other person or body. Advice on how this this should work can be found in the DfE guidance; www.gov.uk/government/publications/multi-academy-trusts-establishing-and-developing-your-trust.

[91] Governance handbook, Department for Education and National College for Teaching and Leadership, 2019; www.gov.uk/government/publications/governance-handbook.

[92] 'Keeping children safe in education', Department for Education, September 2018; www.gov.uk/government/publications/keeping-children-safe-in-education--2.

[93] 'Working together to safeguard children', Department for Education, February 2019; www.gov.uk/government/publications/working-together-to-safeguard-children--2.

[94] 'Positive environments where children can flourish: a guide for inspectors about physical intervention and restrictions of liberty', Ofsted, March 2018; www.gov.uk/government/publications/positive-environments-where-children-can-flourish.

[95] Section 5.6 of 'Inspecting safeguarding in early years, education and skills settings', Ofsted, September 2018; www.gov.uk/government/publications/inspecting-safeguarding-in-early-years- education-and-skills-from-september-2015/inspecting-safeguarding-in-early-years-education-and- skills-settings.

[96] 'Safeguarding concerns: guidance for inspectors', Ofsted, March 2018; www.gov.uk/government/publications/safeguarding-concerns-guidance-for-inspectors.

[97] 'Safeguarding concerns: guidance for inspectors', Ofsted, March 2018; www.gov.uk/government/publications/safeguarding-concerns-guidance-for-inspectors.

[98] 'Inspecting safeguarding in early years, education and skills settings', Ofsted, September 2018; www.gov.uk/government/publications/inspecting-safeguarding-in-early-years-education-and-skills- from-september-2015/inspecting-safeguarding-in-early-years-education-and-skills-settings.

[99] MAT support within a trust is not considered external support.

[100] Taking into account any exemptions from the learning and development requirements of the EYFS.

[101] Synthetic phonics teach children to recognise the sounds that individual letters and combinations of letters make. Pupils learn to blend these sounds together to read words. They go on to use this knowledge when writing. A systematic approach starts with the easiest sounds, progressing to the most complex.

[102] Teaching should not be taken to imply a 'top down' or formal way of working. It is a broad term that covers the many different ways in which adults help young children learn. It includes: their interactions with children during planned and child-initiated play and activities, communicating and modelling language, showing, explaining, demonstrating, exploring ideas, encouraging, questioning, recalling, providing a narrative for what they are doing, facilitating and setting challenges. It takes account of the equipment that adults provide and the attention given to the physical environment, as well as the structure and routines of the day that establish expectations. Integral to teaching is how practitioners assess what children know, understand and can do, as well as taking account of their interests and dispositions to learn (characteristics of effective learning), and how practitioners use this information to plan children's next steps in learning and to monitor their progress.

[103] Non-qualification activities may include tutorials, work to develop study, leadership teamwork, self-management skills and volunteering.

[104] Wherever possible, inspectors should listen to children read in a classroom or in an open area with which

pupils are familiar. The length of time a pupil has attended the school should be taken into consideration.

[105] Maintained nursery schools in the early years sector: role and contribution. DFE-RR895 February 2019

[106] The handbook for the inspection of local areas' effectiveness in identifying and meeting the needs of children and young people with special educational needs and/or disabilities, Ofsted, April 2016; www.gov.uk/government/publications/local-area-send-inspection-guidance-for-inspectors.

[107] Special educational needs and disability code of practice: 0 to 25 years, DfE and Department of Health, January 2015, section 8, preparing for adulthood from the earliest years.

[108] All registered children's homes will undergo at least one inspection in a year. Every children's home receives a full inspection, and some children's homes will also be subject to an interim inspection. All inspections are carried out in line with the 'Social care common inspection framework (SCCIF): children's homes, including secure children's homes' Ofsted, May 2018; www.gov.uk/government/publications/inspecting-childrens-homes-framework.

[109] 'Social care common inspection framework (SCCIF): boarding schools and residential special', Ofsted, April 2018; www.gov.uk/government/publications/the-framework-for-inspecting-boarding-and- residential-provision-in-schools.

SECTION C – School inspection handbook – section 8

Handbook for inspecting schools in England under section 8 of the Education Act 2005

This handbook brings together guidance for inspectors and schools about inspections carried out under section 8 of the Education Act 2005.

Introduction

1.   This handbook brings together guidance for inspectors and schools about inspections carried out under section 8[1] of the Education Act 2005.[2] Section 8 enables Her Majesty's Chief Inspector (HMCI) to conduct inspections for a range of purposes, including monitoring visits by Her Majesty's Inspectors (HMI) to schools that are in a category of concern following a section 5 inspection. HMI may also visit schools to aid HMCI in keeping the Secretary of State informed or to contribute to reports on, for example, teaching in a curriculum subject or a particular aspect of the work of schools. Section 8 is also used to enable HMCI, where she has concerns, to carry out an inspection of those outstanding schools that are exempt from routine inspection under section 5.

2.   Section 8 also provides the statutory basis for the Secretary of State to request an inspection. Section 8(1)[3] of the Education Act 2005 requires HMCI to inspect and report on any school or class of school in England, when requested to do so by the Secretary of State.

3.   Part 1 of this handbook covers the general policy and principles that apply to inspections carried out under section 8.

4.   Part 2 of this handbook sets out the arrangements for carrying out inspections under section 8 in the following circumstances:

- section 8 inspections of schools judged to be good at their most recent section 5 inspection and those outstanding schools that are not exempt from section 5
- monitoring inspections of schools judged as requires improvement
- monitoring inspections of schools judged to have serious weaknesses
- monitoring inspections of schools judged to require special measures
- any inspection that is carried out in other circumstances where the inspection has no specific designation, known as 'section 8 no formal designation inspection'
- unannounced behaviour inspections.

Privacy notice

5.　　　During inspection, inspectors will collect information about staff and children at the school by looking at school records, responses to the pupil survey and responses to the staff survey where appropriate, and by observing the everyday life of the school. We use this information to prepare our report and for the purposes set out in our privacy policy.[4] In most cases, we will not record names. However, some of the information may make it possible to identify a particular individual. We will not publish any information that identifies an individual in the report, but we will usually name the headteacher and the proprietor (where applicable).

6.　　　Individuals and organisations have legal requirements to provide information to Ofsted. The Education Act 2005 gives our inspectors the power to inspect and take copies of any relevant records kept by schools. Regulations enable the Department for Education (DfE) to provide Ofsted with individual pupils' information that relates to school inspections.[5]

7.　　　In the vast majority of settings, we will gather evidence electronically using a range of devices, including laptops, mobile phones and tablets. All evidence is securely transferred to Ofsted's systems. Our inspectors may take photographs of pupils' work. These will be stored as evidence, but not retained by the inspector personally.

Part 1. Inspection policy and principles for inspection conducted under Section 8 of the Education Act 2005

8.   The handbook is primarily a guide for inspectors on how to carry out inspections in the circumstances described in the introduction under HMCI's discretionary power to inspect. However, it is made available to schools and other organisations to ensure that they are informed about the policy and procedures for using the section 8 inspection power in particular situations. It applies to school inspections carried out from September 2019 under the education inspection framework (EIF).

Before the inspection
Requests for deferrals

9.   A school may request a deferral of its inspection. It may make a request to the inspection support administrator at the time when it is notified of the inspection, or to the lead inspector on the day it is notified of the inspection. We will not normally consider deferrals if we receive them after 4.30pm on the day the school is notified. The inspection support administrator or lead inspector must immediately make us aware by contacting the relevant regional duty desk. We will decide whether a deferral should be granted in accordance with our policy.[6]

10.   Normally, if pupils are receiving education in the school, an inspection will go ahead. In exceptional circumstances, however, an inspection might be cancelled or deferred after the school has been notified, following a request made by the school. We will aim to let the school know whether a request is granted on the same day it is made, but in some cases it may happen by 8 the next morning.

11.   If a school is within six months of confirmed closure, but does not request a cancellation when the inspector makes contact, the inspection support administrator will call the regional duty desk to highlight this and get advice about whether the inspection should still be carried out. Decisions will be made on a case-by-case basis.

12.   In the case of unannounced inspections, any requests for a deferral will be passed to the relevant regional director, who will decide whether the request will be granted.

During the inspection

13.   On arrival at the school, each inspector will show their identity badge and ask to see the headteacher. The headteacher should be advised that they may telephone the applications, regulatory and contact (ARC) team (telephone: 0300 123 4234) to check on the identity of the inspectors if they wish to do so.
Safeguarding

14.   Inspectors will always consider how well children, pupils and learners are helped and protected so that they are kept safe. Section 8 inspections of good and non-exempt outstanding schools will always report on the effectiveness of safeguarding.

15.   For all other section 8 inspections, inspectors are not required to report specifically

on the effectiveness of safeguarding, unless it is a specified focus of the inspection. In these cases, the judgement that will be reported in the letter, where safeguarding is judged to be effective, will be:

- safeguarding is effective.

16. If safeguarding is not effective or if pupils are considered to be at risk, the lead inspector will convert the inspection to a section 5 inspection (unless the school is already inadequate).

17. We have published a document setting out the approach that inspectors should take to inspecting safeguarding in all the settings covered by the EIF:

- 'Inspecting safeguarding in early years, education and skills settings'.[7] It should be read alongside this handbook.

18. It is also essential that inspectors are familiar with the following guidance in relation to safeguarding:

- 'Keeping children safe in education: statutory guidance for schools and colleges'[8]
- 'Working together to safeguard children'[9]
- 'Positive environments where children can flourish'.[10]

19. In the event of concerns or queries about safeguarding, inspectors should contact their regional duty desk.

20. In the event of a current or ongoing incident coming to light during the inspection, inspectors should refer to 'Inspecting safeguarding in early years, education and skills settings', which contains guidance on what to include in the inspection report.

21. When evaluating the effectiveness of a school's safeguarding procedures, inspectors should also ask whether there have been any safeguarding incidents since the previous inspection of the school. Inspectors must record the school's response as part of the evidence gathered.

22. On a very small number of occasions, inspectors may come across evidence of child abuse, or allegations of child abuse that are currently being investigated, within a school. Inspectors should consult all relevant guidance referred to above and seek advice where appropriate. Inspectors must not attempt to investigate any incident of child abuse but will ensure that concerns about a child's safety are referred, as appropriate, to the relevant local authority's children's services department. The referral will normally be made by the safeguarding lead for the school.

Providing feedback

23. At the end of all section 8 inspections, feedback will be provided to the school by the lead inspector. The final feedback meeting will be chaired by the lead inspector and she or he will agree with the headteacher who should attend.

24. Normally, the final feedback meeting will be attended by:

- the headteacher/principal and other senior leaders, agreed by the lead inspector and headteacher

- for maintained schools, the chair of the school's governing body and as many governors as possible
- for academies, including academies that are part of a multi-academy trust (MAT), the chair of the board of trustees, and as many governors or trustees as possible
- in an academy that is part of a MAT, the chief executive officer (CEO)/their delegate or equivalent
- a representative from the local authority (for maintained schools), or the academy sponsor.

25.   During the final feedback meeting, the lead inspector will ensure that the headteacher, those responsible for governance and all attendees are clear:

- about the judgements made
- that the main findings of the inspection and the main points provided orally in the feedback, subject to any change, will be reflected in the text of the report
- about any recommendations for improvement
- may be subject to change as a result of quality assurance procedures or moderation and must, therefore, be treated as restricted and confidential to the relevant senior personnel (as determined by the school). They may be shared with school staff and all those responsible for the governance of the school, irrespective of whether they attended the meeting, so long as they are clearly marked as provisional and subject to quality assurance. Information about the inspection outcomes should be shared more widely only when the school receives a copy of the final inspection report
- about the procedure for making a complaint about the inspection.

After the inspection
Arrangements for publishing the report[11]

26.   The process for the writing, quality assurance and publication of reports from all types of inspections outlined in this handbook mirrors that for section 5 inspections.[12]

27.   The lead inspector is responsible for writing the inspection report and submitting the evidence to us shortly after the inspection ends. The text of the report will explain our findings and reflect the evidence. The findings in the report should be consistent with the feedback given to the school at the end of the inspection.

28.   Inspection reports will be quality assured before we send a draft copy to the school. The draft report is restricted and confidential to the relevant personnel (as determined by the school), including those responsible for governance, and should not be shared more widely or published.

29.   The school will be invited to comment on the draft report and informed of the timescales in which to do so. This is usually one working day. Comments must be limited to the factual accuracy of the report. We will notify the school of the lead inspector's response to the factual accuracy check.

30.   Ofsted may share a draft of the inspection report with the DfE, funding bodies or regional schools commissioners where HMCI considers it necessary to do this. This will only take place following moderation. If a section 8 inspection has been deemed to be a section 5 inspection and the judgement is that the school has serious weaknesses or requires special measures, the Secretary of State must be informed.[13]

31.   Typically, schools will receive an electronic version of the final report within 25 working days after the end of the inspection. In most circumstances, the final report will be published on our website within 30 working days.

32.   Ofsted will notify the DfE and/or the relevant funding body before final publication. In all cases, the inspection process should not be treated as complete until all inspection activity has been carried out and the final version of the report has been sent to the school.

The inspection evidence base

33.   The evidence base for the inspection must be retained in line with Ofsted's retention and disposal policy. This is normally six years from when the report is published. We may decide that retaining it for longer is warranted for research purposes.

Quality assurance and complaints

Quality assurance

34.   All inspectors are responsible for the quality of their work. The lead inspector must ensure that inspections are carried out in accordance with the principles of inspection and the Ofsted code of conduct.

35.   We monitor the quality of inspections through a range of formal processes. HMI/Senior HMI visit some schools, or monitor remotely to quality assure inspections, and we may also evaluate the quality of an inspection evidence base. The lead inspector will be responsible for feeding back to team inspectors about the quality of their work and their conduct.

36.   All schools are invited to take part in a post-inspection evaluation in order to contribute to inspection development.

Handling concerns and complaints

37.   The great majority of our work is carried out smoothly and without incident. If concerns do arise during an inspection, they should be raised with the lead inspector as soon as possible, in order to resolve issues before the inspection is completed. The lead inspector will seek advice where necessary. Any concerns raised and actions taken will be recorded in the inspection evidence.

38.   If it is not possible to resolve concerns during the inspection, the school may wish to lodge a formal complaint. The lead inspector will ensure that the school is informed that it is able to make a formal complaint and that information about how to complain is available on our website.[14]

39.   This section sets out in more detail the approach inspectors should take when carrying out section 8 inspections in a variety of different contexts.

Part 2. Inspections carried out under section 8
Section 8 inspections of good and non-exempt outstanding schools

Introduction

40.   This section explains how we will conduct section 8 inspections of good and non-exempt outstanding schools that have not been otherwise selected for a section 5 inspection following risk assessment.

41.   The EIF provides for inspection to be proportionate to the performance and circumstances of schools. Consequently, good schools will normally receive a two-day section 8 inspection approximately every four years.

42.   However, some good schools will be subject to a section 5 inspection instead of a section 8 inspection when the risk assessment process identifies that the quality of provision may have deteriorated significantly. Some other good schools will be subject to a section 5 inspection. This will happen, for example, if a school has undergone significant change, such as in its age range, or through merging with another school.

43.   Special schools, pupil referral units (PRUs) and maintained nursery schools that are judged good or outstanding will also receive a two-day section 8 inspection approximately every four years. These schools are not exempt from routine inspections if they are judged outstanding; they are referred to here as 'non- exempt outstanding schools'.

44.   The purpose of a section 8 inspection of a good or non-exempt outstanding school is to confirm whether the school remains good or outstanding under the definition of overall effectiveness set out in the 'school inspection handbook'.[15]

45.   In order to confirm whether the school remains good or outstanding, inspectors will refer closely to the criteria below (from paragraph 53). They will not be expected to carry out a full section 5 inspection within a reduced timeframe. Instead, they will focus on particular aspects of the school's provision. These aspects are drawn principally from the 'quality of education' judgement, but also include specific elements of pupil behaviour, personal development, potential gaming and off-rolling, and safeguarding.

46.   A section 8 inspection of a good or non-exempt outstanding school will not result in individual graded judgements. It cannot change the overall effectiveness grade of the school. If the inspection is converted to a section 5 inspection (see paragraph 82 for the circumstances in which this may happen), then inspectors will make the full set of graded judgements using the four-point grading scale required under section 5.

47.   Once a school has received its first section 8 inspection of a good or non- exempt outstanding school, further of these section 8 inspections will normally be conducted at approximately four-year intervals.[16]

Days allocated to inspection and inspection team members

48.   In almost all cases, a section 8 inspection of a good or non-exempt outstanding school will last for two days. However, a section 8 inspection of any good primary school or

a good/outstanding maintained nursery school that has fewer than 150 pupils or children on its roll will last for one day.

49.   Regardless of number on roll, section 8 inspections of special schools and PRUs will last for two days, given the often complex nature of the provision.

50.   HMI or Ofsted Inspectors (OIs) will lead section 8 inspections of good or non-exempt outstanding schools. Section 8 inspections of all of these secondary schools and large primary schools (600 pupils or more on roll), will be led by an HMI or OI, normally accompanied by one team inspector. In secondary schools of more than 1,100 pupils, there will normally be two team inspectors. In primary schools with fewer than 600 pupils on roll, the inspection will normally be conducted by one inspector. For PRUs and special schools (including maintained residential special schools and non-maintained special schools with residential provision), the inspection will be led by an HMI or OI, who will usually be accompanied by one team inspector. Depending on the complexity of the provision, size and number of sites in use, up to two more inspectors may be assigned as a team for the inspection.

51.   The lead inspector will be on site for both inspection days, unless the school is a maintained nursery school, primary, first, infant or junior school and there are fewer than 150 pupils on roll. Any team inspectors will normally be on site for the first inspection day only.

52.   If the lead inspector decides to convert the section 8 inspection to a section 5 inspection, the size of the inspection team may increase.

Quality of education

53.   Inspectors will focus primarily on the 'quality of education' during a section 8 inspection of a good or non-exempt outstanding school. Inspectors will form a secure view of whether the quality of education as defined in the 'school inspection handbook' remains good at this school. In order to do this, inspectors will focus on key aspects of the school's provision. They will:

- always consider and evaluate all aspects of the aims of the school's curriculum, including the degree to which the school's overall curriculum is coherently sequenced and structured

- consider the extent to which teachers have good knowledge of the subjects they teach, present subject matter clearly, check pupils' understanding systematically, identify misconceptions accurately and provide clear, direct feedback to pupils

- consider the extent to which pupils develop detailed knowledge and skills across the curriculum and, as a result, achieve well and are ready for the next stage of education, employment or training

- always consider whether there is any evidence that the school's curriculum has been narrowed inappropriately

- observe, where it exists, provision for two- and three-year-olds, and assess whether staff are knowledgeable about the typical development and characteristics of two- and three-year-olds, are focused on teaching children through the three prime areas of learning and are attentive to children's needs

- in primary schools, always consider how well reading and early mathematics are taught in early years foundation stage and key stage 1 as part of a wide-ranging curriculum that prepares children well for the next stage in their education
- in primary schools, explore how well a broad range of subjects (exemplified by the national curriculum) is taught in key stage 2. Inspectors will focus first and foremost on the teaching of reading, particularly on how children gain access to the whole of the national curriculum through learning to read fluently and with comprehension
- in secondary schools, explore how well the school teaches a broad range of subjects (exemplified by the national curriculum) throughout years 7 to 9, or whether the school is in the process of bringing this about. Inspectors will also explore whether the school is aware of the DfE's national EBacc ambition and what it is doing to prepare to achieve this through its key stage 4 curriculum.

54.   Inspectors will gather evidence about the implementation of the curriculum so that they can form a view about the degree to which series of lessons follow the curriculum intent of the school. They will also look at the degree to which these series of lessons are well sequenced within the intended curriculum and how well they provide purposeful opportunities for pupils' progression through it.

55.   If the school is not performing well against these criteria, this could be considered evidence that the school would no longer receive a 'good' judgement at a section 5 inspection. If the lead inspector has serious concerns about the quality of education, the inspection will be converted to a section 5 inspection.

Inspectors will not look at internal progress or attainment data

56.   Inspectors will review nationally published performance information about pupils' progress and attainment. They will ask school leaders to set out their understanding of pupils' educational performance. However, inspectors will not themselves look directly at schools' internal progress or attainment data in relation to current pupils as evidence. For full guidance on this see the 'school inspection handbook'.

Behaviour

57.   Inspectors will **not** make a judgement on all the criteria contained in the 'behaviour and attitudes' judgement. Nevertheless, they will consider two key factors:

- whether the school has high expectations for pupils' behaviour and conduct and applies these expectations consistently and fairly. Inspectors will also consider whether this is reflected in pupils' positive behaviour and conduct.

They will consider whether staff make sure that pupils follow appropriate routines, whether low-level disruption is not tolerated and whether pupils' behaviour does not disrupt lessons or the day-to-day life of the school

- whether leaders, staff and pupils create an environment in which bullying is not tolerated. When harassment, violence, bullying, aggression, discrimination and use of derogatory language occur, inspectors will consider whether they are dealt with quickly, in line with statutory guidance, effectively and are not allowed to spread.

58.   Where behaviour is not being managed well, this could be evidence that the school would no longer receive a 'good' judgement if it received a section 5 inspection. Where the lead inspector has serious concerns about behaviour, the inspection will be converted to a section 5 inspection.

Gaming and off-rolling

59.   When conducting these inspection activities, inspectors will be particularly alert to any evidence that suggests that the school may be:

- gaming – entering pupils for courses or qualifications that are not in their educational best interest in order to achieve apparently better performance for the school
- off-rolling – removing a pupil or pupils from the school roll without a formal, permanent exclusion when the removal is primarily in the interests of the school rather than in the best interests of the pupil. Please refer to the 'school inspection handbook' for further explanation.

60.   Where inspectors uncover any evidence that gaming or off-rolling may be taking place, this could be evidence that the school would no longer receive a 'good' judgement if it received a section 5 inspection. Where the lead inspector has serious concerns about gaming or off-rolling, the inspection will be converted to a section 5 inspection.

Pupils' wider development

61.   Inspectors will consider the extent to which the curriculum goes beyond the academic, vocational or technical, whether the school provides effectively for pupils' broader development and whether the school's work to enhance pupils' spiritual, moral, social and cultural development is of a high quality.

62.   Inspectors will not make a judgement on the criteria contained in the 'personal development' judgement.

Workload

63.   Inspectors will consider the extent to which leaders engage with staff and are aware and take account of the main pressures on them, engaging with them realistically and constructively. They will consider the extent to which staff are free from bullying and harassment. Inspectors will also consider whether leaders and staff understand the

limitations of assessment and use it in a way that will avoid creating unnecessary burdens.

64.   If these issues are not being managed well, this could be considered as evidence that the school would no longer receive a 'good' judgement if it received a section 5 inspection. Where the lead inspector has serious concerns about workload or the bullying or harassment of staff, the inspection will be converted to a section 5 inspection.

Safeguarding

65.   All schools should have a good culture of safeguarding. This means that they should have effective arrangements to:

- always act in the best interests of pupils to protect them online and offline;
- **identify** pupils who may need early help and those who are at risk of harm or have been harmed. This harm can include, but is not limited to, neglect, abuse (including by their peers, in school or outside school), grooming or exploitation
- secure the **help** that pupils need, and, if required, refer pupils in a timely way to those who have the expertise to help
- **manage** safe recruitment and allegations about adults who may be a risk to children, pupils, students and vulnerable adults.

66.   Inspectors will not grade this key aspect of a school's work. However, inspectors will always make a written judgement in the report about whether the arrangements for safeguarding children and pupils are effective.

67.   Inspectors must go beyond simply reviewing documents in order to evaluate the safeguarding culture of the school.

68.   In addition to understanding Ofsted's inspecting safeguarding policies, inspectors should be familiar with relevant, including statutory, guidance in relation to safeguarding:

- 'Keeping children safe in education: statutory guidance for schools and colleges'[17] (all parts)
- 'Working together to safeguard children'[18]
- 'Positive environments where children can flourish'. [19]

69.   For a full explanation of the methodology inspectors will adopt in relation to safeguarding, see the 'school inspection handbook'.

Methodology for gathering evidence

70.   Inspectors will normally adopt the same methodology for inspecting the quality of education and safeguarding as that used on a section 5 inspection. However, in all other areas they will not gather the same depth of evidence on a section 8 inspection as a full team conducting a section 5 inspection, as this would not be possible.

71.   For a full explanation of the methodology inspectors will adopt, see the 'school inspection handbook.

Potential inspection outcomes

72.   There are four possible outcomes for a section 8 inspection of a good or non-exempt outstanding school. See Annex A for a diagram of this process.

■ **Outcome 1** – the school continues to be a good/outstanding school. This is the most common outcome

or

■ **Outcome 2** – the school remains good and there is sufficient evidence of improved performance to suggest that the school might be judged outstanding if it received a section 5 inspection at the time of the section 8 inspection. The school will be informed that its next inspection will be a section 5 inspection, which will typically take place within one to two years of the publication of the section 8 inspection report

or

■ **Outcome 3** – the lead inspector is not satisfied that the school would receive at least its current grade if a section 5 inspection were carried out at the time of the section 8 inspection. The school will be informed that its next inspection will be a section 5 inspection within the statutory timeframe, which will typically take place within one to two years of the publication of the section 8 inspection report, depending on how near to the end of the statutory timeframe the section 8 inspection has taken place

or

■ **Outcome 4** – the lead inspector has gathered evidence that suggests that the school may be inadequate in one or more of the graded judgements under section 5 inspection, and there are serious concerns about the quality of education, pupils' behaviour or safeguarding. For outstanding non-exempt schools, there are concerns that the performance of the school could be declining to 'requires improvement'.[20] The section 8 inspection will be converted to a section 5 inspection, usually within 48 hours.

73.   Inspectors **will always** report on whether safeguarding is effective. If there is evidence that safeguarding may be ineffective, the lead inspector **will always** convert the section 8 inspection to a section 5 inspection.

Schools that remain good/outstanding (outcome 1)

74.   Where the lead inspector judges that a school remains good/outstanding, they will confirm this judgement in the final feedback to the school at the end of the section 8 inspection. The lead inspector will notify their Ofsted regional support team as soon as this decision is made.

Schools that remain good, with marked improvement (outcome 2)

75.   Where the lead inspector considers that, based on the evidence seen, a school remains good and inspectors have reason to believe that the quality of education might be better than good if it received a section 5 inspection at the time of the section 8 inspection,

the lead inspector will indicate that this is likely to be their conclusion (subject to quality assurance of the inspection). The lead inspector will then discuss with the school which subjects, topics or areas of provision may usefully serve as the focus of a subsequent section 5 inspection, and record this in their summary evidence.

76. The school will then receive a report that makes clear that its next inspection will be carried out under section 5 of the Education Act 2005. The report will confirm that the school remains good and will highlight the reasons why inspectors believe that the quality of education is better than good.

77. The section 5 inspection will usually take place within one to two years after the publication of the section 8 inspection report, giving the school time for the strong practice and marked improvements to be consolidated. The decision on the timing of the full section 5 inspection will be for the relevant Ofsted regional director to determine. Schools may request an early inspection and these requests will be considered by the relevant Ofsted region.

Schools that may no longer be good/outstanding (outcome 3)

78. Where the lead inspector is not satisfied that the school would receive its current grade if a section 5 inspection were carried out at the time of the section 8 inspection, the lead inspector will indicate that this is likely to be their conclusion (subject to quality assurance of the inspection). The lead inspector will then discuss with the school which subjects, topics or areas of provision may usefully serve as the focus of a subsequent section 5 inspection, and record this in their summary evidence.

79. The school will then receive a letter setting out what the school is doing well and what it needs to improve. The school's current overall effectiveness judgement will not change as a result of this inspection. The school will subsequently receive a section 5 inspection within the prescribed statutory timeframe.[21]

80. In line with regulations, the prescribed timeframe will not be reset by the section 8 inspection because the essential test of those regulations has not been met.[22] The section 5 inspection will typically take place within one to two years of the publication of the section 8 inspection report, although this could be sooner if the section 8 inspection has been carried out nearer to the end of the statutory timeframe.

81. For outcomes 2 and 3, if a maintained school converts to become an academy before the section 5 inspection has been carried out, the school's first inspection as an academy will be a section 5 inspection at least one year after the school becomes an academy.

Section 8 inspection is converted to a section 5 inspection (outcome 4)

82. The section 8 inspection will be converted to a section 5 inspection, usually within 48 hours, if there are serious concerns about the quality of education, behaviour, potential gaming (including off-rolling) or safeguarding. This will occur if inspectors:

- find evidence that suggests that the 'quality of education' might be judged to be inadequate were a full section 5 inspection to take place at the time of the section 8 inspection. This may include a situation where the range of subjects being taught is very narrow

- find evidence relating to behaviour that suggests that 'behaviour and attitudes' might be judged to be inadequate were a full section 5 inspection to be taking place at the time of the section 8 inspection[23]
- find evidence that suggests that the school has removed pupils from the school roll without a formal, permanent exclusion, or encouraged parents to remove their child from the school roll, when the removal is primarily in the interests of the school rather than in the best interests of the pupil
- find evidence that deliberate, substantial gaming is taking place
- find evidence indicating that safeguarding may be ineffective.

83.   The section 8 inspection will also be converted when the lead inspector has gathered evidence that suggests the school may be inadequate in one or more of the graded judgements were a section 5 inspection carried out at the time of the section 8 inspection.[24]

84.   A decision to convert the inspection does not predetermine the outcome of the section 5 inspection. At the end of the section 5 inspection, the school may receive any grade along the four-point grading scale.

85.   If inspectors gather evidence that suggests an outstanding non-exempt school's performance may have declined so that, were a section 5 inspection to be carried out at the time of the section 8 inspection, the school would be likely to be judged as requires improvement, inspectors will convert the section 8 inspection, usually within 48 hours. This group of non-exempt outstanding schools caters for those who are at a most critical stage of their education (in the case of nursery schools) as well as some of our most vulnerable pupils.

86.   Where the section 8 inspection is HMI-led and converts to a section 5 inspection, the HMI will remain the lead inspector for the full inspection. However, where the section 8 inspection has been led by an OI, the OI may either remain as the lead inspector for the full inspection or an HMI may lead the full inspection. More inspectors may join the lead inspector. The section 8 inspection will become a section 5 inspection and the team will gather and evaluate evidence in order to make a full set of graded judgements.

87.   A section 8 inspection report will not be produced when the section 8 inspection converts to a section 5 inspection. Instead, the school will receive a section 5 inspection report.

Principles for working with the headteacher, senior leaders and governors
88.   Section 8 inspections of good and non-exempt outstanding schools are designed to promote constructive, challenging, professional dialogue between the lead inspector and school leaders. The lead inspector will start the section 8 inspection on the assumption that the school remains good/outstanding. They will test this over the course of the inspection

through their inspection activities and ongoing discussion with leaders and governors.

89.   Section 8 inspections provide schools with the opportunity to share with the lead inspector how they are sustaining and continuing to improve the overall good quality of education for pupils. Section 8 inspections also provide leaders and governors with the opportunity to demonstrate their capacity for driving further improvement in their school. The lead inspector will test whether leaders and governors have identified weaknesses or areas needing development at the school.

90.   The lead inspector will plan the inspection so that leaders and governors have time to present evidence about key improvements at the school, their assessment of the current performance of the school and action planning that supports improvement. During the pre-inspection call between the lead inspector and the headteacher and/or other senior leaders, school leaders will summarise their evaluation of the school's current performance and the lead inspector will discuss the key issues to be considered during the inspection. They will include these issues in the schedule for the inspection.

91.   Leaders and governors are not required to:

■ prepare documentary evidence that is in addition to any standard documents or policies that they use for the normal day-to-day business of the school

■ prepare a self-evaluation or equivalent in a specified format or with any specific wording. Any assessment that they provide should be part of the school's usual evaluation work and not be generated solely for inspection purposes.

Seeking the views of registered parents, pupils and other stakeholders

92.   When a school is notified of the section 8 inspection, leaders and those responsible for governance should take steps that are reasonably practicable to inform all registered parents of registered pupils at the school, including those who are on fixed-term or internal exclusion, those who attend alternative provision or those who are away from school. Schools should also be invited to notify relevant bodies of the inspection, including providers of alternative provision.

93.   The views of staff and pupils in schools will usually be gathered through an online questionnaire. The inspection support administrator sends online links to the school along with the formal notification of inspection. The school is asked to encourage staff and pupils to complete the online questionnaire, with the exception of those in any boarding provision (whose views will have already been sought through the point-in-time survey). Staff and pupils should complete and submit their questionnaires by 3pm on the first[25] day of the inspection.

94.   Our email confirming the inspection includes a letter that can be used to notify parents formally. It explains how to use Parent View and how parents can contact inspectors. Schools should actively encourage parents to complete Parent View as early as possible by placing a link on their website to the Parent View website.[26] Inspectors

should encourage the school to notify parents using its own systems (such as text messages) where these are available.

95.   The lead inspector will review the evidence from Parent View throughout the section 8 inspection to ensure that all online responses received during the inspection are taken into account. If the response rate for Parent View is low, inspectors may take further steps during the inspection to gather parents' views.

96.   The lead inspector will also take into account any other evidence from parents, including the results of any past surveys that the school has carried out or commissioned. If individual parents raise serious issues, inspectors should follow these up with the school and record its response as part of the evidence gathered during the inspection. Inspectors will not investigate complaints.

Before the inspection
Notification and introduction

97.   For maintained schools and academies (including PRUs, special schools and maintained nursery schools), Ofsted will normally contact the school by telephone to announce the inspection between 10.30am and 2pm on the school day before the section 8 inspection.

98.   Requests for a deferral will be handled in accordance with our deferral policy.[27] During a notification call, if the headteacher is unavailable, we will ask to speak to the next most senior member of staff. Once it has been confirmed that the section 8 inspection will take place, we will send confirmation to the school by email.

Information that schools must provide by 8am on the first day of inspection

99.   The inspection support administrator will also send the school a note requesting that the following information is available to inspectors by 8am the next day, at the formal start of the inspection:

- the school timetable, current staff list (indicating newly qualified teachers (NQTs)) and times of the school day
- any information about previously planned interruptions to normal school routines during the inspection
- records and analysis of exclusions, pupils taken off roll, incidents of poor behaviour and any use of internal isolation
- records and analysis of sexual harassment and/or sexual violence
- records and analysis of bullying, discriminatory and prejudiced behaviour, either directly or indirectly, including racist, sexist, disability and homophobic/biphobic/transphobic bullying, use of derogatory language and racist incidents
- a list of referrals made to the designated person for safeguarding in the school and those who were subsequently referred to the local authority, along with brief details of the resolution

- a list of all pupils who have open cases with children's services/social care and for whom there is a multi-agency plan
- up-to-date attendance analysis for all groups of pupils
- documented evidence of the work of those responsible for governance and their priorities, including any written scheme of delegation for an academy in a MAT
- a summary of any school self-evaluation or equivalent
- the current school improvement plan or equivalent, including any planning that sets out the longer-term vision for the school, such as the school or the trust's strategy
- any reports from external evaluation of the school.

Preparation

100.   Once we have informed the school of the inspection, the lead inspector will contact the school by telephone and ask to speak to the headteacher. Inspectors' preparatory telephone conversations with headteachers will have two elements:

- a reflective, educationally focused conversation about the school's context and challenges and progress made since the last inspection
- a shorter inspection planning conversation that focuses on practical and logistical issues.

101.   It may be that both these elements are discussed in a single telephone conversation. Alternatively, they may be conducted as two separate conversations with a break in-between as mutually agreed by the lead inspector and the headteacher. In total, these conversations are likely to last around 90 minutes.

Discussing the school's progress since the last inspection

102.   Inspectors will hold an introductory telephone conversation with school leaders on the day before the inspection begins. Inspectors should give school leaders the opportunity to explain their school's specific context and challenges. Inspection experience, including our pilots for this framework, shows that this helps both leaders and inspectors build stronger professional relationships.

103.   Inspectors will use this conversation to understand:

- the school's context, and the progress it has made since the previous inspection, including any specific progress made in areas for improvement that were identified at previous inspections and that remain relevant under the current inspection framework
- the headteacher's assessment of the school's current strengths and weaknesses, particularly in relation to the curriculum, the way teaching supports pupils to learn the curriculum, the standards pupils achieve, pupils' behaviour and attitudes, and the personal development of pupils
- the specific areas of the school (subjects, year groups, aspects of provision, and so on) that will be focused on during inspection.

104.   This conversation will normally last up to 90 minutes. It will help inspectors to form an initial understanding of the leaders' view of the school's progress and also help them to shape the inspection plan. Our experience from piloting the EIF shows that this is the part of preparation that school leaders and inspectors often find to be the most helpful and constructive.

Inspection planning discussion

105.   This discussion will be short and focused on practical issues. The lead inspector will:

- make the school aware of its statutory duty to inform parents of the inspection and that Parent View is the main method for gathering the views of parents at the point of inspection. Inspectors will remind the school that Ofsted's letter to parents containing the link to Parent View may be sent electronically, or as a paper copy via pupils
- discuss the nature of any SEND resource base, where applicable
- establish whether the school has any pupils who attend off-site alternative provision, either full time or part time. Inspectors must ask the school about the registration status of any alternative providers that they use. Any provider of alternative provision must be registered as an independent school if it caters full time for five or more pupils of compulsory school age, or one pupil of compulsory school age who is looked after or has an education, health and care (EHC) plan. Where a school uses alternative provision that should be registered but is not, inspectors will carefully consider whether pupils at this provision are effectively safeguarded and may decide to convert the inspection to a section 5 inspection.
- visit alternative providers during the inspection as directed by the relevant Ofsted region. Any alternative provision site that has not yet been inspected should be visited during the inspection
- discuss any off-site units that cater for pupils with behaviour or attendance difficulties, run either by the school or in partnership with other schools
- discuss any nursery provision, before- and/or after-school care or holiday clubs led and managed directly by the school, particularly where these take two- to eight-year-olds[28]
- invite the headteacher, curriculum leaders and other leaders to take part in joint visits to lessons and to observe the main inspection team meetings
- make arrangements for meetings with relevant staff
- provide an opportunity for the school to ask any questions or to raise any concerns, for example perceived conflicts of interest.

106.   The lead inspector will also request the school to provide certain information as early as possible to aid preparation. This will include:

- the single central record for the school

- a list of staff and a note of whether any relevant staff are absent
- a copy of the school timetable
- whether any teachers cannot be observed for any reason (for example, where they are subject to capability procedures)
- whether there is anyone working on site who is normally employed elsewhere in the MAT (where relevant)
- maps and other practical information (see resource bases below)
- access to the school's Wi-Fi, where it exists, so that inspectors can connect to the internet.

107.   It is important that inspectors speak to those responsible for leadership and governance during the inspection. Since schools, and especially MATs, operate a wide variety of leadership and governance models, it is essential that inspectors establish who is responsible for leadership and governance. The lead inspector will therefore:

- establish what the governance structure of the school or academy is,[29] with reference to the range of functions delegated to local governing bodies or other committees
- confirm arrangements for meetings with the school and, where appropriate, MAT executive leaders, as well as representatives of those responsible for the governance of the school and anyone else they think is relevant. The lead inspector should be guided by the school on who they need to meet from a MAT
- make arrangements for a meeting with the chair of the governing body or, where appropriate, the chair of the board of trustees and as many governors/trustees as possible. Inspectors will also ask the school to invite as many governors/trustees as possible to attend the final feedback meeting
- request either a face-to-face meeting or a telephone call with a representative from the local authority, diocese, sponsor or other relevant responsible body as appropriate
- request that a representative from the local authority, diocese, MAT, sponsor or other relevant responsible body is present at the final inspection feedback meeting as appropriate

108.   If any issues arise, the lead inspector may also need further clarification from the school, for example where information is not available on the school's website or there are anomalies with the single central record that may be resolved.

Further inspection preparation carried out by the lead inspector

109.   In addition to the information requested from the school, inspectors will review and consider the following information:

- all relevant information held by Ofsted, including:
  - data from our inspection data summary report (IDSR)[30]
  - inspection reports on the school

- any surveys or monitoring letters
- any complaints made about the school to Ofsted[31]
- replies to questionnaires
- information on our provider information portal,[32] including any warning notices[33]
- the most recent inspection report on the relevant local authority's children's services[34]
- the main findings from the relevant local area's SEND inspection[35]

- relevant publicly available information, such as the school's website[36]
- information published by local authorities, the DfE (including the Education and Skills Funding Agency and regional school commissioners) and the police.

Resource bases

110. If the school has a SEND resource base delegated to it or the local authority maintains direct responsibility for the period when the pupils in the provision are in mainstream classes at the school being inspected, the resource base must be inspected. Inspectors must consider evidence about the resourced provision when making judgements about the school overall.

111. During the lead inspector's planning conversation with the school, they will obtain specific information about any resource base, including:

- the number of pupils and the range of the needs of pupils placed in additionally resourced provision, together with pupils' timetables, including when they are taught in mainstream classes (with and without support) and when they receive specialist support in separate resourced provision
- the type(s) of language/communication systems used. If the specialist provision is for deaf pupils, it is important to establish, where British sign language is used, whether a British sign language interpreter will be provided by the school when inspectors are meeting with the pupils. The lead inspector will contact the inspection support administrator as soon as possible if this support is needed. Details will be available in the team room
- staffing arrangements and details of any outreach services provided by the resourced provision.

During the inspection

Typical inspection day

112. The lead inspector will devise a timetable for the section 8 inspection based on their pre-inspection analysis and conversations with school leaders. This timetable may be adapted as new evidence becomes available or other issues emerge.

113. Inspectors **must** always judge whether the school's arrangements for **safeguarding** are effective.

114. The section 8 inspection will also focus on evidence of how effectively the school's leaders and managers, including those responsible for governance, are:

- sustaining a good quality of education for pupils
- demonstrating capacity to remedy any weaknesses that are not of sufficient concern for the lead inspector to convert the inspection from a section 8 to a section 5 inspection.

Feedback at the end of the section 8 inspection

115. At the end of the section 8 inspection, the lead inspector will provide brief oral feedback that will typically:

- report the range of evidence gathered
- provide the school with a judgement about whether it remains good or outstanding (as relevant)
- report whether safeguarding is effective
- make clear that the text of the section 8 inspection report will differ from the oral feedback as the feedback is for the school and the report is written for parents
- ensure that leaders are clear about the procedures for publishing the report.

After the inspection
Reporting on the section 8 inspection

116. The school will receive a report setting out the inspection findings that will be published on the Ofsted website. Schools should inform parents that this report has been published.

Monitoring inspections for schools that require improvement in order to become good or outstanding

117. This section of the handbook sets out Ofsted's approach to challenging and supporting schools that are judged as requires improvement at their last section 5 inspection. The guidance outlines the main activities that may be undertaken by the lead inspector when conducting a monitoring inspection of a school judged as requires improvement until it is re-inspected under section 5 of the Education Act 2005.

118. Schools judged as requires improvement will usually be re-inspected under section 5 within 30 months after the publication of the section 5 report. The timing of the re-inspection will be at the discretion of Ofsted's relevant regional director.[37]

119. Although not in a formal category of concern, schools judged as requires improvement may be subject to monitoring. This will not normally apply to a school that has been judged as requires improvement for the first time. However, a school that receives two or more successive 'overall effectiveness' judgements of requires improvement will normally be monitored for between 12 and 30 months following publication of the report which resulted in the most recent 'requires improvement' judgement.

120.   Where a school's most recent 'leadership and management' judgement was good, or where leadership has changed since the last section 5 inspection, the relevant regional director may decide that a school that would otherwise have had a monitoring inspection does not require one. However, these decisions will be by exception, having taken account of all relevant information about the current position in the school.

121.   Where, following a monitoring inspection, the lead inspector considers that a school is ready for re-inspection because it has made good progress, they may recommend that the next section 5 inspection is brought forward. Conversely, when the lead inspector feels that the school would benefit from further time to improve to a judgement of good, they may recommend that the school is re- inspected later in the 30-month inspection window.

122.   If, at the section 5 re-inspection, the school has not demonstrated that it has improved to good, the lead inspector will need to consider whether the school continues to require improvement or whether it is inadequate. If the school has demonstrated improvement in some areas and there is a general upward trend, but key aspects of performance remain less than good, the school may be judged as requires improvement again, in which case there may be monitoring before another section 5 inspection takes place, which would normally be within 30 months after the publication of the previous section 5 report. These considerations will be made at each section 5 re-inspection of a school that was previously judged as requires improvement.

Before the inspection
Staffing

123.   An HMI will normally carry out the monitoring inspection, which lasts one day. On occasion, an OI may lead the monitoring inspection.

124.   Where a school that requires improvement has residential or boarding provision, the lead inspector should inform the Senior HMI for social care in the relevant region.[38]
Planning the first monitoring inspection

125.   Schools judged to require improvement are not required to prepare a separate action plan, but are expected to amend their existing plans to address the areas for improvement identified at the section 5 inspection.

126.   The lead inspector will prepare for the monitoring inspection by reviewing the inspection history and other relevant information in order to build a picture of what has been happening to the school over time. This includes:

- the previous section 5 inspection reports, paying particular attention to the areas recommended for further improvement
- any performance information published since the section 5 inspection
- information from Parent View[39]
- the school's self-evaluation or brief summary, as appropriate. This should include any specific information about curriculum and governance.

127.   During the monitoring inspection, the lead inspector will seek to identify the

barriers that appear to be preventing the school from progressing to good. The lead inspector will decide where to focus inspection activities in order to gather evidence about how quickly and effectively leaders, managers and those responsible for governance are tackling the key areas for improvement identified at the most recent section 5 inspection. Evidence will also be gathered to assess and report on progress made over time since the school was first judged to require improvement and the inspection will report on any barriers that are preventing the school becoming good.

Notification

128.   The lead inspector will telephone the school up to two days in advance of the monitoring inspection. If the headteacher is unavailable, the lead inspector should ask to speak to the next most senior member of staff and explain the arrangements for the monitoring inspection.

129.   This notification period is designed to ensure that those responsible for governance and representatives of the local authority or other appropriate authority are available when the monitoring inspection takes place. In academies that are part of a MAT, the lead inspector should also arrange to speak to the CEO/their delegate or equivalent during the inspection where these roles are part of the structure.[40]

130.   The lead inspector should seek to ensure that the headteacher will be present on the day of the inspection. Once the inspection has been confirmed, the lead inspector will inform the inspection support team at Ofsted, who will send formal notification to the school by email.

131.   During the initial telephone call with the school, the lead inspector will:
- confirm the date of the inspection
- explain the purpose of the monitoring inspection
- confirm that the school will inform the governing body and the local authority/proprietor/trust (as relevant) and that the lead inspector will wish to speak to them during the inspection[41]
- provide the opportunity to discuss any specific issues that the lead inspector should be made aware of before arriving to start the monitoring inspection the next day.

During the inspection

Focus of the monitoring inspection

132.   The monitoring inspection will focus on:
- examining with school leaders and those responsible for governance whether the fundamental actions needed to improve the school are being taken quickly and robustly. Pupils are unlikely to be served well by a school that has focused on peripheral matters or only on planning, rather than directly on the core issues that need tackling
- examining whether school leaders and those responsible for governance are taking action to ensure that pupils receive a good quality of education, and

136

particularly whether they are building or adopting an effective curriculum

- considering the impact of the support provided to the school, with particular reference to the proprietor's or the trust's statement of action and, as appropriate, the impact of any support and challenge provided by any external partners on school improvement
- identifying with the school any barriers to progress towards becoming a good or outstanding school
- reviewing the impact of any support to the school on its improvement
- determining the extent of progress that has been made over time since the school was first judged to require improvement
- where applicable, recommending whether or not the school is ready for a section 5 re-inspection.

Monitoring inspection activities

133.   During the telephone call with the school, the lead inspector will discuss the inspection activities needed to gather evidence of the impact of leaders', managers' and governors' actions since the last section 5 inspection, as well as the progress that has been made since that inspection, and over time.

134.   While the lead inspector will consider the progress made in implementing the school's action plan and the impact of leaders', managers' and governors' actions, lead inspectors are **not** visiting simply to evaluate action plans, but to challenge and support the school. Through inspection activities, the lead inspector will gather evidence about the pace of improvement and ensure that leaders, managers and governors are making the necessary improvements swiftly and sustainably.

135.   It is likely that one or more of the areas for improvement identified at the previous section 5 inspection will be for the school to address specific areas of curriculum weakness. In evaluating the progress that the school is making to address these areas for improvement, inspectors will take account of the 'quality of education' section of the 'school inspection handbook'. Inspectors will also draw on the inspection methodology set out in that handbook in order to support them form a picture of this area.

136.   During the monitoring inspection, the lead inspector will:

- meet the headteacher and other senior leaders (including, where appropriate, the CEO of the MAT/their delegate or equivalent) to establish a purposeful and productive working relationship and focus on discussing the actions taken so far to tackle issues from the section 5 inspection
- hold meetings with representatives of the local authority/proprietor/trust, the chair and members of the governing board, or, where appropriate, the chair of the board of trustees, to establish what action is being taken
- gather any other evidence needed. This may include discussions with staff and pupils, reviewing minutes of governing body meetings, observing learning and pupils' behaviour, and talking to pupils about their work and

their progress

- consider views expressed on Parent View. Where possible, inspectors will talk to parents about their views about the school
- discuss with the headteacher the next steps
- plan time to reflect on and summarise the evidence, draft the monitoring report and consider what, if any, further challenge or support is required.

Arriving at final judgements

137.   At the end of the monitoring inspection, the lead inspector will make a single overarching judgement stating:

- 'senior leaders and governors/the responsible authority/the proprietor/the trust are/is taking effective action to tackle the areas requiring improvement identified at the last section 5 inspection in order to become a good school'

or

- 'senior leaders and governors/the responsible authority/the proprietor/the trust are/is not taking effective action to tackle the areas requiring improvement identified at the last section 5 inspection in order to become a good school.'

At the end of the inspection
Final feedback

138.   The lead inspector will hold a feedback meeting with key stakeholders, including as many governor representatives as possible, at the end of the monitoring inspection. If there are serious concerns about the lack of urgency in tackling weakness at the school, the lead inspector will expect to speak to the governing board/board of trustees, or as many governors/trustees as possible. If needed, they will arrange to do this after the inspection. The lead inspector should also invite the CEO/their delegate or equivalent of a MAT to the final feedback meeting.

139.   Where the lead inspector has concerns about the school, the effectiveness of leadership and/or governance or the lack of urgency with which weaknesses are being tackled, they will share the concerns with the school and make specific recommendations for more urgent action or intervention.

140.   If a monitoring inspection identifies serious concerns about aspects of the school's performance that were not identified in the previous section 5 inspection or in any earlier monitoring visits, these will be reported to us and may lead to the next section 5 inspection being brought forward.

141.   In exceptional circumstances, where the concerns are such that the school requires immediate inspection under section 5, the section 8 inspection may be deemed a section 5 inspection.[42] Where this is the case, all the judgements required by the evaluation schedule will be made and a section 5 inspection report will be produced. Where necessary, more inspectors may be deployed to complete the inspection.

Reporting on the monitoring inspection

142.   The monitoring report letter which is written at the end of the monitoring inspection will include:

- the date of the inspection
- a summary of the type of evidence gathered during the inspection and the context of the school
- the judgement on whether the areas for improvement identified at the section 5 inspection are being tackled effectively
- the relevance, speed and impact of the work being carried out to improve the school since the last section 5 inspection, with particular reference to the inspection findings and including, in all cases, the improvement of teaching and learning and the effectiveness of school leadership, management and governance
- a judgement on the effectiveness of the action taken and the progress made by the school over time towards becoming good
- the suitability of the school's plans to tackle the areas requiring improvement that were identified at the recent inspection and any recommendations from a previous monitoring inspection
- an evaluation of whether school leaders and those responsible for governance are taking effective action to ensure that pupils receive a good quality of education, and particularly whether they are building or adopting an effective curriculum
- any additional priorities for improvement arising from the monitoring inspection.

Monitoring inspections for schools judged inadequate

143.   Schools that are judged inadequate fall into one of two categories, both of which are formally defined in legislation as categories of concern:[43]

- special measures or
- serious weaknesses (defined in law as 'requires significant improvement').

144.   A school requires **special measures** if it is failing to give its pupils an acceptable standard of education, and the persons responsible for leading, managing or governing are not demonstrating the capacity to secure the necessary improvement in the school.[44] If inspectors consider that the evidence shows that the overall effectiveness of the school is inadequate, they must conclude that the school is failing to give an acceptable standard of education. Inspectors must then consider whether leaders, managers and governors are failing to demonstrate the capacity to improve the school. If so, then the school requires special measures.

145.   If inspectors consider that the evidence shows that the overall effectiveness of the school is inadequate, but consider that leaders, managers and governors demonstrate the capacity to improve the school, the school will instead be judged to have **serious weaknesses**. A school with serious weaknesses will have one or more of the key judgements graded inadequate (grade 4) and/or have important weaknesses in the provision for pupils' spiritual, moral, social and cultural development.

146.   Maintained schools and PRUs that are judged to be causing concern will be subject to an academy order. The Secretary of State has a duty to make an academy order for all maintained schools judged to have serious weaknesses ('requiring significant improvement') and those that require special measures. This includes maintained special schools, but excludes maintained nursery schools and non-maintained special schools. For academies that are causing concern, the Secretary of State has a power to terminate the funding agreement, and the academy may become part of a trust or be 'rebrokered' to another trust.

147.   Maintained schools or PRUs that have been issued with an academy order and academies that are being brokered or 'rebrokered' to new sponsors following termination of their funding agreements will normally receive monitoring inspections if they have not been brokered or 'rebrokered' after nine months.

148.   Whether they become a new academy or are brokered or 'rebrokered', these schools will become new sponsored academies and will subsequently be inspected as new schools within three years of operation and normally in the third year. However, in exceptional circumstances, schools that become new academies or are 'rebrokered' may receive a section 8 inspection before their next section 5 inspection.

149.   Academies judged to have serious weaknesses and which are not brokered or 'rebrokered' will be subject to monitoring by us. They will normally be re- inspected within 30 months of the publication of the inspection report in which they were judged to have serious weaknesses.

150.	Academies judged to require special measures, and which are not 'rebrokered', will be subject to monitoring by us. The timing of the next section 5 inspection will be determined by the academy's rate of improvement. However, it will normally take place within 30 months of the publication of the inspection report that judged it to require special measures.

151.	Maintained nursery schools and non-maintained special schools judged inadequate are not subject to academy orders and will be monitored by Ofsted as set out in this section of the handbook.

Appointment of newly qualified teachers (NQTs)

152.	With regard to the appointment of NQTs in maintained schools and PRUs, regulations governing the induction of teachers provide that induction may not be served in a school that has been judged to require special measures, unless HMCI has given permission in writing.

153.	Where the lead inspector at the latest section 5 inspection has informed a maintained school that it may not appoint NQTs, and no monitoring inspections are taking place, the school must seek approval in writing from the relevant Ofsted regional director if it later wishes to appoint NQTs, stating the reasons for the request. The restriction on the appointment of NQTs does not extend to trainee teachers on employment-based training programmes.

Exceptions to routine monitoring of inadequate schools

154.	Maintained schools or PRUs that have been issued with an academy order and academies that are being 'rebrokered' to new sponsors following termination of their funding agreements will not normally receive monitoring inspections.

155.	There is still a requirement for the local authority, proprietor or trust to prepare a statement of action, even though these schools will become new sponsored academies once the new funding agreements are in place. However, with the exception of any safeguarding concerns, which the statement of action must address, the purpose of the statement should be to set out how the relevant local authority and the school will facilitate the transition to the new academy.

156.	In the case of schools where serious safeguarding concerns have been identified, it is essential that early action is taken to ensure that pupils are safe. Ofsted may, in some cases, conduct a section 8 inspection within three to six months after the publication of the section 5 report to ensure that the actions relating to safeguarding that were specified in the statement of action have been implemented. These inspections will not include checks on the extent to which the school and the relevant authority is supporting the transition to sponsored academy status.

157.	Once an inadequate maintained school or PRU has become a sponsored academy, or an inadequate academy has been moved to a new sponsor with a new funding agreement, it will be inspected as a new school, with its first inspection being a section 5 inspection. This will usually take place during the third year of operation.[45] If there is a delay in any school judged inadequate becoming a sponsored academy or being 'rebrokered' to be sponsored by a new trust, Ofsted may initiate monitoring of the school to check on what progress has been made in tackling the areas for improvement.

Notification

158.   The lead inspector will telephone the school up to two days in advance of the monitoring inspection. If the headteacher is unavailable, the lead inspector should ask to speak to the next most senior member of staff and explain the arrangements for the monitoring inspection.

159.   This notification period is designed to ensure that those responsible for governance as well as representatives of the local authority or other appropriate authority are available when the monitoring inspection takes place. In academies that are part of a MAT, the lead inspector should also arrange to speak to the CEO/their delegate or equivalent during the inspection where these roles are part of the structure.[46]

160.   During the initial telephone call with the school, the lead inspector will:
- confirm the date of the inspection
- explain the purpose of the monitoring inspection
- confirm that the school will inform the governing body and the local authority/proprietor/trust (as relevant) and that the lead inspector will wish to speak to them during the inspection[47]
- provide the opportunity to discuss any specific issues that the lead inspector should be made aware of before arriving to start the monitoring inspection the next day.

161.   Requests for a deferral will be handled in accordance with our policy about the deferral of inspections.[48] If a school requests a deferral, HMI must contact the relevant regional duty desk immediately. The deferral policy makes clear that the absence of the headteacher is not normally a reason for deferring an inspection.

Guidance for inspecting schools that have serious weaknesses
Introduction

162.   Schools are judged to have serious weaknesses where HMCI is of the opinion that:

'The school requires significant improvement because it is performing significantly less well than it might in all the circumstances reasonably be expected to perform.'[49]

163.   Schools judged to have serious weaknesses are not required to prepare a separate action plan. They are expected to amend their existing plans or develop a new plan to tackle the areas for improvement identified by the section 5 inspection. The local authority,[50] the proprietor or the trust board[51] must submit a statement of action[52] to HMCI[53] within 10 working days of the school receiving the final section 5 inspection report. An inspector will review the statement of action. Inspectors will provide initial feedback in writing on the fitness for

purpose of the statement within 10 working days of receiving the statement. If the statement of action is judged to be not fit for purpose, the local authority, the proprietor or the trust will be informed. They will be asked to address the weaknesses urgently and to ensure that the revised version is resubmitted to us. Inspectors will re-evaluate the revised statement of action and confirm its fitness for purpose. This will also be reported in the first monitoring letter.

164.   Inspectors will usually conduct the first monitoring inspection within three to six months of the publication of the section 5 inspection report.

165.   During the first monitoring inspection, inspectors will meet with the headteacher, the chair of the governing body or board of trustees, an appropriate representative of the local authority, or the CEO/their delegate or equivalent where an academy is part of a MAT. Inspectors will look for evidence of how well leaders are implementing the statement of action and the school's improvement plan. If any concerns remained following the initial review and feedback of these, inspectors should check to ensure that the current statement of action and improvement plans are fit for purpose and report on this in the first monitoring inspection.

166.   If, after a programme of monitoring inspections lasting up to 30 months, the school has not been removed from the serious weaknesses category of concern, it must be re-inspected under section 5.

The monitoring inspection(s)

167.   Monitoring inspections will focus on the actions taken by the school's leaders and those responsible for governance to tackle the areas for improvement identified in the section 5 inspection that judged the school to have serious weaknesses. Monitoring inspections must also focus on the progress that the school has made since being judged as having serious weaknesses.

168.   The monitoring inspection report must include an assessment of the effectiveness of the action taken by the school towards removal of the serious weaknesses designation.

169.   An overarching judgement will be made stating whether:

- leaders and managers are taking effective action towards the removal of the serious weaknesses designation

or

- leaders and managers are not taking effective action towards the removal of the serious weaknesses designation.

170.   The crucial factor is the anticipated timescale for the removal of the serious weaknesses designation given the current rate of improvement. A school in which leaders and managers are taking effective action is one that will be on course to have the serious weaknesses designation removed within 30 months after the publication of the previous section 5 report. A school that is not taking effective action will be likely to continue to have serious weaknesses, or may require special measures, when the section 5 re-inspection takes place.

171.   The purpose of the monitoring inspection(s) is to evaluate how much progress the school has made by considering:

- the school's response to being judged as having serious weaknesses and how well placed it is to secure rapid improvement based on the actions taken since the previous section 5 inspection
- the extent to which the school's actions are rigorously focused on tackling the key areas for improvement identified at the section 5 inspection
- how effectively the school is adapting its existing school development or improvement plans to meet the challenge of moving out of the serious weaknesses category
- the impact that governors at the school are having on bringing about the necessary improvements
- whether school leaders and those responsible for governance are taking action to ensure that pupils receive an improved quality of education, and particularly whether they have steps in place towards building or taking up an effective curriculum

172.   Monitoring inspections cover aspects of the section 5 evaluation schedule, but are selective and focused sharply on the areas for improvement identified by the section 5 inspection that judged the school to have serious weaknesses.

173.   The work of those responsible for governance should be evaluated to assess the extent to which they are making an effective contribution to leadership and management and the school's performance.

174.   If governance was not identified as an area for improvement at the section 5 inspection but the monitoring inspection raises concerns about weak governance, inspectors must say this in the report. Similarly, where inspectors have concerns about the school's use of the pupil premium, they must highlight this in the report.

175.   Inspectors should consider whether the school's leaders continue to demonstrate convincingly that the school's capacity to improve is strengthening. It is important that the school's leaders are having a significant impact on all of the school's areas of weakness and are capable of securing further improvement.

176.   There should be clear evidence that leaders and managers are having an impact on accelerating learners' progress and thereby raising attainment, particularly in schools where attainment is low. Inspectors must also consider the impact of the external support provided to the school, with particular reference to the proprietor's or the trust's statement of action and, as appropriate, any support and challenge provided by external partners on school improvement.

177.   Not all schools will receive a second or third monitoring inspection. This will depend on the inspectors' evaluation of the quality of leadership and management and the school's rate of improvement towards becoming a good school.

178.   If a second or third monitoring inspection is carried out, inspectors will continue to

evaluate the effectiveness of the school's actions towards the removal of the serious weaknesses designation. An overarching judgement will be made in the same format as specified above for the first monitoring inspection.

179.   While, generally, the judgement will be informed by the school's progress in dealing with each of the areas for improvement identified by the section 5 inspection, other factors that arise during the monitoring period must not be ignored. Inspectors should make the key judgement about the school's overall progress towards the removal of the serious weaknesses designation by considering the evidence they have gathered and using their professional judgement.

180.   Where inspectors are satisfied that the school is taking effective action and making enough progress for the likely removal of the serious weaknesses designation, they will take the decision to deem the section 8 monitoring inspection to be a section 5 inspection. This may result in the school being judged as no longer having serious weaknesses. Where a monitoring inspection identifies significant concerns about aspects of the school's performance that were not identified in the previous section 5 inspection or any earlier monitoring inspections, these must be considered by inspectors and will affect the judgement about the progress made by the school.

181.   When the serious weaknesses designation is removed, whether through a section 8 deemed section 5 inspection or when the next section 5 inspection takes place, the lead inspector must, on the final day of the inspection, notify our relevant regional duty desk.

182.   Where the section 5 inspection team has reached the judgement that the school no longer has serious weaknesses, the oral feedback and written report must include the formal statement that: 'In accordance with section 13 (5) of the Education Act 2005, Her Majesty's Chief Inspector is of the opinion that the school no longer requires significant improvement.'

183.   The introduction to the report should explain why the school was inspected. For example:

'When xx school was inspected in xx 20xx, it was judged to have serious weaknesses. Subsequently, the school was inspected on xxx occasions. At the last monitoring inspection, leaders and managers were judged to be taking/not taking effective action.' After the inspection

Feedback at the end of the monitoringinspection(s)

184.   The school will receive verbal feedback at the end of each monitoring inspection on the fitness for purpose of the statement of action and of the school's improvement plan. Feedback at the end of any monitoring inspections must:

- report the range of evidence gathered
- include the judgement made about the effectiveness of actions towards the removal of serious weaknesses, describing the progress made against the areas for improvement identified during the section 5 inspection that deemed the school to have serious weaknesses

- comment on the impact of any support on school improvement
- cover any specific issues identified by the lead inspector in the pre- inspection preparation and during the inspection
- make clear that the text of the letter or report may differ from the verbal feedback, but that the judgements will not change unless quality assurance deems that appropriate.

185.   The lead inspector should identify additional priorities only where they are essential to the school's further development. Progress against these priorities has to be evaluated at the next monitoring inspection and reported in the monitoring report. They are not to be added to the list of judgements to be made as set out in the annex to the covering letter. The priorities should help the school focus on what needs to be done next to improve the quality of education.

The monitoring inspection letter and report

186.   For all monitoring inspections, the school will receive a brief covering letter with the judgements included and a monitoring report, both of which will be published on the Ofsted website. The first and possibly the second monitoring letter will need to comment on the fitness for purpose of the statement of action and of the school's improvement plan.

187.   When a monitoring inspection focuses on only one or two aspects of provision, this should be clearly explained in the evidence section.

188.   The monitoring letter and report must include:
- a summary of the evidence gathered by inspectors
- a brief summary of any significant changes to the context of the school
- a judgement about the effectiveness of actions towards the removal of the serious weaknesses designation
- a judgement about the effectiveness of leadership and management, with specific reference to the impact that governors'/trustees' actions are having on improvements
- an evaluation of whether school leaders and those responsible for governance are taking effective action to ensure that pupils receive a good quality of education, and particularly whether they are building or adopting an effective curriculum
- brief bullet points evaluating the progress made by the school in tackling the key areas for improvement, and brief bullet points setting out:
  - strengths in the school's approaches to securing improvement
  - weaknesses in the school's approaches to securing improvement
- reference to the impact of any support provided to the school.

Guidance for inspecting schools that are subject to special measures
Introduction

189.   Schools are made subject to special measures under section 44(1) of the

Education Act 2005, where the Chief Inspector is of the opinion that:

'The school is failing to give its pupils an acceptable standard of education and the persons responsible for leading, managing or governing the school are not demonstrating the capacity to secure the necessary improvement in the school.'[54]

190.   Schools that are subject to special measures are not required to prepare a separate action plan. These schools should review their existing plans to tackle the areas for improvement identified by the section 5 inspection.

191.   The local authority,[55] the proprietor or the trust board[56] must submit a statement of action[57] to HMCI[58] within 10 working days of the school receiving the section 5 inspection report. An inspector will review the statement of action. Inspectors will provide initial feedback in writing on the fitness for purpose of the statement within 10 working days of receiving the statement. If the statement of action is judged to be not fit for purpose, the local authority, proprietor or trust will be informed and asked to address the weaknesses urgently. The revised version is resubmitted to Ofsted. An inspector will re- evaluate the revised statement of action and confirm its fitness for purpose.

The monitoring inspections

192.   Inspectors will usually conduct the first monitoring inspection within three to six months of the publication of the section 5 inspection report.

193.   A school may receive up to five monitoring inspections over the 30 months following the publication of the section 5 inspection report that placed it in special measures. The focus will be on getting schools out of a category of concern and the expectation is for schools subject to special measures to improve within 18 to 24 months. Re-inspecting such schools at 30 months should be the exception.

194.   At the end of a monitoring inspection, inspectors will consider whether the school has made sufficient progress and no longer requires special measures. Where this is the case, the section 8 inspection will be deemed a section 5 inspection. All the judgements required by the section 5 school inspection handbook will be made and a full inspection report produced.

195.   If, after a programme of monitoring lasting up to 30 months, a school continues to be subject to special measures, it must be re-inspected under section 5.

During the inspection

196.   During the monitoring inspections, inspectors are required to evaluate the school's progress towards the removal of special measures. Inspectors will make an overarching judgement on whether:

■ leaders and managers are taking effective action towards the removal of special measures

or

■ leaders and managers are not taking effective action towards the removal of special measures.

197.   While this judgement will be informed by the school's progress in dealing with each

of the areas for improvement identified by the section 5 inspection, other factors that arise during the monitoring period must not be ignored.

198.   The crucial factor is the anticipated timescale for the removal of special measures given the current rate of improvement. A school that is taking effective action will be on course to have special measures removed within 18 to 24 months of the monitoring period following publication of the inspection report that placed the school in special measures. A school that is not taking effective action will be likely to continue to require special measures when the section 5 re-inspection takes place.

199.   At the final meeting, the inspection team must:

- judge the progress that the school is making towards the removal of special measures, weighing the progress made against the areas for improvement identified during the section 5 inspection that placed the school in special measures
- decide whether the school should be permitted to appoint NQTs or, in the case of academies, make appropriate recommendations regarding such appointments.

Evaluating support

200.   During the first monitoring inspection, inspectors will meet with the headteacher, the CEO/their delegate or equivalent in a MAT, the chair of the governing body/board of trustees and as many governors/trustees as possible. Inspectors will look for evidence of how well relevant leaders and those responsible for governance are implementing the statement of action and the school's improvement plan.

201.   On subsequent inspections, inspectors will also report on the impact of the trust's support for the school, along with any other external support and challenge on school improvement.

202.   At the conclusion of each monitoring inspection, inspectors should consider whether the school continues to require special measures.

203.   Whatever the outcome, during the feedback at the end of the inspection inspectors should explain clearly the reasons for the decision to remove or not to remove the special measures judgement.

204.   The judgement that special measures are no longer required may involve reference to:

- evidence from previous monitoring inspections
- the best interests of the pupils. This is paramount
- the school's ability to demonstrate that it meets the needs of all pupils and has the capacity for sustained improvement. This determines the timing of removal of special measures
- the extent to which capacity for sustained improvement has been demonstrated by leaders and managers at all levels, rather than through an over-reliance on external support or on one or two individuals in the school

- the overall rate of improvement. Some schools may not be making enough progress for the removal of special measures before the re-inspection.

205. When special measures are removed, inspectors must, on the final day of the inspection, notify the relevant Ofsted regional duty desk to log the necessary details.

After the inspection

Feedback at the end of the monitoring inspection

206. At the end of the first monitoring inspection, inspectors will provide oral feedback and make clear whether the judgement or recommendation about the appointment of NQTs should remain.

207. At the end of each monitoring inspection, oral feedback must include the judgement made about the effectiveness of actions and the progress towards the removal of special measures, describing the progress made against the area(s) for improvement that formed the focus for each monitoring inspection.

208. Inspectors should identify additional priorities only where they are essential to the school's further development. Progress against these priorities has to be evaluated and reported on at the next monitoring inspection. They are not to be added to the list of judgements to be made as set out in the report. Any new priorities should help the school focus on what needs to be done next to improve the quality of education.

209. Where the inspection team has reached the judgement that special measures are no longer required, the oral feedback and written report should include the formal statement that:

'In accordance with section 13(4) of the Education Act 2005, Her Majesty's Chief Inspector is of the opinion that the school no longer requires special measures.'

210. This judgement is not subject to moderation. However, as with all inspections, it should remain confidential until the final report is sent to the school. Where special measures are removed, a full section 5 report must be written.

211. The monitoring letter and report for each of the monitoring inspections must include:

- the judgement about the effectiveness of actions towards the removal of special measures
- a judgement about whether the school should be permitted to employ NQTs
- a brief summary of any significant changes to the context of the school
- an evaluation of the progress made by the school in tackling the key areas for improvement and brief bullet points setting out:
  - strengths in the school's approaches to securing improvement
  - weaknesses in the school's approaches to securing improvement
- where applicable, a judgement on the impact of any support provided to the school.

212. In addition to the above, the monitoring letter and report for the first monitoring inspection must include:

- a judgement on the fitness for purpose of the statement of action and of the school's improvement plan
- an evaluation of whether school leaders and those responsible for governance are taking effective action to ensure that pupils receive a good quality of education, and particularly whether they are building or adopting an effective curriculum
- when a monitoring inspection focuses on only one or two aspects of provision, this should be clearly explained in the evidence section.

213. Progress made on additional priorities for further improvement, identified in previous monitoring inspections, should be reported in the monitoring report. They should not be added as bullet points alongside the original areas for improvement identified at the section 5 inspection.

214. When it is judged that the school no longer requires special measures, the section 8 monitoring inspection is deemed to be a section 5 inspection. A full inspection report must be written and published in accordance with the section 5 school inspection handbook.

215. The school details page of the report must include the statement:

'This inspection was carried out under section 8 of the Education Act 2005. The inspection was deemed a section 5 inspection under the same Act.'

216. The introduction to the report should explain why the school was inspected. For example:

'When xxx School was inspected in xx 20xx, it was judged to require special measures. Subsequently, the school was inspected on xxx occasions. At the previous monitoring inspection, leaders and managers were judged to be taking/not to be taking effective action towards the removal of special measures.'

217. A report that removes special measures should include the following statement in accordance with the section 5 report template guidance:

'In accordance with section 13(4) of the Education Act 2005, Her Majesty's Chief Inspector is of the opinion that the school no longer requires special measures'.

Inspections with no formal designation

218. Under section 8(2) of the Education Act 2005 (the Act), Ofsted can carry out inspections to follow up concerns about schools that are not in a category of concern but that have been brought to our attention through, for example, a qualifying complaint made to us or by other means.

219. This part of the section 8 handbook provides guidance for school inspections with a specific focus. This could include a focus on the effectiveness of safeguarding arrangements and/or aspects of:

- quality of education (or, for example, a subject survey visit examining a particular subject through the lens of quality of education)
- personal development
- behaviour and attitudes
- leadership and management (including governance).

220. Inspectors will follow this guidance where Ofsted has concerns that the safety of pupils and/or staff is at risk or where information suggests that there has been a serious breakdown in leadership and management or a decline in standards. Where we receive information about a school that causes us concern, we will weigh this carefully against all other data and information we hold before making a decision on whether to inspect the school under 'no formal designation' procedures. The decision on whether to inspect the school is made by the relevant Ofsted regional director. Where an inspection takes place as a result of a qualifying complaint, inspectors must also take account of guidance issued by the national complaints team.[59]

221. Certain types of outstanding school are exempt from inspection under section 5 of the Act. If an exempt school undergoes significant change, for example through merging with another school or by adding a new phase or a key stage, we will select it for inspection under section 8(2) of the Act. Under section 9 of the Act, HMCI may elect to treat such inspection as if it were an inspection under section 5. In such circumstances, if the expanded school is judged outstanding it will be exempt from future inspection under section 5. These inspections are also carried out under the no formal designation guidance.

222. These inspections are selective and focus sharply on the issues brought to Ofsted's attention that caused the school to be inspected. As a result, inspectors should not make judgements that consider the whole of the evaluation schedule for the areas inspected. The judgements are made based on the areas of focus. Where the inspection focus is on the school's safeguarding arrangements, inspectors will take account of the guidance on inspecting safeguarding.[60]

223. It is important to note that those leading, managing and governing a school are responsible for the effectiveness of safeguarding arrangements. Governors in particular must ensure that the school's arrangements for safeguarding meet statutory requirements. Concerns about safeguarding may raise wider questions about the effectiveness of

leadership and management and governors' ability to hold the school to account. Therefore, in some cases, inspections with no formal designation will focus on both elements and may be expanded as appropriate. It is the responsibility of the lead inspector, using their professional judgement, to determine the precise focus of the inspection and make sure that leaders are fully aware of this when the inspection begins. An inspection may begin with a specific focus on safeguarding, but its scope may be widened to cover leadership and management or other aspects of the provision where appropriate.

224.   If, during the inspection, inspectors are sufficiently concerned about the overall standard of education provided by the school, the inspection may, under section 9 of the Act, be treated as ('deemed') a section 5 inspection. In these cases, all the judgements required by the full evaluation schedule will be made and a section 5 inspection report produced and published.

Before the inspection
Staffing and scheduling the inspection

225.   These inspections are normally led by an HMI, regardless of the size of the school. However, more inspectors may be required depending on the complexity of the issues that were brought to Ofsted's attention and that caused the school to be inspected. The inspection will normally last for two days. However, it may in some instances be shorter or longer, depending on the circumstances of the school and the nature of the concerns that led to the inspection.

226.   Inspections being carried out as a result of a qualifying complaint made to Ofsted will normally be led by an HMI.

227.   Once we receive information that causes concern and leads to a decision to inspect, the inspection should take place as soon as is practicable. The exact timing is, however, at the discretion of the relevant regional director.

Notification

228.   The notice given to the school of the inspection will be half a day, the same as that for section 5 inspections. However, Ofsted may conduct the inspection without notice. Where this is the case, the HMI will normally telephone the school about 15 minutes before arriving on site.

229.   Where notice of inspection is given, the HMI will make the initial telephone call to the school to inform them that an inspection will take place. If required, the HMI may arrange a time for a second longer telephone conversation with the headteacher to discuss the inspection. The HMI will make the purpose of the inspection clear during the initial telephone call with the headteacher. If the inspection is conducted without notice, the HMI must make the focus of the inspection and the reasons that led to it clear to the headteacher at the earliest opportunity after she or he arrives at the school.

230.   If the school is being inspected because of a qualifying complaint made to Ofsted

about the school under section 11A of the Act, the HMI will inform the school of this, as well as that, as a result of the wider issues raised by the complaint, a decision has been taken to inspect the school.

231.   The HMI will explain that the inspection will focus on the wider issues raised by the complaint and will not investigate the complaint itself. If the complainant has requested confidentiality, the HMI must take all practicable steps to ensure that the complainant's identity is not disclosed to the school. At times, the nature of the complaint may mean that the headteacher is able to discern the identity of the complainant. Regardless, HMI should not confirm the complainant's identity.

232.   The headteacher, at the end of the telephone conversation, should be in a position to understand the reasons for, and the purpose and focus of, the inspection and the judgements that will be made. There is no mandatory requirement for a school to inform parents about the inspection. The HMI should invite the school to inform parents so that there is an opportunity for parents to contribute their views about the school through Parent View.

233.   Following the pre-inspection telephone conversation, Ofsted will confirm the arrangements for the inspection by sending a notification letter to the school. Where no prior notice of the inspection is given, formal notification of the inspection by Ofsted will be provided to the school following the arrival of the inspector/s.

234.   Schools are not required to provide copies of any information in advance of the inspection, but if these are offered, the HMI should accept them.

Preparing for the inspection

235.   The HMI must check the provider information portal (PIP) for information relevant to the inspection. The HMI will brief any team inspectors about the inspection and ensure that the key lines of enquiry and key issues to pursue are understood. Where an inspection is carried out as a result of issues raised in a qualifying complaint made to Ofsted, inspectors must not investigate the complaint itself during the inspection or seek parents' views on the complaint itself. It is the whole-school issues raised in the complaint that will be followed up during inspection.

236.   To prepare for the inspection, inspectors will review:
- copies of any qualifying complaint(s) received, other information on the PIP and any response letters
- issues raised by the investigation of any qualifying complaints[61] about the school
- the previous section 5 inspection report, where one exists, and any section 8 reports from, for example, surveys or monitoring inspections
- Ofsted's IDSR
- information from the pre-inspection telephone conversation with the headteacher
- any documentation emailed to the HMI in advance of the inspection, as

agreed between the headteacher and the HMI.

During the inspection

Engagement with the school's senior leadership team

237. The meeting at the start of the inspection may or may not involve the whole of the school's senior leadership team. The headteacher may be of the view that a meeting with her or him alone, or with one or two senior leaders, will be sufficient to limit any potential interruption to the school's normal routines.

238. The meeting with school leaders at the start of the inspection will cover pertinent issues about the school and the focus of the inspection. It must give the headteacher and others the opportunity to present an oral summary evaluation of the school's position on the issues, and identify where evidence may be found.

Evidence gathering during the inspection

239. The kinds of activities conducted during these inspections are no different to section 5 inspections. However, where the focus of the inspection is on the school's safeguarding arrangements, activities should focus on safeguarding issues, including but not exclusively:

- a review of the single central record and safeguarding policy
- a review of referrals made to the designated person for safeguarding in the school and those that were subsequently referred to the designated officer, and their resolution
- a review of records of staff training on child protection and the prevention of radicalisation and extremism
- a review of the school's procedures for dealing with relevant staffing issues, for example suspensions or disciplinary investigations/actions over issues of child protection and/or safety. This is not a review of individual cases, but of school procedures in dealing with such issues
- discussions with pupils and staff
- a check of the school's internet safety procedures
- a review of the personal, social and health education curriculum and how it links to issues of safety and pupils' welfare
- a review of persistent absence cases and exclusions data
- consideration of the views of parents and carers through Parent View and, where practicable, through discussions/meetings with parents or groups of parents during the inspection
- any relevant issues that appear to be of greatest concern from pre-inspection evidence
- any other issues that affect care, safety or child protection and that do not appear to have been tackled fully
- any issues that relate to poor pupil behaviour.

240. The exact structure of the day will depend on the issues to be followed up and is

likely to be drawn from the sources of evidence described in the 'school inspection handbook'.[62]

241.   During the inspection, the HMI will maintain an ongoing dialogue with the headteacher and senior managers. It is especially important to make sure that the headteacher and senior managers understand any emerging issues. The final feedback to the school, especially when it is challenging, should not be a surprise to the headteacher and senior leaders.

242.   If inspectors conduct observations in lessons, the lead inspector will discuss with the headteacher the strategy for providing feedback to individual teachers. The feedback will be offered in accordance with the 'school inspection handbook'.

Judgements

243.   Inspectors should not make judgements that consider the whole of the evaluation schedule for the areas of focus inspected; this is only necessary for section 5 inspections. If there are weaknesses in a specific area, inspectors may make specific recommendations about what the school needs to do to tackle the weaknesses in that area.

244.   If, however, inspectors have sufficient evidence that some of the core reporting areas for judging a school under section 5 have declined significantly, then they will need to consider whether the effectiveness of the provision as a whole has declined. In such circumstances, it may be necessary for the inspection to be deemed a section 5 inspection, under section 9 of the Act. In these cases, all the judgements required by the evaluation schedule will be made and a section 5 inspection report published.

245.   Alternatively (for schools that are not exempt from routine inspection), where evidence prompts concerns that overall standards may no longer be as last reported under section 5, but where no serious concerns have been identified, the lead inspector may recommend to the relevant regional director that the next section 5 inspection be brought forward. The timing of any such inspection should not be indicated to the school. If the inspection raises concerns, these concerns should be reported at the feedback meeting.

246.   Where safeguarding is a focus for the inspection or where it becomes a focus during the course the inspection, the lead inspector, having reviewed all the evidence gathered during the inspection, will report in the letter whether safeguarding is effective.

247.   If there are relatively minor shortcomings in a school's procedures and the school is able to resolve them on the day of the inspection, then inspectors can make an assessment that safeguarding is effective. If safeguarding is not effective and/or if pupils are considered to be at risk, the lead inspector will convert the inspection to a section 5 inspection.

At the end of the inspection
Final feedback

248.   The HMI and headteacher should discuss which other members of staff, if any, will attend the feedback session, especially if the feedback is likely to be challenging or is likely

to raise sensitive issues.

249. The oral feedback at the end of the inspection, typically towards the end of the second day of a two-day inspection, must:

- report the extent of the evidence base
- cover the issues brought to Ofsted's attention that caused the school to be inspected
- be clear about whether the school's safeguarding arrangements are effective
- be clear about the judgements being made on the specific areas of focus for the inspection
- identify the school's areas of strength and any aspects that the school needs to improve in relation to safeguarding and child protection, and the specific areas of focus for the inspection
- make clear that the text of the report may differ from the oral feedback.

Unannounced behaviour inspections

250. Schools will be selected for a section 8 unannounced behaviour inspection because Ofsted has cause for concern about behaviour and attitudes. Concerns may arise from previous inspection reports, parents' views, complaints, information from the local authority or data about exclusions or attendance.

251. The inspection will focus on the factors that research and inspection evidence indicates contribute most strongly to pupils' positive behaviour and attitudes. These factors are:

- a calm and orderly environment in the school and the classroom, as this is essential for pupils to be able to learn
- the setting of clear routines and expectations for the behaviour of pupils across all aspects of school life, not just in the classroom
- a strong focus on attendance and punctuality to minimise disruption
- clear and effective behaviour and attendance policies with clearly defined consequences that are applied consistently and fairly by all staff
- pupils' motivation and positive attitudes to learning as important predictors of attainment. The development of positive attitudes can also have a longer-term impact on how pupils approach learning tasks in later stages of education
- a positive and respectful school culture in which staff know and care about pupils
- an environment in which pupils feel safe, and in which bullying, discrimination and peer-on-peer abuse – online or face-to-face – are not accepted and are dealt with quickly, consistently and effectively whenever they occur.

252. The inspection will make a judgement on the effectiveness of the actions taken by leaders and managers, including governors, since the previous inspection (where applicable) to improve behaviour. This will include evaluating how well leaders are securing consistently positive attitudes to learning or maintaining previously high standards of behaviour and attitudes to learning.

253. If the evidence gathered and scrutinised during the inspection indicates that behaviour, welfare and safety or any other aspects of the school may be inadequate, and pupils are at risk of harm, the lead inspector may, under section 9 of the Act, deem the inspection as a section 5 inspection. If the inspection converts to a section 5 inspection, all of the judgements required by the full evaluation schedule will be made and a section 5 inspection report will be produced and published. In such cases, the lead inspector must contact the regional duty desk to confirm that they are deeming the inspection a section 5 inspection.

254. A monitoring report should be written unless the relevant regional director confirms that the section 8 is deemed a section 5 inspection.

Before the inspection

Staffing and scheduling the inspection

255.　Unannounced behaviour inspections will usually be conducted by one inspector for one day. These inspections may be led by HMI or by OIs.

Notification

256.　The inspector will contact the school 15 minutes before arriving to announce the inspection to the headteacher or other senior member of staff if the headteacher is unavailable. This notification call is simply to inform the school that the inspection is about to begin and the lead inspector will leave all other arrangements until they arrive at the school.

257.　If no one from the school answers the telephone, inspectors will arrive at the school and announce the inspection on arrival.

258.　Inspections should begin at around 8.15am and not before 8am.

259.　On arrival, the lead inspector will begin their observation of the start of the school day, keeping the initial meeting with the headteacher brief. The lead inspector will agree with the headteacher a time to meet after observing the start of the school day.

260.　If the school is being inspected as a result of a qualifying complaint about the school, the lead inspector should inform the headteacher in line with the guidance in paragraphs 218–249.

Preparing for the inspection

261.　The lead inspector will prepare for the inspection by:

- reading and recording any comments about behaviour and attendance in the school's latest section 5 inspection report and any section 8 inspection reports, for example from survey visits
- evaluating the school's behaviour policy, which should be available on the school's website
- identifying, from the previous section 5 report, whether the school has any pupils who attend alternative provision, and noting any comments about how well these pupils are progressing and behaving
- analysing the most up-to-date information about permanent and fixed- term exclusions available in analyse school performance (ASP) and the IDSR, paying particular attention to the repeated use of fixed-term exclusions and to any groups that are excluded disproportionately[63]
- analysing the most up-to-date information about overall and persistent absence available in ASP and the IDSR, again paying particular attention to groups of pupils[64]
- checking Ofsted's PIP for information about any complaints about the school.

262.　From their initial analysis, the lead inspector will arrive at key lines of enquiry and key issues that will be shared with the headteacher and senior leaders at a brief meeting once the inspection begins. The key issues and lines of enquiry that are the focus of the inspection may change as evidence is gathered during the inspection.

During the inspection

263. The majority of the inspection activity must focus on observing short parts of lessons and observing informal times of the school day in order to evaluate pupils' behaviour and attitudes. In addition, inspectors will be guided by Annex B, which sets out in more detail the types of activities that inspectors will typically conduct during the inspection.

264. The lead inspector will meet with senior staff briefly to inform them of the key issues and lines of enquiry from pre-inspection analysis and then arrange a further meeting to discuss emerging findings and follow up any issues that arise during the day. This meeting must not overlap with lunchtime periods, break times or with the time pupils leave the school, as these times of the day must be observed. The lead inspector may also request that a senior member of staff be present during the scrutiny of documentation in order to answer questions as they arise.

265. As it is important that the lead inspector sees pupils' typical behaviour throughout the day, the lead inspector will not jointly observe short extracts or whole classes with the headteacher, senior leaders or staff.

266. To gather and evaluate evidence about the impact of actions taken by leaders and managers, including governors, to improve behaviour, inspectors will evaluate pupils' behaviour, the management of behaviour and the culture of the school.

267. Inspectors will carry out evidence-gathering activities that include, but are not limited to:

- observations of pupils' behaviour and their attitudes to learning in lessons (including, where relevant, with new, temporary or less experienced teachers). A particular focus will be placed on low-level disruption, for example pupils:
  - calling out without permission
  - being late to lessons or slow to start work or follow instructions
  - showing a lack of respect for each other and staff
  - not bringing the right equipment
  - chatting when they are supposed to be working or listening to the teacher
  - using mobile devices inappropriately in lessons
  - wasting time, through teachers having to deal with inappropriate uniform
  - packing up well before the end of the lesson
- observations of pupils' behaviour throughout the day, including discussions with pupils during break times and lunchtimes, arriving and leaving the school
- observation of any system of 'internal exclusion' that the school uses to manage behaviour

- at least one planned discussion with a group of pupils whose behaviour the school has helped to improve over time
- scrutiny of documentary evidence[65]
- discussions with leaders and staff
- gathering evidence about the typical behaviour of pupils who are not in the school on the day of the inspection
- visiting any off-site unit that the schools runs for pupils whose behaviour is poor, or who have low attendance.

268.   Inspectors must take account of the following:

- pupils' attitudes to learning and their conduct in lessons
- pupils' conduct around the school, including the way in which they speak to each other and to staff
- how well leaders and staff model good behaviour to pupils
- how well leaders and managers model good behaviour management techniques to staff
- the effectiveness of the management of pupils' behaviour, including how well leaders, managers and governors analyse and use documentary evidence to improve the way behaviour is managed
- if the school uses fixed-term or internal exclusion, the impact of this on improving behaviour
- pupils' views about behaviour and all types of bullying (these views must be gathered from a range of pupils at informal times, not just from a formal discussion)
- any specific issues raised in the previous inspection report about pupils' behaviour and whether these have been tackled effectively and are showing clear and sustainable signs of improvement.

Judgement

269.   Inspectors will make a judgement on the effectiveness of the actions taken by leaders and managers, including governors, since the previous inspection, to improve behaviour. This includes securing consistently positive attitudes to learning, or maintaining previously high standards of behaviour and attitudes to learning.

270.   The inspection report will state one of the following:

■   For schools where behaviour was judged to require improvement at their previous section 5 inspection:

'Leaders and managers have/have not taken effective action to improve behaviour and secure consistently positive attitudes to learning.'

■   For schools where behaviour was judged to be good or outstanding at their previous section 5 inspection:

'Leaders and managers have/have not taken effective action to maintain the high standards of behaviour and attitudes identified at the school's previous inspection.'

271. The monitoring report should cover the following, with specific examples:

- pupils' conduct around the school during the inspection, including the way in which they move around the school, speak to each other and to staff, conform with the school's dress code; and pupils' typical conduct around the school, evidenced by pupils' views, staff's views, and the school's documentary evidence
- pupils' attitudes to learning during the lessons observed and pupils' typical attitudes to learning, evidenced by pupils' views, staff's views and the school's documentary evidence
- how well pupils' behaviour is managed by leaders and staff on a day-to-day basis
- the extent to which the school's culture promotes and supports good behaviour, including:
  - the way in which staff speak to pupils and to parents and carers
  - how consistently staff reinforce the school's expectations of pupils' behaviour
  - the way in which the headteacher and other leaders model the behaviour that is expected of all staff
  - the way in which the headteacher and other leaders support staff to promote good behaviour.

272. The monitoring report will include recommendations that set out what the school needs to do to improve the way it manages pupils' behaviour. How well the school has addressed these recommendations will be followed up during the school's next inspection.

At the end of the inspection
Final feedback

273. Feedback should be offered at the end of the day.[66] Normally, the final feedback meeting will be attended by:

- the headteacher/principal
- other senior staff as appropriate
- the chair of the school's governing board/academy board of trustees and as many governors/trustees as possible
- in an academy that is part of a MAT, the CEO/their delegate or equivalent
- a representative from the local authority (for maintained schools) or academy sponsor.

Annex A – Section 8 inspection outcomes of a good or non-exempt outstanding school

Is the school still at least good?

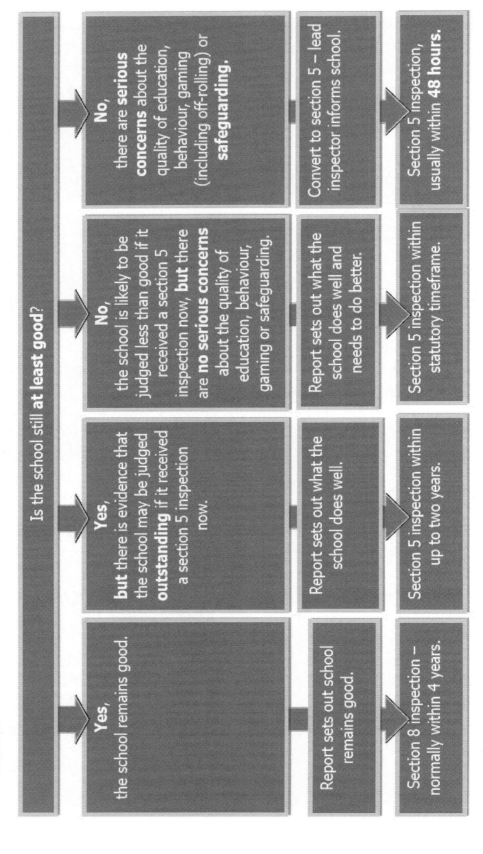

Yes, the school remains good.	Yes, but there is evidence that the school may be judged outstanding if it received a section 5 inspection now.	No, the school is likely to be judged less than good if it received a section 5 inspection now, but there are no serious concerns about the quality of education, behaviour, gaming or safeguarding.	No, there are serious concerns about the quality of education, behaviour, gaming (including off-rolling) or safeguarding.
Report sets out school remains good.	Report sets out what the school does well.	Report sets out what the school does well and needs to do better.	Convert to section 5 – lead inspector informs school.
Section 8 inspection – normally within 4 years.	Section 5 inspection within up to two years.	Section 5 inspection within statutory timeframe.	Section 5 inspection, usually within 48 hours.

Annex B – Inspection activities relating to behaviour

Observations of behaviour and informal discussions with pupils

1.   Inspectors must observe behaviour at the following times:
- pupils' arrival at school
- in lessons
- in between lessons
- break-time
- lunchtime
- as pupils leave the school.

2.   During these times, inspectors should talk to pupils about behaviour, their welfare and their safety.

Pupils' arrival at school

3.   Inspectors will:
- observe interactions between pupils, for example whether they are pleasant and relaxed or aggressive. Consider whether different groups of pupils look comfortable together and whether there are any tensions
- ask different pupils about their journey to and from school, for example how safe they feel; whether they encounter any bullying during that time; what they would do to seek help from the school if they did
- evaluate whether there are sufficient numbers of staff on duty. Consider where staff are situated and whether they are actively supervising
- observe interactions between staff and parents, and between staff and pupils, for example how staff greet pupils and speak to them and whether this provides a good role model
- consider pupils' vulnerability in the playground, for example whether pupils have to wait for a long time before entering the school, whether they are in full view of the school or whether there are areas where pupils might be vulnerable
- in special schools and PRUs, observe pupils as they get out of taxis and minibuses and ask them about their journey. Consider aspects of safety, such as supervision and bullying
- if parents and carers are available, ask them their views about behaviour and safety
- consider how well staff uphold the school's expectations, for example by reminding pupils about how they should treat each other in the playground, move around the school and make sure their uniform is correct
- consider whether pupils are dressed according to the school's uniform or dress code.

Pupils' behaviour between lessons and on arrival at lessons

4.   Inspectors will:

- consider what interactions are like between pupils, and between staff and pupils, as pupils move from one lesson to the next, for example whether staff remind pupils of expectations, convey a sense of urgency in getting to the next lesson promptly and greet them as they arrive
- evaluate the extent to which pupils are aware of and respect each other's physical space
- consider how well staff model the behaviour expected from pupils
- consider how promptly and calmly pupils enter classrooms and how quickly they respond to staff's instructions.

Pupils' behaviour at break time

5.   Inspectors will:

- consider how pupils are grouped, and observe whether there are any tensions or if certain pupils are excluded
- seek pupils' views about bullying, for example whether they experience bullying, what they do to seek help, how they feel about break-times, whether there are any 'no go areas' for different year groups. Include any pupils who are by themselves
- evaluate the structure of break-times and how well the structure supports good behaviour. In primary and special schools, consider how well pupils are being taught to play and interact well together. In secondary schools, consider whether the outdoor space allows all groups to be safe
- go to the far reaches of the school site to consider how well supervised these are and whether there are any spaces where bullying could easily occur
- evaluate the appropriateness of the language pupils use towards each other, for example whether it is respectful or includes derogatory language.[67] Evaluate how well staff challenge such language if they hear it
- consider behaviour in and around the toilets, especially in secondary schools, and how well supervised they are.

Pupils' behaviour at lunchtimes

6.   Inspectors will:

- observe the same aspects as for break-times, such as interactions, supervision, safety and organisation, and check that pupils have an appropriate place to eat their lunch if they bring their own
- evaluate how well pupils conduct themselves in the dining room and how well staff model desired behaviours to the pupils
- establish whether pupils who are eligible for free school meals have a different payment system to others and whether this marks them out as different

- ask the lunchtime staff about bullying, for example what they see and how they help to prevent it

- ask the lunchtime staff about behaviour in general. What they see and how pupils respond to them, for example when lunchtime staff ask pupils to pick up litter or clear their table.

Observations of pupils' behaviour and their attitudes to learning in lessons

7.   Inspectors should carry out short visits to a range of lessons. Observations should include some starts and ends of lessons in order to evaluate how well teachers manage transition between lessons, how quickly pupils settle, and whether pupils remain focused to the end of lessons.

8.   Evaluations should include consideration of the following:

- whether pupils arrive promptly at lessons and with the equipment they need for the lesson

- how promptly pupils respond to staff's instructions

- how clear the school's expectations of behaviour are, for example through classroom displays

- how well teachers use the school's behaviour management system, including issuing rewards as well as sanctions if these are part of the procedures, and how effective this system is in supporting staff to manage behaviour and helping pupils to behave well

- how well pupils respond to teaching assistants and other support staff

- how well pupils interact with each other, and whether they work cooperatively in groups or pairs as required

- whether pupils are supportive of each other's learning, for example not making derogatory comments about other pupils' answers to questions

- how well staff help pupils to interact positively with each other, for example whether they model appropriate ways to talk to other people, tolerate or ignore put-downs or tackle them, and are explicit about the need to respect others.

9.   Inspectors should ask pupils questions about typical behaviour in lessons, if it is possible to do so without disturbing learning.

Observation of 'internal exclusion' room, 'remove room' or equivalent

10.   If the school uses this type of provision, inspectors should visit this during lesson time to evaluate:

- leaders' intended purpose for the room

- the appropriateness of the room as a place for pupils to learn, considering pupils' age and particular needs

- pupils' behaviour while in the room

- the use of the room, for example how many pupils are present and whether this is typical (through scrutiny of records)

- how well the room is used to improve behaviour, for example whether there is any follow-up action after the pupil has attended the room
- whether the school informs and involves parents and carers when their child has been placed in the room
- whether any patterns shown by the room's use are used to provide appropriate support and challenge to staff.

Discussions with pupils

11.   Inspectors should hold at least one discussion about behaviour and safety with a group of pupils that the school has worked with to improve their behaviour. These pupils might include those who:

- have previously been excluded more than once
- attend some alternative provision
- have moved from another school on a managed move
- were previously involved in bullying other pupils
- were previously disruptive in lessons but are now 'back on track'.

12.   During the discussions, inspectors should explore pupils' views about:

- what behaviour is typically like in school and in their lessons
- variations in behaviour from lesson to lesson
- behaviour outside lessons
- the school's reward and sanction system, including what difference this has made to their behaviour
- if they or any of their friends attend an alternative provision for part of the week, why they were selected and how it has helped them
- their understanding of the school's stance on bullying, including what happens if someone bullies or is bullied
- how the school has helped them to improve their behaviour
- how the school is helping them to maintain the improvements
- how well the school has worked with their parents or carers to lead to these improvements
- how often and where they hear derogatory language – including homophobic, biphobic, transphobic, racist, sexist or discriminatory language – and the school's response to this.

Scrutiny of documentary evidence

13.   Inspectors should scrutinise the school's records of behaviour and the school's analysis of behaviour in order to evaluate how well leaders and managers analyse documentary evidence and then use it to improve the way in which behaviour is managed.

14.   Documents should include records and analysis of:

- bullying incidents
- pupils being removed from lessons

- permanent, fixed-term and internal exclusion
- pupils leaving the school roll
- rewards and sanctions, including how senior leaders check that rewards and sanctions are used consistently by all staff.

15.   Inspectors should consider any patterns shown by such records and analysis, for example pupils being removed more from certain lessons or at a particular time of day, pupils with SEND or pupils from a particular year group or ethnic group receiving more sanctions than others do.

16.   Inspectors should use the school's documentation and its analysis to inform their judgements about typical behaviour around the school and in lessons.

Discussion with staff and leaders

17.   Inspectors should talk briefly to staff when appropriate, including NQTs where applicable, support staff, cover supervisors, lunchtime supervisors and other non-teaching staff, for example when they are on duty in the playground or in the corridors, to ascertain their views on behaviour. Inspectors must hold a discussion with senior leaders towards the end of the day in order to follow up any issues that have arisen and to discuss leaders' evaluation of behaviour. This discussion should include a focus on how new staff and inexperienced staff are informed of the school's expectations and how they are supported in the management of behaviour.

1 Education Act 2005, section 8; www.legislation.gov.uk/ukpga/2005/18/section/8.

2 In this handbook, any reference to the Education Act 2005 includes any amendments made by the Education and Inspections Act 2006, the Education and Skills Act 2008, the Academies Act 2010 and the Education Act 2011.

3 Education Act 2005, section 8; www.legislation.gov.uk/ukpga/2005/18/section/8.

4 'Schools: Ofsted privacy notice', Ofsted, June 2018; www.gov.uk/government/publications/ofsted-privacy-notices/schools-ofsted-privacy-notice.

5 Section 3(5)(b) of the Education (Individual Pupil Information) (Prescribed Persons) (England) Regulations 2009 (Amended).

6 'Deferring Ofsted inspections', Ofsted, June 2016; www.gov.uk/government/publications/deferring- ofsted-inspections.

7 'Inspecting safeguarding in early years, education and skills', Ofsted, August 2016; www.gov.uk/government/publications/inspecting-safeguarding-in-early-years-education-and-skills- from-september-2015.

8 'Keeping children safe in education', Department for Education, 2018; www.gov.uk/government/publications/keeping-children-safe-in-education--2. 9 'Working together to safeguard children', Department for Education, 2018; www.gov.uk/government/publications/working-together-to-safeguard-children--2.

10 Positive environments where children can flourish: guidance for inspectors about how to approach the use of physical intervention, restraint and restrictions of liberty in social care settings and schools, Ofsted, March 2018; www.gov.uk/government/publications/positive-environments-where-children- can-flourish.

11 The term 'report' is used to describe the formal published outcome of the inspection. For section 8 inspections, except where the inspection is deemed to be a section 5 inspection, the report will take the form of a letter.

12 'School inspection handbook', Ofsted, 2019

13 Education Act 2005, Section 13; www.legislation.gov.uk/ukpga/2005/18/section/13.

14 'Complaints about Ofsted', Ofsted, 2018; www.gov.uk/government/publications/complaints-about- ofsted.

15 'School inspection handbook, Ofsted, 2019

16 In certain circumstances, any school may be selected for a section 8 'no formal designation' or section 5 inspection rather than a section 8 inspection of a good or non-exempt outstanding school. This might arise if, for example, concerns are raised by a qualifying complaint about the school. A school may be subject to a section 5 inspection if it has undergone significant change, such as in its age range, or where the quality of provision may have deteriorated significantly.

17 'Keeping children safe in education', Department for Education, 2018; www.gov.uk/government/publications/keeping-children-safe-in-education--2. 18 'Working together to safeguard children', Department for Education, 2018; www.gov.uk/government/publications/working-together-to-safeguard-children--2.

19 Positive environments where children can flourish: a guide for inspectors about physical intervention and restrictions of liberty, Ofsted, March 2018; www.gov.uk/government/publications/positive- environments-where-children-can-flourish.

20 Non-exempt schools are maintained nursery schools, pupil referral units and special schools.

21 The timeframe is within five school years from the end of the school year in which the previous section 5 inspection (or the previous section 8 inspection) took place. This means that, for a small number of schools, the follow-on section 5 inspection may be carried out sooner than the usual one to two years after the inspection has taken place, in order to comply with the prescribed interval for section 5 inspections (The Education (School Inspection) (England) (Amendment) Regulations 2015;

www.legislation.gov.uk/uksi/2015/170/contents/made).

[22] In accordance with the requirements of The Education (School Inspection) (England) (Amendment) Regulations 2015. In order for the inspection to be a 'relevant inspection' under the regulations, it must be conducted for the purpose of determining that the school remains good or outstanding, and having been so conducted, Her Majesty's Chief Inspector is satisfied that the evidence does not suggest that the school would not achieve such a grade if a section 5 inspection were carried out.

[23] This statement should not be taken to imply that inspectors are expected to gather a full range of evidence in a section 8 inspection of a good school. They are not. However, if they see evidence of this nature then they should convert the inspection.

[24] Section 9 of the Education Act 2005 states that these section 8 inspections can be treated as section 5 inspections.

[25] For one day inspections, questionnaires should be completed by 11am on the day of inspection.

[26] https://parentview.ofsted.gov.uk.

[28] 'Deferring Ofsted inspections', Ofsted, June 2016; www.gov.uk/government/publications/deferring- ofsted-inspections.

[28] www.gov.uk/government/publications/factsheet-childcare-registering-school-based-provision

[29] This must be checked with the headteacher as part of the call. Where MATs have delegated responsibility to local governing bodies, this should be set out in a scheme of delegation. Academies should also set out their governance structure in their annual financial statements, which can generally be found through the DfE performance tables' site. Inspectors should clarify where responsibility lies and who they should talk to during the inspection, especially where a school is part of a MAT.

[30] Inspection Data Summary Report; www.gov.uk/government/collections/using-ofsteds-inspection-dashboard.

[31] Further internal guidance is available to inspectors on obtaining information on complaints in preparation for inspections.

[32] The provider information portal (PIP) provides a high-level view for Ofsted inspectors of information about providers that Ofsted inspects and regulates.

[33] Warning notices for academies are listed at www.gov.uk/government/publications/list-of-letters-to-academy-trusts-about-poor-performance. Inspectors should also note that they can locate individual warning notices by conducting a search on GOV.UK by typing the name of the academy followed by the words 'warning notice' into the search facility.

[34] Framework, evaluation criteria and inspector guidance for the inspections of local authority children's services, Ofsted, November 2017; www.gov.uk/government/publications/inspecting-local- authority-childrens-services-from-2018.

[35] Handbook for inspecting local areas in England under section 20 of the Children Act 2004, Ofsted, April 2016; www.gov.uk/government/publications/local-area-send-inspection-guidance-for-inspectors. [36] Guidance for schools about information required on a maintained school's website is available at www.gov.uk/guidance/what-maintained-schools-must-publish-online. Non-statutory guidance for academies and free schools about information on their websites is available at www.gov.uk/guidance/what-academies-free-schools-and-colleges-should-publish-online.

[37] Headteachers of schools judged to require improvement who may have concerns about the scheduling of their school's next section 5 inspection may write to the relevant Ofsted regional director to set out the context of their school's present position.

[38] Further guidance for education and social care inspectors on conducting integrated monitoring inspections is available at www.gov.uk/government/collections/ofsted-inspections-of-boarding-and- residential-provision-in-schools.

[39] www.parentview.ofsted.gov.uk.

[40] In larger MATs that have regional accountability structures, it may be appropriate to speak to other relevant

intermediate leaders or managers in the delegated structure.

[41] The lead inspector may need to explain to the governing board and the local authority/the proprietor/the trust that the monitoring inspection is being carried out under section 8 of the Education Act 2005.

[42] A section 8 inspection may be treated as if it were an inspection under section 5, using Her Majesty's Chief Inspector's discretionary power under section 9 of the Education Act 2005: www.legislation.gov.uk/ukpga/2005/18/section/9.

[43] Education Act 2005, section 44; www.legislation.gov.uk/ukpga/2005/18/section/44.

[44] As set out under section 44 of the Education Act 2005.

[45] The policy statement about the inspection of new schools can be found here: www.gov.uk/government/publications/how-ofsted-will-inspect-academy-schools-including-free- schools.

[46] In larger MATs that have regional accountability structures, it may be appropriate to speak to other relevant intermediate leaders or managers in the delegated structure.

[47] The lead inspector may need to explain to the governing board and the local authority/ the proprietor/the trust that the monitoring inspection is being carried out under section 8 of the Education Act 2005.

[48] Deferring Ofsted inspections', Ofsted, 2016 www.gov.uk/government/publications/deferring-ofsted-inspections.

[49] Education Act 2005, section 44(2); www.legislation.gov.uk/ukpga/2005/18/section/44.

[50] Education Act 2005, sections 15(2)(d) and 15(2)(e); www.legislation.gov.uk/ukpga/2005/18/section/15.

[51] Education Act 2005, sections 17(1A)(d) and 17(3)(a); www.legislation.gov.uk/ukpga/2005/18/section/17.

[52] Education and Inspections Act 2006, schedule 7; www.legislation.gov.uk/ukpga/2006/40/schedule/7.

[53] Statements of action must be sent to QALAstatementsofaction@ofsted.gov.uk.

[54] Education Act 2005, section 44(1); www.legislation.gov.uk/ukpga/2005/18/contents. [55] Education Act 2005, sections 15(2)(d) and 15(2)(e); www.legislation.gov.uk/ukpga/2005/18/section/15.

[56] Education Act 2005, sections 17(1A)(d) and 17(3)(a); www.legislation.gov.uk/ukpga/2005/18/section/17.

[57] Education and Inspections Act 2006, schedule 7; www.legislation.gov.uk/ukpga/2006/40/schedule/7.

[58] Statements of action must be sent to QALAstatementsofaction@ofsted.gov.uk.

[59] Ofsted does not have the power to investigate individual complaints or incidents of a safeguarding and/or child protection nature. However, such matters may raise whole-school issues, for example about the school's arrangements to keep pupils safe. It is the whole-school issues that will be the focus of these inspections.

[60] 'Inspecting safeguarding in early years, education and skills settings', Ofsted, August 2016; www.gov.uk/government/publications/inspecting-safeguarding-in-early-years-education-and-skills- from-september-2015.

[61] Ofsted has specific powers (under section 11A-C) of the Education Act 2005 to investigate certain complaints known as qualifying complaints. Further guidance is available at: www.gov.uk/complain- about-school.

[62] 'School inspection handbook', Ofsted, 2019.

[63] Note: for different groups of pupils, such as pupils with SEND, inspectors must compare the school's figure for that group to the national figure for **all pupils**, not the national figure for the group.

[64] As above.

[65] This should include records and analysis of bullying incidents, pupils being removed from lessons, the use of rewards and sanctions, exclusion and 'internal exclusion'.

[66] The time should be arranged according to when pupils leave the school – this aspect of the school day should be observed so inspectors need to plan accordingly.

[67] For example, racist, sexist, homophobic, biphobic, transphobic, or sexual language, or language that is derogatory about people with SEND or any other group, or aggressive personal comments about physical appearance or ability.

SECTION D – Early years inspection handbook for Ofsted registered provision

Handbook for inspecting early years provision registered by Ofsted in England under sections 49 and 50 of the Childcare Act 2006

This handbook describes the main activities inspectors undertake when they conduct inspections of early years providers in England registered under sections 49 and 50 of the Childcare Act 2006.

Introduction

1.   This handbook describes the main activities that inspectors undertake when they conduct inspections of early years providers in England registered under sections 49 and 50 of the Childcare Act 2006. The handbook also sets out the judgements that inspectors will make and on which they will report.

2.   The handbook has two parts:

☐   Part 1. How we will inspect Ofsted registered early years providers

This contains instructions and guidance for inspectors on preparing for and conducting early years registered inspections.

☐   Part 2. The evaluation schedule

This contains guidance for inspectors on judging the quality and standards of Ofsted registered early years settings and indicates the main types of evidence used.

3.   This handbook is available to providers and other organisations to make sure that they know about inspection processes and procedures. It balances the need for consistent inspection with the flexibility needed to respond to each provider's particular circumstances. It should be regarded as an explanation of normal procedures, as inspections will vary according to the evidence provided. This handbook applies from September 2019.

Privacy notice

4.   During an inspection, inspectors will collect information about staff and children at the setting by looking at records and observing the everyday life of the setting. Ofsted uses this information to prepare its report and for the purposes set out in its privacy policy.[1]

Part 1. How we will inspect early years providers registered with Ofsted

How we select providers for inspection

5.   Once a provider is registered on the Ofsted Early Years Register, we carry out regular inspections to evaluate the overall quality and standards of its early years provision in line with the principles and requirements of the 'Statutory framework for the early years foundation stage (EYFS)'.[2] The current inspection cycle runs from 1 August 2016 to 31 July 2020. Providers on the Early Years Register will normally have their setting inspected at least once within this four- year cycle. Newly registered providers will normally be inspected within 30 months of their registration date.

6.   Ofsted prioritises inspections and/or inspects more frequently when it receives a concern about a setting, and risk assessment concludes that an inspection is needed.

7.   All provision judged as inadequate will be re-inspected within six months.

8.   All pre-school and nursery provision judged as requires improvement will be re-inspected within 12 months. Where possible, we will also inspect childminders judged as requires improvement within 12 months.

9.   Provision that has been given two previous 'requires improvement' judgements is likely to be judged inadequate if there is no improvement at the next inspection. Provision that has been given two previous 'inadequate' judgements is likely to have its registration cancelled if there is no improvement at the next inspection. We may also take steps to cancel a provider's registration at any point if we find that they are no longer meeting requirements.[3]

10.   We risk-assess any information we receive about early years provision. If this shows that the information is significant enough, it will trigger an inspection or a regulatory visit. We may carry out an inspection within seven days of receiving the information. Depending on the urgency, regulatory visits may take place on the day the information is received. Information about regulatory visits is available in the early years compliance handbook.

11.   Where we prioritise an inspection as a result of the risk assessment, inspectors must, as part of the inspection, gather evidence that relates back to the concern. They should plan activities – including a discussion with the provider – and observations that enable them to gather sufficient evidence to complete the inspection. The provision may subsequently be judged to be outstanding, good, requires improvement or inadequate, according to the evidence, even if the inspection is taking place because of possible previous non-compliance. Judgements are not pre-determined. If a provider notifies us of an incident and uses the learning from it to improve the quality of the provision, this is generally considered to be a sign of a responsible provider. However, a number of notifications, particularly within a short space of time, or that relate to similar incidents, may be indicative of wider leadership weaknesses within the setting. The inspector should consider this when reaching their judgement.

12.   When the inspection follows other regulatory action we have taken, the inspector should check that the provider is compliant with any actions or other enforcement measures that result from that previous action.

No children on roll or present on the day of inspection

13.   Some childcare providers and childminders may have no children on roll at the time the inspection is carried out, or may not have any children present, even though they have children on roll.

14.   In either circumstance, the inspection must **not** be deferred. However, if it becomes clear during the initial notification telephone call that the provider cares for children only on certain days or part-days, the inspection should be scheduled on a day where children are present, if practicable. While the provider remains registered with us, they should expect to be inspected at any time.

15.   Where there are no children on roll or present, the inspector must make it clear at the start of the inspection or during the initial notification telephone call that the inspection will not be a full inspection but will be a check that the provider continues to be suitable to remain registered. As a result, no grades will be given against the four key judgements. The inspector will make a judgement only on the 'Overall quality and standards of the early years provision', with one of three possible outcomes:

    ▯   met
    ▯   not met with actions
    ▯   not met with enforcement.

16.   Where a judgement is 'met', the inspector will not make recommendations.

17.   If the provider does not meet one or more of the learning and development requirements and/or safeguarding and welfare requirements, the inspector must consider a judgement of 'not met' and either issue actions for the provider to take or consider enforcement action. In these cases, the inspector must follow the guidance for inadequate judgements set out later in this handbook.

18.   The majority of inspections affected by no children on roll will be of childminders. A small number may be childcare providers. The main purpose of the inspection is to fulfil our legal duty to inspect registered providers within a defined period and to report in writing on certain matters. The inspection will report on whether the provider continues to demonstrate suitability to remain on the Early Years Register and, if applicable, the Childcare Register.

19.   For these inspections, the inspector must assess whether the provider:

    ▯   has premises suitable for the education and care of children
    ▯   can demonstrate sufficient understanding of the EYFS requirements
    ▯   is able to meet the care, learning and development needs of children.

20.   Providers must confirm that they meet the requirements of the Childcare Register, if applicable.

21.   The provider must demonstrate how they will:

 meet the learning and development requirements, if appropriate[4]

 meet the safeguarding and welfare requirements

 develop and deliver the educational programmes, if appropriate

 identify children's starting points and ensure that children make progress in their learning through effective planning, observation and assessment, if appropriate

 safeguard children

 work in partnership with parents, carers and others

 offer an inclusive service

 evaluate their service and strive for continuous improvement.

22.   The provider should tell the inspector how they have addressed any actions and/or recommendations from the last inspection and how this will improve the provision for children's care and learning.

23.   If, during the inspection, the provider decides to resign from the Early Years Register and remain registered only on the Childcare Register, the inspector must collect sufficient evidence of compliance with the Childcare Register requirements by referring to the 'Childcare Register requirements: childcare providers on non-domestic or domestic premises'.

Early years or childcare provision on a school site[5]

24.   Schools that take children aged two years and over as part of their early years provision cannot normally register that provision with Ofsted. We will inspect the provision for these children under the school inspection arrangements.[6]

25.   Schools that take children younger than two years must register with Ofsted. We will inspect this provision under the early years inspection arrangements set out in this handbook.

Before the inspection

Inspectors' planning and preparation

26.   The inspector must prepare for the inspection by gaining a broad overview of the setting, its context and history. As part of this preparation, inspectors must check and evaluate information to inform their areas of inspection focus.

27.   As part of their preparation, inspectors must consider:

 which register(s) the provider is on and confirm the registration details; if there is any uncertainty about the registration, the inspector must contact their regional duty desk and try to resolve the issue promptly; if this is not possible, the inspector may delay carrying out the inspection until the matter is resolved

 the accuracy of the information about individuals connected with the registration

 all the information held on our database

- details of any concerns received and specifically those they have been asked to follow up
- previous inspection reports
- any published information, such as outcome summaries and monitoring letters
- the progress the provider has made with any actions or recommendations raised at the last inspection or visit
- the provider's website, if they have one
- the internet, to see whether there are any safeguarding or other issues relating to the provider may need to be followed up during the inspection
- any other contextual information we may hold about the provider or the setting.

28. Inspectors **must** update the information about the setting in their evidence base and agree this with the provider at the start of the inspection.

29. Inspectors must take account of the provider's regulatory history when planning the inspection and note any concerns in their evidence. These will normally be shared with the provider.

Notification of inspection

30. Group provision will normally receive a telephone call at around midday on the working day before the start of the inspection.

31. In group provision, if the provider or their representative is unavailable when the inspection notification call is made to the setting, the inspector should ask to speak to the most senior member of staff available.

32. If all reasonable steps have been taken to make contact with the setting but the inspector has not been able to speak to anyone, then the inspection will continue the following day without notice.

33. Childminders, or group providers that do not operate regularly, such as summer play schemes, will usually receive a call no more than five days before the inspection to check which days they are operating and whether there are children on roll and present. The inspector must not specify any proposed dates for the inspection but should indicate the time of day the inspection will start. This will allow the childminder to leave the house if the inspector has not arrived by that time.

34. The telephone call is the first opportunity to initiate a professional relationship between the inspector and the provider or their representative. It should be short and focused on practical issues. Inspectors should not use this conversation to start inspecting. The purpose of the notification call is to provide an opportunity for the setting to ask questions about the inspection and to confirm that:

- the setting is aware of Ofsted's privacy notice
- the setting's registration status and clarify any issues relating to the registration
- the setting knows about its statutory duty to inform parents of the inspection
- arrangements for the inspection; this includes informing the provider or their

representative (normally the manager) that they will usually be required to take part in joint observations

- discussions with particular staff members, including the manager or the named deputy in the manager's absence
- the nominated person, where appropriate, giving them the opportunity to be present at the feedback meeting
- that relevant documents are made available as soon as possible from the start of the inspection (see paragraph 35)
- the age range of children, numbers on roll and the times at which the setting is open and any other contextual information
- whether the setting provides any funded places and/or receives early years pupil premium funding
- any additional support and/or arrangements for children with special educational needs and/or disabilities (SEND)
- whether any children attending the setting are subject to a child protection plan or child in need plan.

35.   Inspectors should tell the provider that the relevant documentation or information they may need access to includes:

- a list of current staff and their qualifications, including in paediatric first aid
- a register/list showing the date of birth of all children on roll and routine staffing arrangements
- a list of children present at the setting during the inspection (if not shown on the register)
- the Disclosure and Barring Service (DBS) records and any other documents summarising the checks on, and the vetting and employment arrangements of, all staff working at the setting
- all logs that record accidents, exclusions, children taken off roll and incidents of poor behaviour
- all logs of incidents of discrimination, including racist incidents
- complaints log and/or evidence of any complaints and their resolutions
- safeguarding and child protection policies
- fire-safety arrangements and other statutory policies relating to health and safety
- a list of any referrals made to the local authority designated person for safeguarding, with brief details of the resolutions
- details of all children who are an open case to social care/children's services and for whom there is a multi-agency plan.

36.   Childminders are not required to provide inspectors with written policies and procedures but must be able to explain them in relation to the requirements in the EYFS.

Requests for deferral or rescheduled inspection

37.   If a setting requests a deferral of its inspection, the inspector must immediately tell the regional duty desk. We will decide whether the request should be granted in line with our deferral policy.[7] The absence of the provider or manager, or having no children on roll, are not valid reasons for deferral. Decisions will be made on a case-by-case basis.

38.   Where possible, a setting that has no children present on the planned day of inspection, but is operating at other times during the week, should have its inspection rescheduled for one of those days.

39.   Inspections that are prioritised as a result of risk assessment will not usually be deferred, even if there are no children on roll or present at the time of the visit.

Inspection without prior notification

40.   We may conduct inspections without notice. This normally, but not exclusively, happens when inspections are prioritised. We prioritise inspections of settings that are judged as inadequate and/or because of concerns that have been expressed about a setting. When the inspection is conducted without notice, the inspector will:

- introduce themselves and show the provider their identification; the inspector must allow the provider time to look at their identification and to contact us to confirm the identity of the inspector should they wish to do so
- ask the provider to display the **notice of inspection** so that parents are aware that an inspection is taking place
- make arrangements to talk to parents; this may be almost immediately if parents are present
- confirm the accuracy of – or any changes to – the information about the setting
- agree a timetable for inspection activities, including joint observations
- conduct a learning walk of the premises and follow up any issues that arise
- check staff qualifications, including paediatric first aid, and record them in their evidence base
- arrange meetings with the provider and/or their representative at a mutually convenient time during the inspection
- refer to any concerns that have led to the inspection being prioritised, remaining mindful of the need to maintain confidentiality and to protect sensitive information and the identities of any complainants
- arrange meetings with staff.

Safeguarding

41.   Inspectors will always have regard to how well children are helped and protected so that they are kept safe. Although inspectors will not provide a separate grade for this crucial aspect of a provider's work, they will always make a written judgement in the report about whether the arrangements for safeguarding children are effective.

42.   We have published a document that sets out the approach inspectors should take to inspecting safeguarding in all the settings covered by the framework. It should be read

alongside the EYFS and the early years handbooks:

- 'Inspecting safeguarding in early years, education and skills settings'.[8]

43.   It is also essential that inspectors are familiar with and take into account the statutory guidance in relation to safeguarding:

- 'Working together to safeguard children'.[9]
- Where the expectations in the 'Inspecting safeguarding in the early years, education and skills settings' differ from those set out in the EYFS, settings should follow the EYFS requirements.

During the inspection

Days allocated to inspection and inspection team members

44.   The time spent on inspection normally depends on the size of the provision. Most inspections are carried out by one inspector.

45.   When inspecting:

- a childminder, the inspector will normally be on site for about three hours
- group provision that operates only for restricted daily hours, the inspector will normally be present for about four hours
- group provision open for a full day, the inspector will normally be on site for at least six hours
- the inspection may be carried out by more than one inspector or be carried out over more than one day, at the discretion of the region.

The start of the on-site inspection

46.   On entering the setting, inspectors must introduce themselves and show the provider their identification. The inspector must allow the provider time to check the identification and to contact us to confirm it, should they wish to do so. In group settings, the inspector must ensure that the provider has been informed of their arrival.

47.   The inspector should meet the provider or representative briefly on arrival to confirm arrangements for the inspection, including:

- checking the accuracy of – or any changes to – the information about the setting
- gathering any information about staff absences, children on roll and other practical matters
- asking the provider to display the notice of inspection – if this has not already been done – so that parents are aware that an inspection is taking place
- agreeing the timetable for inspection activities, including a learning walk; joint observations; inspectors must offer the provider or their representative the opportunity to take part in joint observations and their response must be recorded
- making arrangements for a longer meeting at a convenient time with the provider or their representative to discuss the setting's evaluation of the quality of provision and other matters relating to leadership and management

- making arrangements for providing feedback at the end of the inspection and, for group provision, request that the nominated individual or their representative is invited
- making arrangements to talk to parents – this may be almost immediately if parents are present – and to check that the provider has informed them about the inspection
- checking staff qualifications and record them in the evidence base.

48.   If the inspection is being conducted without notice, the inspector should refer to any concerns that have led to the inspection being prioritised. The inspector should be aware of the need to maintain confidentiality and to protect fully any sensitive information relating to complainants.

49.   If there is more than one inspector, a short team meeting should clarify inspection activities, the areas to be explored initially and individual roles and responsibilities.

Gathering and recording evidence

50.   Inspectors must spend as much time as possible gathering evidence about the quality of care, teaching and learning by:
- observing the children at play
- talking to the children and practitioners about the activities provided
- talking to parents to gain their views on the quality of care and education provided
- observing the interactions between practitioners and children
- gauging children's levels of understanding and their engagement in learning
- talking to practitioners about their assessment of what children know and can do and how they are building on it
- observing care routines and how they are used to support children's personal development, including the setting's approach to toilet training
- evaluating the practitioners' knowledge of the EYFS curriculum.

51.   In **group provision**, the inspector **must** track a representative sample of two or more children across the inspection. The inspector should discuss with the provider what they intend the relevant children to learn and remember based on what those children know and can already do. The evidence collected **must** refer to:
- the practitioner's knowledge of each child
- the progress check for any children aged two
- the impact of any early years pupil premium funding on the children's development
- the quality of support for any children with SEND
- the discussions held with each child's key person and how they decide what to teach
- how well children are developing in the prime and specific areas of learning that help them to be ready for their next stage of education, including school

◻ the reason why children may not receive their full entitlement to early education and the impact that has on them, particularly those from disadvantaged backgrounds and those with SEND.

If any of the children are eligible for the early years pupil premium or subject to a child protection plan or child in need plan, at least one of them must be included in the sample of those tracked.

52. As childminders have only a small number of children, inspectors are not able to track a sample of children in the same way. Nevertheless, the same principles apply in terms of evaluating the childminder's practice and its impact on children's learning, development and well-being.

53. Inspectors must record their evidence clearly and succinctly. All sections of the evidence base must be completed before the end of the inspection. Inspectors may make handwritten notes, but these must be transferred to the electronic evidence as soon as possible after the end of the inspection. It is essential that the evidence accurately reflects discussions with staff and managers. Individuals can be named in inspection evidence if it is necessary to identify them and to avoid confusion. Inspectors should identify clearly any information that was provided in confidence.

54. The evidence underpinning the judgements and areas for improvement must be used to summarise the main points for feedback and to write the report.

55. The electronic evidence and any handwritten notes may be scrutinised for the purposes of retrieval or quality assurance monitoring or as a source of evidence in the event of a complaint or a Freedom of Information request.

Using the setting's own analysis of its strengths and weaknesses during the inspection

56. Leaders and managers of settings should have an accurate view of the quality of their provision and know what to improve. They do not need to produce a written self-evaluation but should be prepared to discuss the quality of education and care they provide – and how well they meet the needs of the children – with the inspector. Inspectors will consider how well leaders and managers evaluate their provision and know how they can improve it or maintain its high standards.

57. The inspector must meet the provider or their representative to discuss how they evaluate their practice. Normally, the discussion should be at a point in the inspection that gives the inspector enough time to follow up any matters discussed. To test the accuracy of the setting's analysis, the inspector will observe children learning, staff caring and teaching, and the safety and suitability of the premises. The inspector will discuss how the provider evaluates the quality of its provision, checking whether they take account of the views of parents and the progress made by the children to determine what it needs to improve.

58. During the inspection, inspectors will use the information provided to test whether the provider's view of the quality of the setting is realistic and to gauge what needs to improve.

Observation and discussion

59.   Inspectors will complete a learning walk around the premises with the provider or their representative at the start inspection. This provides an opportunity for leaders to explain how they organise the early years provision, including the aims and rationale for their EYFS curriculum.

60.   Inspectors must discuss with leaders and practitioners what they intend children to learn, know and do as a result of the EYFS curriculum they offer. They must follow this discussion through in their observations and discussions with children at play and staff interactions.

61.   Inspectors must not advocate a particular method of planning, teaching or assessment. They must not look for a preferred methodology but must record aspects of teaching and learning that they observe to be effective and identify what needs to improve.

62.   Inspectors do not expect to see documentation other than that set out in the EYFS. They will use the evidence gathered from discussions and their own observations to help judge the overall quality of the curriculum provided for children.

63.   Inspectors must spend most of the inspection time gathering first-hand evidence by observing the quality of the daily routines and activities of children and staff. These observations enable inspectors to judge the contribution practitioners make to children's learning, progress, safety and well-being. The observations should also enable them to collect sufficient evidence to support detailed and specific recommendations about improvements needed to the quality of education, behaviour and attitudes, personal development, and leadership and management.

64.   In group settings, inspectors should observe as many staff as possible to ensure that an accurate picture of the overall quality of interactions between practitioners and children can be gained.

65.   When observing interactions between staff and children, inspectors should consider how well staff:

- engage in dialogue with children
- watch, listen and respond to children
- model language well
- read aloud and tell stories to children
- encourage children to sing songs, nursery rhymes and musical games
- encourage children to express their thoughts and use new words
- support independence and confidence
- encourage children to speculate and test ideas through trial and error
- enable children to explore and solve problems
- behave as an excellent role model for children
- support children to recognise and respond to their own physical needs
- attend to children's personal needs
- deal with children's care arrangements, including intimate care, the levels of

privacy afforded to children and the supervision arrangements when undertaking personal hygiene tasks.

66.   Inspectors will also discuss children's learning and development with staff as part of the inspection. Much of this will be through incidental conversations prompted by observing the children at play and the interactions between them and adults.

67.   Where the quality of practice is weak, the inspector must talk to the provider about what has been observed. The inspector should also ask about any action the provider is taking to bring about improvement.

68.   The inspector should always invite the provider or a nominated senior member of staff – such as the manager or early years professional – to take part in one or more **joint observations** of activities, care routines and/or scrutiny of the progress children make. If the provider declines the opportunity to take part in joint observations, this should be recorded in the evidence base, along with the reason given.

69.   Joint observations should enable the inspector to:
   ▯ gain an insight into the effectiveness of the provision's professional development programme for practitioners
   ▯ learn about the provider's view of staff's interactions with children
   ▯ see the quality of the implementation of the **curriculum**/educational programmes
   ▯ consider how effectively the manager supports staff to promote the learning and development of all children.

70.   Following a joint observation, the inspector should note any similarities or differences between the provider's evaluation and their own.

71.   When childminders work alone, it is not possible to carry out joint observations in the same way. However, it is possible for the inspector and childminder to observe individual children together and discuss their learning, progress and behaviour as part of the activities that the children are engaged in. The inspector should follow this up with a further discussion about what the child has learned and how the childminder intends to build on it to help the child make progress. If childminders have assistants, a joint observation of one assistant may be possible.

Evaluating policies and procedures

72.   Childcare providers are required to have policies and procedures, as set out in the EYFS. Childminders are **not** required to have written policies, but they must make sure that they have effective procedures in place as set out in the EYFS. They must ensure that any assistants are aware of and follow the statutory policies and can explain them to parents and others when requested.

73.   All providers, including childminders, are expected to keep any written records in English.

74.   Some providers may have agreement from us to keep some documents required by EYFS requirements off site. The EYFS is clear that records must be easily accessible

and available. It is for the provider to demonstrate their rationale for seeking agreement from us to keep any such records off site. If, during an inspection, providers ask whether they may keep certain records off the premises, the inspector may agree to this as long as records required by the safeguarding and welfare requirements of the EYFS, are easily accessible and available by the end of any visit or inspection, as appropriate. Inspectors should make a record of this agreement and liaise with the regional duty desk to confirm these arrangements are in place.

75.   In addition to meeting the EYFS requirements, providers must comply with other legislation. This includes legislation relating to **safeguarding**, employment, anti-discrimination, health and safety, and data processing and storage. If the inspector identifies concerns that may relate to other legislation, they must notify the regional duty desk. A decision will then be made about what action should be taken and whether there should be liaison with the other agencies.

76.   The inspector **must** check all DBS records and paediatric first-aid certificates, and record in the evidence base that they have done so.

77.   Inspectors are unlikely to check all policies held by the provider. However, they should consider:
  - recruitment records
  - staff qualifications and deployment
  - staff training for safeguarding practice and procedures
  - records of complaints.

78.   The inspector is likely to talk to leaders and staff about how they implement their policies in practice, particularly where it relates to the training and development of staff. Where potential non-compliance with the EYFS is identified, inspectors are likely to check staff's knowledge of the setting's policies.

Meetings with parents

79.   Wherever possible, the inspector must find out the views of parents during the inspection, including those of any parents who ask to speak to them. This will contribute to judgements about how well the provision works in partnership with parents to support children's learning and development, and the promotion of their well-being.

80.   Where the provision has been notified in advance, parents will know that an inspection is taking place. The inspector should consider the arrival times of children and parents to the setting and should set aside time to speak to parents.

81.   If the inspection is carried out with no notice, the inspector must check how the provider obtains and uses their views to improve its service. If there is no evidence relating to this, the inspector must consider whether the partnership with parents is good enough and the inspector may choose to contact parents by phone to request their views.

Meeting with the provider and/or their representative

82.   The inspector must meet the provider or, if the provider is not present, the manager. The inspector should consider the best time to hold this meeting. It should be

early enough in the inspection so that matters that are being discussed can be followed up.

83.   If the provision operates from one room or in the provider's home, the meeting will need to take place at appropriate moments during the general observations, when the children are safely occupied. The inspector should be mindful that the provider has to supervise children and continue to meet their needs during any meeting time.

84.   If the provider is not working directly with children and the meeting takes place in a room or office where the inspector cannot see the provision, it should take no longer than one hour. In most cases, it will be much shorter. The main evidence must come from direct observation of children.

85.   The inspector should hold brief discussions with the provider to discuss the findings that are emerging during the inspection and record all these in the inspection evidence.

86.   Before the inspection is complete, the inspector should always check with the provider whether further evidence should be taken into account. If the evidence suggests that the provision might be inadequate, the inspector should give the provider an opportunity to offer further evidence by having early discussions about this.

87.   The inspector should seek to identify where improvements are needed and make recommendations about how the provision might improve.

Performance management and professional development

88.   Inspectors will gather evidence of the effectiveness of staff supervision, performance management, training and continuing professional development, and the impact of these on children's well-being, learning and development. This includes evidence on how effectively leaders engage with staff and make sure they are aware of and manage any of the main pressures on them.

89.   The early years sector is diverse, ranging from single childminders to large day- care settings. This means that inspectors must use their professional judgement to assess how well the provider improves the quality of provision.

90.   Inspectors should consider how effectively senior leaders use performance management and their assessment of strengths and areas for improvement within the setting to provide a focus for professional development activities, particularly in relation to increasing children's vocabulary and cultural capital.

Reaching final judgements

91.   Inspection activity, including observations, should continue throughout the inspection. Inspectors should avoid giving any impression that they have reached final judgements before the inspection has finished.

92.   The inspector must set aside sufficient time towards the end of the inspection to consider the evidence and make the final judgements. Final judgement grades should be recorded and the main points for feedback should be identified. The inspector should also ensure that time is set aside for the final feedback meeting.

93.   Part 2 of this handbook sets out the judgements that the inspector must make and the aspects they should consider when doing so. The inspector must use professional

judgement to weigh up the evidence gathered for each key judgement. It should be considered against the descriptors to reach fair and reliable judgements that reflect the quality of the provision.

94.   Actions and recommendations for improvement should make clear what the provider needs to do to improve. Actions must refer to the requirements in the EYFS but should not simply repeat its wording. Recommendations must focus on areas that are preventing the setting from being judged as good. The inspector is **not** expected to check that each of the statutory requirements set out in the EYFS are met. However, if, in the course of collecting evidence, the inspector finds that a particular requirement is not met, they should take this into account when reaching judgements.

95.   If one or more of the **statutory requirements is not being met**, this should be reflected in the judgement on leadership and management, as well as in any other judgements where it is relevant.

96.   Failure to meet a statutory requirement will not always result in a judgement that the provision is inadequate. Where a statutory requirement is **not** met, the inspector will take into account the impact of this on children's health, safety and well-being as well as their learning and development.

97.   Where the quality of education judgement is judged to be less than good, the overall effectiveness judgement will normally not be higher. There does **not** need to be a failure to meet a statutory requirement of the EYFS for a setting to be judged as less than good.

98.   When a provision does not meet statutory requirements at the time of the inspection, the inspector must take into account any previous non-compliance. A provider may commit a series of minor breaches to EYFS requirements that, taken individually, do not have a significant impact on children's health, safety or welfare or their learning and development. However, a history of previous non-compliance in the same, or different, areas is likely to indicate either that the provider lacks knowledge of the requirements or is unwilling to comply with them. In such cases, the inspector is likely to judge the leadership and management to be inadequate because the provider does not understand the statutory requirements sufficiently.

99.   Minor administrative errors that can be put right before the inspection is over should not necessarily have a negative impact on the judgements. An example might be that the certificate of registration is not properly displayed (paragraph 3.76 of the 'Statutory framework for the early years foundation stage'). However, where the provider is not meeting a number of administrative requirements, the inspector will need to consider whether these failings, taken together, suggest wider weaknesses within the setting. If this is the case, it is likely to have a negative impact on the leadership and management judgement.

100.   The inspector must take account of all failures to meet EYFS requirements when determining the judgements. If the inspector judges the provision not to have an

acceptable standard of care and/or quality of education, the overall effectiveness will be judged **inadequate**. When judging provision as inadequate, the inspector must decide whether the provider has the capacity to put things right through non-statutory actions or whether the failures are serious enough to warrant enforcement action.

101.   Where a provider is not meeting statutory requirements but the inspector judges that leadership has the capacity to remedy this quickly, actions will be set. The actions will be listed in the inspection report. The inspector should raise actions if they find that:

- the provider is not meeting one or more of the learning and development requirements and/or safeguarding and welfare requirements (and the inspection report must show the significant impact on children's learning and development and/or well-being and safety)
- leaders and managers demonstrate an understanding of the requirements and show that they have the ability to make the necessary improvements without the need for statutory enforcement action and this is the first occasion on which the specific requirement(s) has not been met.

102.   When there is a significant failure to meet the safeguarding and welfare requirements, inspectors will normally issue a welfare requirements notice. Inspectors will not normally issue an additional actions letter because any actions will usually be written in the inspection report. Inspectors are likely to issue a welfare requirements notice when a provider is failing to meet one or more of the safeguarding and welfare requirements that has a significant impact on children's health, safety and well-being. This is normally where one or more of the following apply:

- leaders and managers do not demonstrate their understanding of how to meet the safeguarding and welfare requirements of the EYFS
- there have been previous occasions of non-compliance in relation to the same or different requirement(s)
- actions relating to existing failures to meet safeguarding and welfare requirements have not been completed satisfactorily
- the failure to meet the requirement is so serious that the inspector judges that a welfare requirements notice is appropriate.

103.   On making the judgement that the provision is inadequate, the inspector must consult with the regional duty desk if:

- there is evidence of any immediate risk to children or failure to meet any of the conditions placed on the registration
- previous concerns about the provision have not been dealt with in a satisfactory way, including the failure to take satisfactory action to meet actions and/or welfare requirements set at a previous visit
- the inspector considers that they may need to issue a welfare requirements notice or take other enforcement action, such as suspension, cancellation or prosecution

- the provider shows insufficient understanding of their responsibility to meet the safeguarding and welfare and/or learning and development requirements of the EYFS
- the last inspection resulted in a judgement that the overall effectiveness was inadequate.

104.   The purpose of the inspector's consultation with the regional duty desk is to discuss whether – and what type of – enforcement action should be taken and the kind of monitoring that will be required. The Early years compliance handbook has more information about enforcement options and the arrangements for following up enforcement activity. The discussion will determine what the inspection report will say about the enforcement action.

Failure to notify Ofsted and/or meet conditions

105.   It is an offence to fail to notify Ofsted of a significant event or fail to comply with a condition of registration, without good reason. Where the inspector finds non-compliance, they must refer to the compliance handbook and contact the regional duty desk if necessary. The inspector should not set actions for breaches of condition or a failure to notify Ofsted about a significant event. However, the inspector must note any such failure in the report. Where appropriate, this may contribute to an inadequate judgement overall.

Providing feedback

106.   Towards the end of the inspection the inspector should talk to the provider to:
- discuss any inadequate or outstanding practice they have seen
- ensure that the provider understands how the evidence supports the judgements
- allow the provider to raise any concerns, including those related to the conduct of the inspection or the inspector
- alert the provider to any serious concerns that may lead to the provision being judged inadequate.

107.   At the end of the inspection, there must be a feedback meeting that should include the provider and/or their representative. If the provider is not able to attend, the inspector should give feedback to the manager as the provider's representative. The inspector must not defer feedback to another day.

108.   The inspector should allow enough preparation time for feedback, making sure that their evidence is clear and fully supports the judgements. They should be ready to provide examples that illustrate the provision's strengths and weaknesses.

109.   At the feedback meeting, the inspector should explain that its purpose is to share the main findings of the inspection and any areas for improvement. The inspector must make it clear that the findings are restricted and confidential to the relevant senior personnel and that they must remain so until the provider receives the final report. If the provision is judged to be inadequate, however, the provider must inform the local authority immediately after the inspection.

110. Feedback notes must be consistent with the evidence discussed with the provider and the content of the report, and should cover the strengths and areas for improvement about:

- quality of education
- behaviour and attitudes
- personal development
- leadership and management
- actions and/or recommendations for improvement.

111. The inspector must ensure that the provider or their representative is clear about the grades awarded for each judgement. The inspector should:

- refer to specific evidence if any judgements differ from the provider's view of the provision's strengths and areas for improvement
- state clearly the areas are judged as inadequate and the reasons for this
- explain the areas for improvement and be prepared to discuss these with the provider so that they understand what should or must be improved and the reasons why
- state that the grades are provisional and so may be subject to change as a result of quality assurance procedures and should, therefore, be treated as restricted and confidential until the provider receives a copy of the inspection report (except in the case of an inadequate judgement where the provider should inform the local authority)
- where relevant, set out the next steps for provision judged as requires improvement or inadequate
- provide information about Ofsted's complaints procedure.

112. The inspector should summarise in the evidence base the main points raised at the feedback meeting and the responses to these.

Before- and after-school care and holiday provision

113. Providers (including childminders) who only offer care before and after school or during the school holidays for children who normally attend Reception (or older) classes during the school day do not have to meet the learning and development requirements for those children. For children younger than Reception age, the provider must have regard to, but does not have to meet, the learning and development requirements. In both cases, this means they only have to meet the safeguarding and welfare requirements of the EYFS. The arrangements for inspecting this type of provision are set out in annex A.

Provision that primarily educates children in their home language

114. Provision that educates children primarily through the medium of their home language must show inspectors that individuals have a sufficient grasp of English to ensure the children's well-being. For example, providers must demonstrate that, where necessary, they could summon help in English in an emergency or keep records required by the EYFS in English and share them with inspectors. They must also be able to read

and understand safety instructions, other instructions, information about the administration of medication and information about food allergies.

115. If children are not developing a good standard of spoken English, inspectors will consider the impact on their progress and whether this might lead to a judgement that the overall quality of the provision is inadequate.

Educational and philosophical approaches

116. The choice of teaching methods is a decision for providers, within the confines of the EYFS. The inspector will judge the quality of the provision in relation to the impact it has on children's learning, development and well-being.

117. Some providers will be exempt[10] from some or all aspects of the learning and development requirements of the EYFS. The exemptions may modify or fully exempt providers from delivering the educational programmes, meeting individual learning goals and making the assessment arrangements. During the inspection, inspectors should find out if this is the case after reviewing the associated paperwork, which must include confirmation from the Department for Education that the provider is exempt and the extent of any such exemption. Inspectors should use their professional judgement in applying the grade descriptors in these cases and report accordingly. They should expect to gather evidence for the parts of the learning and development requirements that are not exempt.

118. If provision follows a specific philosophical or pedagogical approach, or reflects a particular faith, inspectors must familiarise themselves with it. Where relevant, inspectors should note the provision's educational or philosophical approach in the report section 'Information about the setting'.

After the inspection

Arrangements for publishing the report

119. The inspector must write the report immediately after the inspection. The text, balance and tone of the report should reflect the judgements made, based on the evidence gathered, and correspond to the feedback given. Guidance on the structure and content of the report is available in 'Reporting requirements for early years inspections'.[11]

120. When writing a report relating to an inspection that was prioritised, inspectors should ensure that it explains why the inspection took place and should report accordingly.

121. Where no children are on roll or present at the time of the inspection, inspectors must include a judgement of met/not met only for overall effectiveness. Although there will be no separate supporting judgements, the summary of main findings for parents on the front page must include at least one bullet point for each judgement in the evaluation schedule. The summary must also describe clearly any weaknesses that led to a 'not met' judgement.

Other information to be completed following an inspection

122. As well as submitting the report and evidence, the inspector must update our database with the following information:

  ▯ the number of places the registered provider offers and the ages of children

190

attending

- the level and number of qualifications, including paediatric first aid, held by staff at the setting
- any previous actions that are complete and need to be closed
- any new actions or recommendations
- any changes to the people connected with the registration, including a note of any failure to notify us of changes
- any errors in the registration details, including those relating to the registered person and the register(s) on which the provider is placed.

The inspection evidence base

123. The evidence base must be retained for the time specified in our guidance.[12] This is normally six years from when the report is published. Information must not be disposed of if it is found that we still require it, and inspection evidence must be kept for longer than six years when:

- an action relates to safeguarding
- the provision is being monitored or regulatory action is linked to the inspection
- there is a potential or current litigation claim against Ofsted, such as a judicial review
- the inspection is of a very sensitive nature or is likely to be of national or regional importance due to a high level of political or press interest
- there is an appeal against enforcement action or an ongoing complaint
- it has been identified for research and evaluation purposes.

Quality assurance and complaints

Quality assurance

124. All inspectors are responsible for the quality of their work. The inspector must ensure that all judgements are supported by the evidence gathered and recorded. All inspections, reports and evidence bases may be subject to quality assurance arrangements. In addition, inspectors may be accompanied by their line manager on an inspection as part of their own performance management. The purpose of these visits will be explained to the provider at the start of the inspection.

Handling concerns and complaints during the inspection

125. The great majority of our work is carried out smoothly and without incident. If concerns do arise during an inspection visit, they should be raised with the inspector present as soon as possible while the inspection is taking place. This provides the opportunity to resolve issues before the inspection is completed.

126. If a provider raises a concern, the inspector should seek to resolve it whenever possible, obtaining advice where necessary. Any concerns raised and actions taken to redress any problems should be recorded in the inspection evidence.

127. If it has not been possible to resolve concerns during the inspection, the provider may wish to lodge a formal complaint. The inspector should ensure that the provider is

informed that the procedure for submitting a complaint is available on the Ofsted website.[13]

Part 2. The evaluation schedule – how early years settings will be judged

Background to the evaluation schedule

128.   The evaluation schedule must be used in conjunction with the guidance set out in Part 1 of this document, 'How we will inspect early years providers', and in the education inspection framework: education, skills and early years (the EIF).

129.   The evaluation schedule is not exhaustive. It does not replace the professional judgement of inspectors. Inspectors must interpret grade descriptors in relation to children's age, development and stage of education.

130.   In line with the EIF, inspectors will make the following judgements:

- overall effectiveness
- the quality of education
- behaviour and attitudes
- personal development
- leadership and management.

131.   The criteria for each of these judgements are drawn from Ofsted's inspection experience, areas of consensus in academic research, and research that Ofsted has itself undertaken. A full note of how the judgement criteria relate to the available research can be found here.[14]

132.   Inspectors use a four-point scale to make all judgements.

- grade 1: outstanding
- grade 2: good
- grade 3: requires improvement
- grade 4: inadequate.

133.   Inspectors must use their professional judgement to interpret and apply the grade descriptors to the setting they are inspecting. In doing so, they consider the following factors:

- a childminder who has only a very small number of children
- settings in which only babies and very young children are present
- settings that provide for funded two-year-olds or groups who may be disadvantaged
- settings that have children who receive their main EYFS experience elsewhere
- children who are no longer in the early years age range.

134.   Inspectors must note any differences in the quality of education for children[15] of different ages. They will use their professional judgement and take into account all their evidence and give clear reasons for their judgements.

Reaching a judgement of outstanding

135.   Outstanding is a challenging and exacting judgement. In order to reach this standard, inspectors will determine whether the early years provision meets **all** the criteria

set out under 'good' for that judgement and does so **securely** and **consistently**. In other words, it is not enough that the provision is strong against some aspects of the judgement and not against others: it must meet each and every criterion. **In addition**, there are further criteria set out under the outstanding judgement, **all of which** the provision will **also** need to meet. Provision should only be judged 'outstanding' in a particular area if it is performing exceptionally, and this exceptional performance in that area is consistent and secure across the whole provision.

Reaching a judgement of good, requires improvement or inadequate

136. A judgement of good or requires improvement will follow the **best fit** approach, with inspectors considering whether the overall quality of the provision is most closely aligned to the descriptions they set out. Inspectors are likely to reach a judgement of inadequate under a particular judgement if **one or more** of the inadequate criteria applies.

Overall effectiveness: the quality and standards of the early years provision

137. Inspectors must use all their evidence to evaluate what it is like to be a child in the provision. In making their judgements about a provider's overall effectiveness, inspectors will consider whether the standard of education and care is good. If it meets all the criteria for good, then inspectors will consider whether it is outstanding. If good is not the best fit, then inspectors will consider whether it requires improvement or is inadequate.

138. In judging the overall effectiveness, inspectors will take account of the four judgements. They will also make a judgement about the effectiveness of the arrangements for safeguarding children.

139. Inspectors should take account of all the judgements made across the evaluation schedule. In particular, they should consider:

    ▢ the extent to which leaders and providers plan, design and implement the EYFS curriculum
    ▢ the extent to which the curriculum and care practices that the setting provides meet the needs of the range of children who attend, particularly children with SEND
    ▢ the progress children make in their learning and development relative to their starting points, and their readiness for the next stage of their education
    ▢ children's personal and emotional development, including whether they feel safe and are secure and happy
    ▢ whether the requirements for children's safeguarding and welfare have been fully met and there is a shared understanding of and responsibility for protecting children
    ▢ the effectiveness of leadership and management in evaluating practice and securing continuous development that improves children's education.

Outstanding (1)

- The quality of education is outstanding.

- All other judgements are likely to be outstanding. In exceptional circumstances, one of the judgements may be good, as long as there is convincing evidence that it is improving this area rapidly and securely towards outstanding.

- Safeguarding is effective.

- There are no breaches of EYFS requirements.

Good (2)

- The quality of education is at least good.

- All other judgements are likely to be good or outstanding. In exceptional circumstances, one of the judgement areas may require improvement, as long as there is convincing evidence that it is improving it rapidly and securely towards good.

- Safeguarding is effective.

Requires improvement (3)

- Where one or more aspects of the provision's work requires improvement, the overall effectiveness is likely to require improvement.

- Safeguarding is effective and any weaknesses are easy to rectify because they do not leave children at risk of harm.

- If there are any breaches of EYFS requirements, they do not have a significant impact on children's safety, well-being or learning and development.

Inadequate (4)

The provision's overall effectiveness is likely to be inadequate if one or more of the following apply.

- Safeguarding is ineffective.

- Any one of the judgements is inadequate.

- Breaches of EYFS requirements have a significant impact on the safety and well-being and/or the learning and development of the children.

- It has been given two previous 'requires improvement' judgements and it is still not good.

Quality of education

140. The EYFS[16] curriculum

    ☐ The EYFS (educational programmes) provides the curriculum framework that leaders build on to decide what they intend children to learn and develop.

    ☐ Leaders and practitioners decide how to implement the curriculum so that children make progress in the seven areas of learning.

    ☐ Leaders and practitioners evaluate the impact of the curriculum by checking what children know and can do.

141. Inspectors will evaluate how well:

    ☐ leaders assure themselves that the setting's curriculum (educational programmes) intentions are met and it is sufficiently challenging for the children it serves

    ☐ leaders use additional funding, including the early years pupil premium where applicable, and measure its impact on disadvantaged children's outcomes.

    ☐ practitioners ensure that the content, sequencing and progression in the areas of learning are secured and whether they demand enough of children

    ☐ children develop, consolidate and deepen their knowledge, understanding and skills across the areas of learning

    ☐ the provider's curriculum prepares children for their next stage.

Cultural capital[17]

142. Cultural capital is the essential knowledge that children need to prepare them for their future success. It is about giving children the best possible start to their early education. As part of making a judgement about the quality of education, inspectors will consider how well leaders use the curriculum to enhance the experience and opportunities available to children, particularly the most disadvantaged.

143. Some children arrive at an early years settings with different experiences from others, in their learning and play. What a setting does, through its EYFS curriculum and interactions with practitioners, potentially makes all the difference for children. It is the role of the setting to help children experience the awe and wonder of the world in which they live, through the seven areas of learning.

Grade descriptors for the quality of education

144. Inspectors will **not** grade intent, implementation and impact separately. Instead, inspectors will reach a single graded judgement for the quality of education, drawing on all the evidence they have gathered, using their professional judgement.

145. To reach a judgement about the quality of education, inspectors must use their professional judgement to consider the ages, development and stages of children in the setting.

146. In order for the quality of education to be judged **outstanding**, it must meet all of the good criteria securely and consistently. It must **also** meet all the outstanding criteria.

Outstanding (1)

The provider meets all the criteria for a good quality of education securely and consistently. The quality of education at this setting is exceptional. In addition, the following apply.

- The provider's curriculum intent and implementation are embedded securely and consistently across the provision. It is evident from what practitioners do that they have a firm and common understanding of the provider's curriculum intent and what it means for their practice. Across all parts of the provision, practitioners' interactions with children are of a high quality and contribute well to delivering the curriculum intent.

- Children's experiences over time are consistently and coherently arranged to build cumulatively sufficient knowledge and skills for their future learning.

- The impact of the curriculum on what children know, can remember and do is highly effective. Children demonstrate this through being deeply engaged in their work and play and sustaining high levels of concentration. Children, including those children from disadvantaged backgrounds, do well. Children with SEND achieve the best possible outcomes.

- Children consistently use new vocabulary that enables them to communicate effectively. They speak with increasing confidence and fluency, which means that they secure strong foundations for future learning, especially in preparation for them to become fluent readers.

147.   Inspectors will use their professional judgement and adopt a 'best fit' approach in order to judge whether an early years provider is **good** or **requires improvement**.

Good (2)

Intent

- Leaders adopt or construct a curriculum that is ambitious and designed to give children, particularly the most disadvantaged, the knowledge and cultural capital they need to succeed in life.
- The provider's curriculum is coherently planned and sequenced. It builds on what children know and can do, towards cumulatively sufficient knowledge and skills for their future learning.
- The provider has the same ambitions for almost all children. For children with particular needs, such as those with high levels of SEND, their curriculum is still ambitious and meets their needs.

Implementation[18]

- Children benefit from meaningful learning across the EYFS curriculum.
- Practitioners understand the areas of learning they teach and the way in

which young children learn. Leaders provide effective support for staff with less experience and knowledge of teaching.

- Practitioners present information clearly to children, promoting appropriate discussion about the subject matter being taught. They communicate well to check children's understanding, identify misconceptions and provide clear explanations to improve their learning. In so doing, they respond and adapt their teaching as necessary.
- Practitioners ensure that their own speaking, listening and reading of English enables children to hear and develop their own language and vocabulary well. They read to children in a way that excites and engages them, introducing new ideas, concepts and vocabulary.
- Over the EYFS, teaching is designed to help children remember long-term what they have been taught and to integrate new knowledge into larger concepts.
- Practitioners and leaders use assessment well to check what children know and can do to inform teaching. This includes planning suitably challenging activities and responding to specific needs. Leaders understand the limitations of assessment and avoid unnecessary burdens for staff or children.
- Practitioners and leaders create an environment that supports the intent of an ambitious and coherently planned and sequenced curriculum. The available resources meet the children's needs and promote their focus on learning.
- Practitioners share information with parents about their child's progress in relation to the EYFS. They help parents to support and extend their child's learning at home, including how to encourage a love of reading.

Impact

- Children develop detailed knowledge and skills across the seven areas of learning and use these in an age-appropriate way. Children develop their vocabulary and understanding of language across the EYFS curriculum.
- Children are ready for the next stage of education, especially school, where applicable. They have the knowledge and skills they need to benefit from what school has to offer when it is time to move on.
- Children enjoy, listen attentively and respond with comprehension to familiar stories, rhymes and songs that are

appropriate to their age and stage of development.

- Children understand securely the early mathematical concepts appropriate to their age and stage that will enable them to move on to the next stage of learning.

- Children articulate what they know, understand and can do in an age- appropriate way, holding thoughtful conversations with adults and their friends.

- From birth onwards, children are physically active in their play, developing their physiological, cardiovascular and motor skills. They show good control and coordination in both large and small movements appropriate for their stage of development.

Requires improvement (3)

- **Provision is not good.**
- Any breaches of the statutory requirements do not have a significant impact on children's learning and development.

Inadequate (4)

The quality of education is likely to be inadequate if one or more of the following applies.

- A poorly designed and implemented curriculum does not meet children's needs. The needs of babies and young children are not met.

- Practitioners have a poor understanding of the areas of learning they teach and the way in which young children learn.

- Assessment is overly burdensome. It is unhelpful in determining what children know, understand and can do.

- Children are not well prepared for school or the next stage of their learning, particularly those who are in receipt of additional funding. Strategies for engaging parents are weak and parents do not know what their child is learning or how they can help them improve.

- Breaches of the statutory requirements have a significant impact on children's learning and development.

Behaviour and attitudes

148.   Inspectors will consider the ways in which children demonstrate their attitudes and behaviour through the characteristics of effective learning:

- playing and exploring
- active learning
- creating and thinking critically.

149.   Although attendance at the setting is not mandatory, inspectors will explore how well providers work with parents to promote children's attendance so that the children form good habits for future learning. In particular, inspectors will consider the attendance of children for whom the provider receives early years pupil premium.

150.   Inspectors will consider the extent to which leaders and practitioners support children's behaviour and attitudes, including how the provision helps children to manage their own feelings and behaviour, and how to relate to others.

151.   To reach a judgement about children's behaviour and attitudes, inspectors must use their professional judgement to **consider the ages, development and stages of children** in the setting.

Grade descriptors for behaviour and attitudes

152.   In order for behaviour and attitudes to be judged **outstanding**, it must meet all of the good criteria securely and consistently. It must **also** meet all the outstanding criteria.

Outstanding (1)

The provider meets all the criteria for good behaviour and attitudes securely and consistently. Behaviour and attitudes in this provision are exceptional.

In addition, the following apply.

- **Children have consistently high levels of respect for others. They increasingly show high levels of confidence in social situations. They confidently demonstrate their understanding of why behaviour rules are in place and recognise the impact that their behaviour has on others.**

- **Children are highly motivated and are very eager to join in, share and cooperate with each other. They have consistently positive attitudes to their play and learning.**

- **Children demonstrate high levels of self-control and consistently keep on trying hard, even if they encounter difficulties. When children struggle with this, leaders and practitioners take intelligent, swift and highly effective action to support them.**

153.   Inspectors will use their professional judgement and adopt a 'best fit' approach in order to judge whether a provider is **good** or **requires improvement**.

Good (2)

- The provider has high expectations for children's behaviour and conduct. These expectations are commonly understood and applied consistently and fairly. This is reflected in children's positive behaviour and conduct. They are beginning to manage their own feelings and behaviour and to understand how these have an impact on others. When children struggle with regulating their behaviour, leaders and practitioners take appropriate action to support them. Children are developing a sense of right and wrong.

- Children demonstrate their positive attitudes to learning through high levels of curiosity, concentration and enjoyment. They listen intently and respond positively to adults and each other. Children are developing their resilience to setbacks and take pride in their achievements.

- Children benefit fully from the early education opportunities available to them by participating and responding promptly to requests and instructions from practitioners.

- Relationships among children, parents and staff reflect a positive and respectful culture. Children feel safe and secure.

Requires improvement (3)

- Children's behaviour and attitudes are not good.

- Any breaches of the statutory requirements do not have a significant impact on children's behaviour and attitudes.

Inadequate (4)

Children's behaviour and attitudes are likely to be inadequate if one or both of the following apply.

- Children's behaviour and attitudes to learning are poor. Their frequent lack of engagement in activities and/or poor behaviour lead to a disorderly environment that hinders children's learning and/or puts them and others at risk.

- Children persistently demonstrate poor self-control and a lack of respect for others, leading to children not feeling safe and secure.

Personal development

154.   Inspectors will evaluate the extent to which the provision is successfully promoting children's personal development. Inspectors must use their professional judgement to consider the effectiveness of the provision on children's all-round development. In doing so, inspectors must be mindful of the **ages** and **stages of development** of the children in the setting.

155.   In order for personal development to be judged **outstanding**, it must meet all of the good criteria securely and consistently. It must **also** meet all the outstanding criteria.

Outstanding (1)

The provider meets all the criteria for good personal development securely and consistently. Personal development in this provision is exceptional. In addition, the following apply.

- **The provider is highly successful at giving children a rich set of experiences that promote an understanding of people, families and communities beyond their own.**

- **Practitioners teach children the language of feelings, helping them to appropriately develop their emotional literacy.**
- **Practitioners value and understand the practice and principles of equality and diversity. They are effective at promoting these in an age-appropriate way, which includes routinely challenging stereotypical behaviours and respecting differences. This helps children to reflect on their differences and understand what makes them unique.**

156.   Inspectors will use their professional judgement and adopt a 'best fit' approach in order to judge whether an early years provider is **good** or **requires improvement**.

Good (2)

- **The curriculum and the provider's effective care practices promote and support children's emotional security and development of their character. Children are gaining a good understanding of what makes them unique.**
- **The curriculum and the provider's effective care practices promote children's confidence, resilience and independence. Practitioners teach children to take appropriate risks and challenges as they play and learn both inside and outdoors, particularly supporting them to develop physical and emotional health.**
- **A well-established key person system helps children form secure attachments and promotes their well-being and independence. Relationships between staff and babies are sensitive, stimulating and responsive.**
- **Practitioners provide a healthy diet and a range of opportunities for physically active play, both inside and outdoors. They give clear and consistent messages to children that support healthy choices around food, rest, exercise and screen time.**
- **Practitioners help children to gain an effective understanding of when**

they might be at risk, including when using the internet, digital technology and social media and where to get support if they need it.

■ Practitioners ensure that policies are implemented consistently. Hygiene practices ensure that the personal needs of children of all ages are met appropriately. Practitioners teach children to become increasingly independent in managing their personal needs.

■ The provider prepares children for life in modern Britain by: equipping them to be respectful and to recognise those who help us and contribute positively to society; developing their understanding of fundamental British values; developing their understanding and appreciation of diversity; celebrating what we have in common and promoting respect for different people.

Requires improvement (3)

■ Provision to support children's personal development is not good.

■ Any breaches of the statutory requirements for safeguarding and welfare and/or learning and development do not have a significant impact on children's safety, well-being and personal development.

Inadequate (4)

Personal development is likely to be inadequate if one or more of the following applies.

■ Breaches of the statutory requirements have a significant impact on children's safety, well-being and personal development.

■ Practitioners do not support children's social and emotional well-being or prepare them for transitions within the setting and/or to other settings and school.

■ The key person system does not work effectively to support children's emotional well-being and children fail to form secure attachments with their carers. Babies are not stimulated.

■ Policies, procedures and practice do not promote the health and welfare of children. As a result, children do not know how to keep themselves safe and healthy.

■ Children have a narrow experience that does not promote their understanding of people and communities beyond their own or help them to recognise and accept each other's differences.

Leadership and management

157. Inspectors will evaluate evidence from the range of different inspection activities set out in Part 1 of the handbook when considering the effectiveness of leadership and management.

158. Inspectors must use their professional judgement to interpret and apply the grade descriptors for leadership and management for childminders.

Grade descriptors for leadership and management

159. In order for leadership and management to be judged **outstanding**, it must meet all of the good criteria securely and consistently. It must **also** meet all the outstanding criteria.

Outstanding (1)

The provider meets all the criteria for good leadership and management securely and consistently. Leadership and management in this provision is exceptional. In addition, the following apply.

- Leaders ensure that they and practitioners receive focused and highly effective professional development. Practitioners' subject, pedagogical content and knowledge consistently builds and develops over time, and this consistently translates into improvements in the teaching of the curriculum.

- Leaders ensure that highly effective and meaningful engagement takes place with staff at all levels and that any issues are identified. When issues are identified – in particular about workload – they are consistently dealt with appropriately and quickly.

- Staff consistently report high levels of support for well-being issues.

160. Inspectors will use their professional judgement and adopt a 'best fit' approach in order to judge whether an early years provider is **good** or **requires improvement**.

Good (2)

In order for the effectiveness of leadership and management to be judged good, it must meet all of the following criteria.

- Leaders have a clear and ambitious vision for providing high-quality, inclusive care and education to all. This is realised through strong shared values, policies and practice.

- Leaders focus on improving practitioners' knowledge of the areas of learning and understanding of how children learn to enhance the teaching of the curriculum and appropriate use of assessment. The practice and subject knowledge of practitioners build and improve over time. Leaders have effective systems in place for the supervision and support of staff.

- Leaders act with integrity to ensure that all children, particularly those with

SEND, have full access to their entitlement to early education.

- Leaders engage effectively with children, their parents and others in their community, including schools and other local services.
- Leaders engage with their staff and are aware of the main pressures on them. They are realistic and constructive in the way they manage staff, including their workload.

- Those with oversight or governance understand their role and carry this out effectively. They have a clear vision and strategy and hold senior leaders to account for the quality of care and education. They ensure that resources are managed sustainably, effectively and efficiently.

- The provider fulfils its statutory duties, for example under the Equality Act 2010, and other duties, for example in relation to the 'Prevent' strategy and safeguarding.

- Leaders protect staff from harassment, bullying and discrimination.

- The provider has a culture of safeguarding that facilitates effective arrangements to: identify children who may need early help or are at risk of neglect, abuse, grooming or exploitation; help children to reduce their risk of harm by securing the support they need, or referring in a timely way to those who have the expertise to help; and manage safe recruitment and allegations about adults who may be a risk to children.

Requires improvement (3)

- Leadership and management are not yet good.

- Any breaches of statutory requirements do not have a significant impact on children's safety, well-being or learning and development.

Inadequate (4)

Leadership and management are likely to be inadequate if one or more of the following applies.

- Leaders do not have the capacity to improve the quality of education and care. Actions taken to tackle areas of identified weakness have been insufficient or ineffective. Training for staff is ineffective.

- Leaders are not doing enough to tackle the poor curriculum or teaching, or the inappropriate use of assessment. This has a significant impact on children's progress, particularly those who are disadvantaged and those with SEND.

- Links with parents, other settings and professionals involved in supporting children's care and education do not identify or meet children's individual needs. Children fail to thrive.

- Leaders do not tackle instances of discrimination. Equality, diversity and British values are not actively promoted in practice.

- Safeguarding and welfare requirements are not met. Breaches have a significant impact on the safety and well-being of children.

Annex A. Inspecting before- and after-school care and holiday provision

1.   Providers (including childminders) registered on the Early Years Register but who **only** provide care exclusively for children at the beginning and end of the school day or in holiday periods will be inspected without receiving grades against the four judgements ('Quality of education', 'Behaviour and attitudes', 'Personal development' and 'Leadership and management') of the inspection framework.

2.   These providers do not need to meet the learning and development requirements of the EYFS. They do have to meet in full the safeguarding and welfare requirements, which are designed to help providers create high-quality settings which are welcoming, safe and stimulating, and where children are able to grow in confidence.

3.   The inspector will make a judgement only on the 'Overall effectiveness: quality and standards of the early years provision'. The inspection will result in one of three possible outcomes:

- met
- not met with actions
- not met with enforcement.

4.   The inspector will consider the criteria for three of the key judgements ('Behaviour and attitudes', 'Personal development' and 'Leadership and management') in reaching a judgement about whether or not the provider is meeting the safeguarding and welfare requirements of the EYFS.

5.   When the provider does not meet one or more of the safeguarding and welfare requirements, the inspector must consider a judgement of 'not met' and either issue actions for the provider to take or consider enforcement action. In these cases, the inspector must follow the guidance for inadequate judgements set out previously in this handbook.

6.   Provision judged as 'not met' will normally be re-inspected within 12 months.

7.   When inspecting before and after school, and holiday care provision, the inspector must assess whether the provider:

- has premises suitable to care for children in the early years age range (as appropriate)
- can demonstrate sufficient understanding of the safeguarding and welfare requirements of the EYFS
- can meet the care, safeguarding and welfare needs of children.

8.   Providers must confirm that they meet the requirements of the Childcare Register, if applicable.

9.   The provider must demonstrate how they:

- meet the safeguarding and welfare requirements
- safeguard children

- work in partnership with parents, carers and others
- offer an inclusive service
- evaluate their service and strive for continuous improvement.

10.   The provider should tell the inspector how they have addressed any actions from the last inspection and how this will improve the provision for children's care and learning.

Gathering and recording evidence

11.   To assess whether the provider is meeting the safeguarding and welfare requirements, the inspector will undertake appropriate inspection activity as set out in part one of the handbook. In particular, inspectors will:
- observe interactions between practitioners and children
- consider how leaders and practitioners create and plan the play environment
- find out how practitioners seek children's views and engage them in planning of activities
- talk with practitioners about performance management and professional development
- met with the provider and/or their representative
- evaluate a sample of policies and procedures and relevant documentation
- where possible, seek the views of parents.

Writing the report

12.   Although there are no separate supporting judgements, the inspection will result in a summary for parents on the front page, which will explain what it is like for a child to attend the setting.

13.   Inspectors will report on what the setting does well and what it needs to do better. This section must include reference to leadership and management, children's behaviour and attitudes and personal development. It must describe clearly any weaknesses that led to a 'not met' judgement and from which actions or enforcement action have been raised.

[1] 'Childcare: Ofsted privacy notice', Ofsted, June 2018; www.gov.uk/government/publications/ofsted- privacy-notices.

[2] 'Statutory framework for the early years foundation stage', Department for Education, 2017; www.gov.uk/government/publications/early-years-foundation-stage-framework--2.

[3] Enforcement requires the provider to take action to remain compliant with the requirements of the 'Statutory framework for the early years foundation stage'. Our enforcement actions are set out in our 'Early years compliance handbook', April 2019 ; www.gov.uk/government/publications/early-years- provider-non-compliance-action-by-ofsted.

[4] Some providers do not have to deliver the learning and development requirements. See the Statutory framework for the early years foundation stage.

[5] 'Registering school-based provision', Ofsted, February 2017; www.gov.uk/government/publications/factsheet-childcare-registering-school-based-provision

[6] 'School inspection handbook', Ofsted, May 2019; www.gov.uk/government/publications/school- inspection-handbook-eif

[7] 'Deferral of Ofsted inspections: information for providers', Ofsted, June 2016; www.gov.uk/government/publications/deferring-ofsted-inspections.

[8] 'Inspecting safeguarding in early years, education and skills settings', Ofsted, October 2018; www.gov.uk/government/publications/inspecting-safeguarding-in-early-years-education-and-skills- from-september-2015.

[9] 'Working together to safeguard children', Department for Education, July 2018; www.gov.uk/government/publications/working-together-to-safeguard-children--2.

[10] The Early Years Foundation Stage (Exemptions from Learning and Development Requirements) Regulations 2008; www.legislation.gov.uk/uksi/2008/1743/contents/made and The Early Years Foundation Stage (Exemptions from Learning and Development Requirements) (Amendment) Regulations 2012; www.legislation.gov.uk/uksi/2012/2463/contents/made.

[11] 'Reporting requirements for early years inspections', Ofsted, January 2015; www.gov.uk/government/publications/report-template-for-early-years-inspections-with-guidance.

[12] Our guidance 'Retention and disposing of information' is available on the Ofsted intranet.

[13] 'Raising concerns and making a complaint about Ofsted', Ofsted, May 2018; www.gov.uk/government/publications/complaints-about-ofsted.

[14] 'Education inspection framework: overview of research', Ofsted, January 2019, www.gov.uk/government/publications/education-inspection-framework-overview-of-research.

[15] The term 'children' should be read to include the different ages and stages of children in the early years age range (birth to 31 August following a child's fifth birthday). Inspectors should interpret the grade descriptors according to a child's age and stage of development, therefore taking into account babies and young children.

[16] The EYFS sets the standards that all early years providers must meet to ensure that children learn and develop well and are kept healthy and safe.

[17] Cultural capital is the essential knowledge that children need to be educated citizens.

[18] Teaching should not be taken to imply a 'top down' or formal way of working. It is a broad term that covers the many different ways in which adults help young children learn. It includes their interactions with children during planned and child-initiated play and activities: communicating and modelling language; showing, explaining, demonstrating, exploring ideas; encouraging, questioning, recalling; providing a narrative for what they are doing; facilitating and setting challenges. It takes account of the equipment adults provide and the attention given to the physical environment, as well as the structure and routines of the day that establish expectations. Integral to teaching is how practitioners assess what children know, understand and can do, as

well as taking account of their interests and dispositions to learn (characteristics of effective learning), and how practitioners use this information to plan children's next steps in learning and monitor their progress.

SECTION E – Further education and skills inspection handbook

Handbook for inspecting further education and skills providers under part 8 of the Education and Inspections Act 2006, for use from September 2019

This handbook describes the main activities that inspectors carry out when they inspect further education and skills providers in England under part 8 of the Education and Inspections Act 2006.

Introduction

1.   This handbook describes the main activities that inspectors carry out when they inspect further education and skills providers in England under part 8 of the Education and Inspections Act 2006. It sets out the evaluation criteria that inspectors use to make their judgements and on which they report.

2.   The handbook has two parts:

- Part 1. How further education and skills providers will be inspected
  This contains information about the processes before, during and after inspection.
- Part 2. The evaluation schedule

This contains the evaluation criteria inspectors use to judge the quality and standards of further education and skills providers and the main types of evidence used.

3.   This handbook is a guide for inspectors on how to carry out inspections of further education and skills providers. It is also available to providers and other organisations to inform them about inspection processes and procedures. It balances the need for consistent inspections with the need to respond to each provider's individual circumstances. This handbook applies to inspections from 1 September 2019 under the education inspection framework (EIF).[1] Inspectors will apply their professional judgement when they use this handbook.

Types of providers subject to inspection covered by this handbook

4.   The providers we inspect under the Education and Inspections Act 2006 and using this handbook are:

- further education colleges
- sixth-form colleges
- independent specialist colleges
- dance and drama colleges[2]
- independent learning providers
- local authority providers
- designated institutions[3]
- employer providers
- higher education institutions that provide further education and/or apprenticeship training up to level 5
- 16 to 19 academies/free schools.

Privacy notice

5.   During an inspection, inspectors will collect information about staff and learners by talking to them, by looking at documents, records and survey responses and other recorded information and by observing everyday life at the provider. Inspectors may also meet with employers where appropriate. Ofsted uses this information to prepare its report

and for the purposes set out in its privacy policy.[4] We will not record names, but some of the information may make it possible to identify an individual.

6.   Individuals and organisations have legal requirements to provide information to Ofsted as part of inspections. Ofsted has legal powers under section 132 of the Education and Inspections Act 2006 that relate to inspecting providers of further education and skills for learners aged 16 and over. Inspectors can 'inspect, take copies of, or take away any documents relating to the education or training' of students from the provider's premises. These powers also enable our inspectors to inspect computers and other devices that may hold this information.

Part 1. How further education and skills providers will be inspected

Before the inspection
How providers are selected for inspection

7.   To decide when we should next inspect a provider, we use the 'frequencies of inspection' set out from page 6. We also use risk assessment to ensure that our approach to inspection is proportionate, so that we can focus our efforts where we can have the greatest impact.

8.   We use a broad range of information to assess risk and performance when selecting providers for inspection. This process also applies in particular to good or outstanding providers. The indicators include:

- previous inspection records
- self-assessment reports
- performance data
- destination data
- information provided, or concerns raised, by a funding body, government regulators, employers, parents and carers, and learners
- the views of learners, parents and carers, and employers, gathered through online questionnaires
- relevant local intelligence, such as changes to leaders or structures
- any information about significant changes to the type of provision and the number of learners in a provider
- the size and complexity of a provider, including the number and types of provision, the geographical spread of education or training centres and any recent changes to these
- the outcomes of monitoring visits or any other related activity.

9.   We can use relevant information received at any point during the year to select providers. We will review this information regularly.[5]

Frequency of inspection
Providers judged outstanding

10.   Providers judged outstanding for overall effectiveness at their most recent inspection are not normally subject to routine inspection.[6] However, a provider judged outstanding may receive a full inspection if its performance declines or if there is another compelling reason, such as potential safeguarding concerns. A provider judged as outstanding may also be inspected as part of our survey or research work, or through a monitoring visit.

Providers judged good

11.   Providers judged good for overall effectiveness at their most recent inspection will usually be inspected within five years of the publication of their previous inspection report. This will normally be a short inspection but may be a full inspection if information suggests

that this is the most appropriate way forward, for example, if the provider's performance has declined. For more information, see the section on short inspections (paragraphs 122 to 152). A good provider may also be inspected as part of our survey or research work, or through a monitoring visit.

Providers judged to require improvement

12.   Providers judged to require improvement at their most recent inspection will normally receive a full inspection within 12 to 30 months of the publication their previous inspection report. These providers will normally be subject to a monitoring visit before the full re-inspection, normally seven to 13 months after the publication of their previous inspection report (see paragraph 32).[7]

Providers judged inadequate

13.   Providers judged inadequate will receive re-inspection monitoring visits, as outlined in paragraphs 33 to 35. These providers will then receive a full inspection (known as a 're-inspection') within 15 months of publication of their previous full inspection report. The major exceptions to this are providers that no longer receive their main funding or that have been removed from the Register of Apprenticeship Training Providers (RoATP) and deliver only apprenticeship provision.[8] From that point, neither a re-inspection monitoring visit nor a full re-inspection will normally take place. If a provider has apprenticeship provision graded inadequate and has also been removed from the RoATP, that apprenticeship provision will not normally be covered as part of the re-inspection monitoring visit and subsequent re-inspection.

New providers

14.   We will normally carry out a monitoring visit to any provider that becomes newly, directly and publicly funded to deliver education and/or training.[9] This funding may either be received from the Education and Skills Funding Agency (ESFA) or through the apprenticeship levy.[10] The monitoring visit will normally take place within 24 months of the provider starting to deliver directly funded provision. For more details about monitoring visits, see paragraphs 27 to 31.

15.   These providers will normally receive their first full inspection within 24 months of the publication of their monitoring visit report.[11] When a provider receives one or more insufficient progress judgements at their monitoring visit, it will normally receive a full inspection within six to 12 months of the publication of the monitoring visit report. We may carry out a full inspection of these providers without carrying out a monitoring visit, where appropriate.[12]

16.   If a provider has made insufficient progress in safeguarding, it will normally receive one further monitoring visit to review only its safeguarding arrangements within four months of the publication date of its previous monitoring visit report.[13]

Newly merged colleges

17.   A newly merged college will normally receive a full inspection within three years of the merger. This will normally be a full inspection. For inspection purposes, regardless of

the type of merger, we view all merged colleges as new colleges.[14] A newly merged college will not carry forward any inspection grades from predecessor colleges. It will have no inspection grade until the first full inspection.

18.   Any newly merged college may receive a monitoring visit at any reasonable time. A newly merged college will normally receive a monitoring visit before the first full inspection if the overall effectiveness grade of one or more of the predecessor colleges was requires improvement or inadequate.[15] These monitoring visits will focus on relevant themes about the progress of the merged college, including from the most recent report(s) of the predecessor college(s). Monitoring visits will normally arrive at progress judgements against these themes as set out in paragraph 25. The monitoring visit report will normally be published. Concerns about risks arising from this or other sources may lead to an earlier full inspection within the three-year window.[16]

Sixth-form colleges that convert to become 16 to 19 academies

19.   Sixth-form colleges that convert to become 16 to 19 academies will be treated according to their most recent inspection outcome. Those that are outstanding will normally only be inspected if their performance drops or there is another compelling reason, such as safeguarding concerns. Those that were good will normally receive a short inspection within five years of the publication of their previous inspection report (but may receive a full inspection within that timeframe if risks are identified). Those judged as requires improvement will normally be inspected within 12 to 30 months of the publication of the previous report. They will normally receive a monitoring visit within seven to 13 months of the publication of the previous report (as set out in paragraphs 12 and 32). Those judged inadequate will normally be inspected within 15 months of the previous inspection of the converted college. They will normally receive re- inspection monitoring visits as set out in paragraphs 13 and 33 to 35.

20.   A 16 to 19 academy/free school that is re-brokered (transferred to a new sponsor) for performance reasons will be treated as a new provider from the point of re-brokerage for the purposes of inspection.

Types of inspection

Full inspection

21.   Providers that are graded as requires improvement or inadequate will undergo a full inspection as outlined in paragraphs 12 and 13. Inspectors grade the overall effectiveness, the types of provision and the other key judgements areas in accordance with the criteria and grade descriptors set out in part 2 of this handbook. Providers judged as outstanding and good may also undergo a full inspection if, for example, their performance has declined. Ofsted reserves the right to carry out a full inspection of any provider at any reasonable time.

Short inspection

22.   Providers judged good at their previous inspection will normally undergo a short inspection. A short inspection will determine primarily whether the quality of

education/training that learners receive is good. For information about short inspections, see paragraphs 122 to 152 of this handbook.

Survey and research visits

23.　We may visit any provider, including those judged good or outstanding, as part of our surveys and research work, based on our national priorities. We may carry out these visits at any reasonable time.

Monitoring visits

24.　A monitoring visit is a type of inspection that explores one or more specific themes. The purpose of a monitoring visit is to assess progress against these themes to encourage improvement and assess risk. We may carry out a monitoring visit of any provider at any reasonable time. Providers will normally receive two working days' notice of a monitoring visit, although they may be unannounced. They will normally last up to two days. They will normally result in a published report. Concerns arising from monitoring visits may lead to an earlier full inspection.

25.　We will normally use one of the following progress judgements on monitoring visits:

- insufficient progress: progress has been either slow or insubstantial or both, and the demonstrable impact on learners has been negligible[17]
- reasonable progress: the provider's actions are already having a beneficial impact on learners, and improvements are sustainable and are based on the provider's thorough quality assurance procedures
- significant progress: progress has been rapid and is already having considerable beneficial impact on learners.

26.　Monitoring visits follow a similar process to that set out in part 1 of this handbook, except where otherwise noted. Inspectors will make progress judgements based on the themes explored on that visit. They will use part 2 of this handbook as the broader context for monitoring visits.

Monitoring visits to providers that are newly directly publicly funded

27.　We will normally carry out a monitoring visit to any provider that becomes newly directly and publicly funded, as set out in paragraph 14. This visit will normally be carried out within 24 months of starting to deliver the directly funded provision by ESFA or through the apprenticeship levy. These monitoring visits will follow themes. In each case, inspectors will review:

- progress in leadership and management in the first theme
- progress in providing a high-quality of education or training in the second theme
- progress towards ensuring effective safeguarding arrangements in the third theme.

The precise wording of the themes for the most commonly recurring types of new provider are as follows.

Type of new provider	Leadership and management theme	Quality of education and/or training theme	Safeguarding theme
Providers newly directly funded to deliver apprenticeship training provision from or after April 2017	How much progress have leaders made in ensuring that the provider is meeting all the requirements of successful apprenticeship provision?	What progress have leaders and managers made in ensuring that apprentices benefit from high-quality training that leads to positive outcomes for apprentices?	How much progress have leaders and managers made in ensuring that effective safeguarding arrangements are in place?
Providers newly directly funded to deliver adult learning provision from or after August 2017[18]	How much progress have leaders and managers made in designing and delivering relevant adult learning provision that has a clearly defined purpose?	How much progress have leaders and managers made to ensure that learners benefit from high-quality adult education that prepares them well for their intended job role, career aim and/or personal goals?	How much progress have leaders and managers made in ensuring that effective safeguarding arrangements are in place?
New independent specialist colleges newly ESFA funded from August 2018 onwards	How much progress have leaders and managers made in designing and delivering relevant learning programmes that are clearly defined and tailored to suit the individual needs of learners?	How much progress have leaders and managers made in ensuring that learners benefit from high-quality learning programmes that develop their independence, communication and skills, and help them to achieve their personal and/or work-related goals?	How much progress have leaders and managers made in ensuring that effective safeguarding arrangements are in place?

28. We will adapt these themes to apply to other types of new providers as necessary to ensure best fit. They will still follow the format and approach set out above.

29. For these new providers, inspectors make progress judgements by taking into account that the provider is newly directly funded and by considering the impact of actions taken to develop the necessary knowledge, skills and behaviours of learners.

30. If the provider has other types of provision, each type of provision will be covered

by a separate theme and progress judgement.

31.   If a provider is judged to have made insufficient progress in the safeguarding theme, it will normally receive one further monitoring visit to review only its safeguarding arrangements within four months of the previous monitoring visit.

Monitoring visits to providers judged to require improvement

32.   We will normally carry out a monitoring visit to a provider that has been judged to require improvement. The visit will normally take place between seven and 13 months from the publication of its inspection report in which it was judged to require improvement. Inspectors will make progress judgements on the main areas for improvement identified in that report. The monitoring visit will result in a published report.[19] Through the monitoring visit, inspectors will challenge the provider to improve so that it can become good by the next full inspection.[20] The report will set out what progress the provider has made since the previous inspection.

Re-inspection monitoring visits to providers judged to be inadequate

33.   We carry out re-inspection monitoring visits to providers found to be inadequate overall after the publication of their inspection report, except when their main funding has been terminated and/or they have been removed from the RoATP and they deliver only apprenticeship provision.[21]

34.   Re-inspection monitoring visit themes will be based on the main areas for improvement identified in the inspection report. Inspectors will make a progress judgement against each theme as set out in paragraph 25. The re-inspection monitoring visit report will be published. Through the monitoring visit, inspectors will challenge the provider to improve. The report will set out what progress the provider has made since the previous inspection.

35.   The first re-inspection monitoring visit will normally take place within six months of the date of publication of the previous inspection report, if the provider continues to be funded. A second re-inspection monitoring visit will normally take place within 10 months of the date of publication of the previous inspection report, if the provider continues to be funded.

Pilot inspections

36.   From time to time, we may pilot different approaches to inspection. We will provide details for this type of inspection on a case-by-case basis.

Scope of inspection

37.   We will normally inspect providers that have one or more of the following that they are directly responsible for:

- direct funding from ESFA
- an advanced learner loans facility from ESFA
- adult education funding from Greater London Authority (GLA) and/or one of the mayoral and combined authorities (MCAs)[22]
- apprenticeship training provision funded through the apprenticeship levy.[23]

38. Subcontracted provision that is part of the directly funded provider's responsibility is also within the scope of inspection. As part of the inspection, inspectors may look at any provision carried out on behalf of the provider by subcontractors or partners. Typically, visits to, or communications with, subcontractors are likely to include inspecting the direct contract holder's arrangements to quality assure and improve the provision.

39. Inspections will not include provision that the provider operates under subcontracted arrangements on behalf of other providers.

40. Ofsted reserves the right to inspect and grade any subcontractor and its provision as a separate entity against the EIF and this handbook.

41. Any provision that is part of a pilot scheme is normally outside the scope for inspection. Provision funded by the European Social Fund is normally outside the scope of inspection.

Inspecting residential provision in colleges

42. We inspect residential accommodation in colleges against the national minimum standards for the accommodation of students aged under 18. The standards apply to 'institutions within the further education sector', as defined by section 91 of the Further and Higher Education Act 1992, which have residential accommodation for 16- and 17-year-olds.[24] These inspections are separate from the inspection of the education and training provision of the college described in this handbook.

43. Our social care inspectors carry out these inspections. The approach is set out in the 'Social care common inspection framework (SCCIF): residential provision of further education colleges'.[25] If a college is registered as a care home, the Care Quality Commission inspects the accommodation.

Inspection of religious education and collective worship in relation to Catholic sixth-form colleges

44. In the case of these colleges, the relevant Catholic diocese will inspect their denominational religious education, Catholic ethos and the content of collective worship. Our inspectors will not comment on the content of religious worship or on denominational religious education. Inspectors may visit lessons and assemblies in order to help them evaluate how these contribute to students' personal development and behaviour and attitudes.

What inspections will cover

45. On a full inspection, inspectors will make an overall effectiveness judgement and key judgements on:

- quality of education
- behaviour and attitudes
- personal development
- leadership and management.

46. They will also make judgements on each major type of provision offered, as set out in the table below.

Type of provision	Description of provision
Education programmes for young people	Provision funded through the ESFA 16 to 18 classroom-based funding stream for study programmes and traineeships for those aged 16 to 18 and for ESFA-funded full-time provision for 14- to 16-year-olds enrolled in colleges.
Adult learning programmes	Provision funded through the adult education budget and/or advanced learning loans, including employability training for learners aged 19 and over referred for training by Jobcentre Plus. This includes community learning provision and traineeships for those aged 19 and over. This may include adult education provision funded by GLA and/or MCAs.
Apprenticeships	Apprenticeships at levels 2 to 5 funded by the ESFA and/or through the apprenticeship levy.[26]
Provision for learners with high needs	Provision for learners for which providers receive high-needs funding in addition to 16 to 18 ESFA funding for study programmes and/or 16 to 18 apprenticeships. Learners up to the age of 24 may be eligible for this funding.

47.   Inspectors will take account of all types of provision within the scope of the inspection. They will grade and report on the types of provision. If the number of learners in a particular type of provision is low, it will normally be inspected, but may not be graded. Provision for learners with high needs will normally be graded if there are learners supported by this funding unless that number is very low.

48.   The quality of provision for learners with high needs and with special educational needs and/or disabilities (SEND), a much broader group than those attracting high-needs funding, will always be considered during the inspection of any type of provision.

49.   Sector subject areas will not be graded or reported on separately. However, inspectors may use their subject expertise to contribute to the evidence base for types of provision and key judgements.[27]

50.   The lead inspector will normally confirm to the provider which types of provision will be graded separately.

Before the inspection

51.   The lead inspector's planning will focus primarily on how inspectors will gather evidence of learners' experiences, to evaluate the different types of provision offered by the provider against the four key judgements of the EIF.

52.   Inspectors' evidence-gathering will be primarily made up of focused curriculum reviews or 'deep dives', including lesson/session visits, scrutinising learners' work/training and assessment, and discussions with learners and teachers/ trainers. Inspectors may carry out some inspection activities jointly with members of the provider's staff.

53.   Inspectors may plan visits to learners at work at their employer's or at subcontractor's premises and carry out inspection activities. These visits give inspectors

the opportunity to hold discussions with learners and employers, to discuss learning programmes and to look at learners' work. Inspectors may carry out interviews/discussions with learners, employers and staff via telephone, video calls or webinars.

The role of the nominee in inspection

54.   Each provider is invited to nominate a senior member of staff to act as the provider's main link with the inspection team. The nominee should:

- have a detailed understanding of the provider's programmes and operations, including, where appropriate, those of subcontractors
- be sufficiently senior to ensure the cooperation of staff at all levels
- have authority to carry out the role with autonomy.

55.   The nominee's responsibilities include:

- providing information for the lead inspector to support inspection planning
- liaising with the lead inspector and ensuring that documents are available, and that staff can attend meetings
- briefing the provider's staff about arrangements
- informing learners and employers about the inspection[28]
- attending team meetings, in particular the final grading/ judgement team meeting
- coordinating feedback arrangements in particular at the end of the inspection.

Notification of inspection

56.   Notification of all types of further education and skills inspections and monitoring visits normally takes place up to two working days before the inspection unless the inspection is unannounced. Ofsted reserves the right to carry out unannounced inspections or monitoring visits.

57.   We will normally notify the provider in the morning of the notification day and will email the notification letter. The lead inspector will then contact the provider, normally by phone, as soon as possible and by the following morning at the latest. The lead inspector should make sure that:

- good communications and effective working relationships are established
- the arrangements for the inspection are confirmed.

Planning for the inspection

58.   As soon as the provider has been notified of the inspection, staff should draw together the information in paragraph 61. These should be working documents and not prepared specifically for the inspection. Inspectors should keep the review of documentation to a minimum. Providers are not expected to prepare anything extra for inspectors.

59.   Inspectors should be aware that the provider will need to accommodate the inspection while still managing day-to-day operations.

60.   Requests for a deferral will be handled in accordance with our policy.[29]

61.　　To ensure that the lead inspector has a clear understanding of the scope and range of provision and information needed to plan the logistics of the inspection, the nominee will send the following information, as applicable, as soon as possible:

- details of the courses/programmes being delivered and their mode of delivery
- timetables for lessons/sessions/workshops or other learning activities during the week
- a list of provider staff and a diagram of the organisational structure
- the geographical spread of training premises and learners, particularly work-based learners and apprentices, according to regions or sub-regions
- the names and location of employers
- the names and location of subcontractors
- contact information for key staff
- the current number of learners in the following age groups: 14 to 16; 16 to 18; 19+
- the current overall number of learners (excluding apprentices) at level 1 or below, level 2, level 3 and level 4/5, by subject area
- the current number of intermediate, advanced and higher-level apprentices, according to age groups: 16 to 18, 19 to 24, and 25+, by subject area and by apprenticeship framework or standard
- the current number of learners following employability programmes and those who have attended in the previous 12 months
- details of learners who are on a study programme but who are not working towards a substantial qualification
- the current number of learners following traineeships and those who have attended in the previous 12 months
- the current number of learners on community learning programmes and those who have attended in the previous 12 months
- the current number of learners with SEND and the number of learners for whom high-needs funding is received, and their particular needs.

62.　　To ensure that the provider understands the inspection process, the lead inspector will hold a telephone planning meeting with the nominee/most senior member of staff.

63.　　The lead inspector will use the telephone planning meeting to arrange how information is made available to inspectors. The provider should inform all subcontractors' staff, current learners, employers and other users about the inspection. It should emphasise that inspectors may visit any sessions involving learners either on the provider's premises or at other locations, including learners' workplaces or online.

64.　　The lead inspector will draw up a pre-inspection team briefing for the inspection team and the nominee. The purpose of this briefing is to focus inspection activity and identify areas for exploration, in particular the areas of the curriculum that will be reviewed through 'deep dives' (focused curriculum reviews).

65.   Inspectors will select the curriculum review areas they will focus on (and associated inspection activities, such as which learners and employers are being visited). They will take into account a range of factors, including:

- the types of provision
- the courses on offer, their subjects and levels
- the relative performance on different courses
- the number, spread and coverage of sites
- the value of the provider's contract(s) with funding agencies or with employers
- the geographical spread of learners
- the geographical spread of employers
- the mode of delivery and attendance
- information from the provider's nominee, learners and employers
- information from commissioning or funding bodies.

66.   The team briefing letter will provide details about the start of the on-site inspection, including the location and timing of the initial meeting and any other relevant arrangements for the first day, including the planned curriculum reviews.

Seeking the views of learners, parents and carers, employers and staff

67.   Learners' views are important to inspection. It is important that all learners can express their views to inspectors. This also applies to employers and any other key stakeholders. Inspectors will consider the views of learners, parents and carers, provider staff and employers. They will do this before and during the inspection. This may have a bearing on which areas of the curriculum they focus on.

68.   Ofsted's online questionnaires, Learner View and Employer View, are intended to gather the views of learners and employers. There is also an online questionnaire for parents and carers of learners. Respondents are able to complete these at any time during the year. There is also a questionnaire for members of the provider's staff, which is only in place from the inspection notification stage. After notifying the provider of the inspection, we ask the nominee to tell all staff, learners, employers and (where appropriate) parents and carers of learners that the inspection is taking place. The nominee should ask them to give their views to the inspection team by using these online questionnaires.[30]

69.   Surveys of the views of learners, employers, parents/carers and staff carried out by the provider, funding bodies or other organisations provide evidence for the inspection and may indicate themes to explore further. They do not replace talking with learners, employers and staff during the inspection or views collected through our online questionnaires.

70.   Inspectors will speak to a range of learners and employers, often as part of the focused curriculum reviews. This may happen face to face or remotely, for instance through a webinar or online meeting. We may use other surveys to capture views.

224

71. Inspectors will take account of views expressed to them by learners, employers, parents, governors, staff and the nominee. Staff and learners must be able to speak to inspectors in private to ensure that their responses are not influenced by the presence of the nominee or senior staff. Meetings during the inspection are likely to include those with samples of learners selected by inspectors and open-invitation meetings.

72. The lead inspector will take account of any external views on the provider's performance, for example through briefings from commissioning and funding bodies.

During the inspection

Days allocated to inspection and inspection team members

73. Inspections and monitoring visits will be led by either one of Her Majesty's Inspectors (HMI) or an Ofsted Inspector (OI) assisted by other HMIs and/or OIs.[31]

74. A full inspection normally lasts between two and five days on site. The number of inspectors involved will vary according to the size and complexity of the provider. Some inspectors may only be required for part of the inspection. How the lead inspector will deploy the team depends on the number of learners and sites, the type(s) of provision and range of learning programmes.

75. Short inspections (see paragraphs 122 to 152) normally last no longer than two days on site. The number of inspectors involved will vary according to the size and complexity of the provider. Some inspectors may only be required for part of the inspection.

76. Monitoring visits usually last between one and two days, depending on the scope of the visit and size of the provider. They will usually involve one or two inspectors (but may sometimes involve more).

Gathering and recording evidence

77. Inspections will normally begin with in-depth discussions with provider leaders and managers about the provider's curriculum to establish the intent of the curriculum. Inspectors will ask about what leaders intend learners to learn; what are the end points and next steps they wish them to reach through this; what are the key concepts that they need to understand; and in what order they will learn them.

78. Although meetings with leaders are important, inspectors' first priority during inspections is to collect first-hand evidence.

79. Inspectors will primarily do this through a range of inspection activities, grouped into focused curriculum reviews, known as 'deep dives'. These will provide evidence of the effective implementation of the curriculum and its intent – but they will also gather evidence which may be relevant to the other key judgement areas and progress judgements. These activities will be focused on curriculum areas selected by the lead inspector (see paragraph 65).

80. These inspection activities include:

■ direct observation of teaching, training and assessment

- meetings and discussions with teachers, trainers and other staff (in particular subject specialists and subject leaders to understand the intent and implementation of the curriculum)
- interviews and discussions with learners (these may happen in formal planned meetings or in more informal settings)
- scrutinising learners' work
- evaluating learning materials and their use by learners
- analysing provider and learner records, showing planning for, and monitoring of, learners' individual progress and destinations from their starting points when they began their courses or apprenticeships
- assessing learners' progress
- examining what learners know, understand, and can do and make as a result of their learning.

81.   Evidence drawn from these different activities and focused on specific curriculum areas should provide valid, reliable and sufficient evidence of the quality of education and training when connected, combined and brought together.

82.   Evidence from these curriculum-related activities will also inform the other key judgements: behaviour and attitudes; personal development; and leadership and management.

83.   Inspectors will also carry out other inspections activities to gather evidence for the key judgements. These may include:
- analysing documents relating to leadership and management (such as records about safeguarding or notes of governors' meetings), or personal development and behaviour (such as records about attendance or enrichment activities)
- analysing learner, employer, parent/carer and staff views provided through questionnaires and other sources
- meeting with learners, employers, staff, governors, board members, councillors, trustees, subcontractors, where appropriate.

84.   During the inspection, inspectors will collect, analyse and record evidence and their judgements on paper or electronic evidence forms. It is essential that the evidence accurately reflects discussions. Inspectors should identify clearly information that was provided in confidence. The evidence forms, together with any briefings, plans or instructions prepared by the lead inspector, and responses from learners and employers (in hard copy, online or other formats) contribute to the evidence base. The lead inspector is responsible for assuring the quality of evidence.

85.   Ofsted has no preferred teaching style. Inspectors judge the quality of education by the ways in which learners acquire knowledge, develop skills and exhibit appropriate behaviours for work and success in life or study. Teaching staff should plan their lessons as usual.[32]

86.   Inspectors may visit employers, to observe learners' on-the-job skills development and speak to employers and staff.

87.   Inspectors will not normally indicate which sessions they plan to observe. The team reserves the right to visit any learner or employer and may cancel or add visits to ensure that enough evidence is collected. Inspectors will not normally give feedback to individual members of staff following these sessions.

Observations of teaching and training

88.   An important element of the inspection approach with be to visit lessons, workshops or sessions where teaching, training, learning and assessment are happening. Inspectors may often invite appropriate staff from the provider to take part in joint observations of these learning sessions.

89.   Observation is primarily useful for gathering evidence about curriculum implementation and how teaching and training sessions contribute to the quality of education and training. Inspectors can use observations to gather evidence about how well staff implement the curriculum by looking at teaching of one or more subjects, and by triangulating observations with evidence collected through discussions with staff, learners, and, where relevant, employers, and through work scrutiny.

90.   Inspectors will connect observation activity to other evidence for triangulation and as part of the focused curriculum reviews. Observation is not about evaluating individual teachers or trainers. Inspectors will not grade the teaching or training they observe. Instead, inspectors will view teaching and training across a sample of the provision to provide part of the evidence base to inform inspection judgements, in particular the quality of education and training.

91.   Observation is also useful for gathering evidence that contributes to other key judgements, including behaviour and attitudes. Observation enables inspectors to see direct evidence about how behaviour is managed and how behaviours and attitudes are developed in individual learning sessions. This evidence will complement the other evidence that inspectors gather about behaviour and attitudes during inspection.

Work scrutiny

92.   Inspectors may scrutinise learners' work across the provider and aggregate insights to provide part of the evidence for an overall view of quality of education, primarily around the impact of the education provided. Inspectors will not evaluate individual pieces of work. Inspectors will connect work scrutiny to lesson observation and, where possible, conversations with learners, staff and, where appropriate, with employers.

93.   Inspectors may invite appropriate staff from the provider to take part in joint scrutiny of learners' work.

94.   Scrutiny is useful primarily for gathering evidence about the curriculum impact of the quality of education. Inspectors can use work scrutiny to evaluate learners' progress and progression through their course of study. Work scrutiny will show whether learners know more and can do more, and whether the knowledge and skills they have learned are

well sequenced and have developed incrementally. Inspectors will synthesise what they find in order to contribute to their overall assessment of the quality of education across the provider.

The use of data

95.   Inspection uses a range of data that is available. Both before and during the inspection, inspectors will analyse the performance of the provider using the most recent validated data. Analysis may be at overall provider level and/or for individual subjects or types of provision. Although data alone will not lead directly to judgements, the primary data that measures success for each type of provision will provide important evidence for judging the impact of the quality of education.

96.   Inspectors will evaluate learners' progress in relation to their starting points, based on their rate of learning, acquisition of knowledge, skills and behaviours and whether they have achieved their individual, challenging targets. They will also take account of data about the destinations learners go to when they leave the provider.

97.   Inspectors will not look at internal progress and attainment data on GCSE and A-level courses where fixed-time terminal examinations comprise the entire assessment of the course. Similarly, inspectors will not normally look at predicted in-year achievement and attainment data more generally. That does not mean providers cannot use this data if they consider it appropriate. Inspectors will, however, put more focus on the curriculum and less on providers' generation, analysis and interpretation of performance data. Inspectors will be interested in the conclusions drawn and actions taken from any internal assessment information but they will not examine or verify that information first hand.

The self-assessment report

98.   Inspectors will use self-assessment reports, or equivalent documents, to assess risk, monitor standards and plan for inspection. If these documents are not available in advance, the provider should share the latest report/plan(s) with the lead inspector following notification of the inspection.

99.   Inspectors will in any case, use other readily available information about the provider.

100.   During the inspection, inspectors will compare their findings with the provider's self-assessment.

101.   Ofsted does not require self-assessment to be provided in a specific format. Any assessment that is provided should be part of the provider's processes and not generated solely for inspection purposes.[33]

Meetings during inspection

102.   Inspectors are likely to have a number of different meetings with provider staff for different purposes. They will try to minimise disruption to the provider's regular business and to the inspection team's focus on assessing the quality of education and training. Therefore, meetings will be kept brief and purposeful.

103.   Inspections will normally begin with in-depth discussion with senior leaders and

managers about the provider's curriculum to establish the intent of the curriculum and quality of education. This initial meeting will also provide useful insights into leadership and management and other areas. There may be other meetings with senior leaders, including the nominee as necessary, as the inspection progresses.

104.	Inspectors carrying out deep dives focusing on specific areas of the curriculum will normally meet with key curriculum staff. This is to understand its intent and implementation before carrying out their inspection activities to review that area of the curriculum. Other types of meeting have been referred to above in paragraphs 80 and 83.

105.	The inspection team itself will hold meetings. They may be meetings of the whole team or between two or more inspectors. They may be held remotely via Skype or telephone or face to face. These may include:

- an initial team meeting to:
  - brief the inspection team on the schedule for the inspection
  - clarify any queries about team members' roles
  - receive a brief update from the provider, including, if appropriate, an initial briefing from the provider's managers with relevant responsibilities for key areas to be covered of the inspection[34]
- a meeting for the nominee to hear the emerging judgements and identify any opportunities to provide additional evidence
- a grading/progress judgement meeting on the last day of the inspection to reach judgements about the provider.

106.	The nominee may attend some inspection team meetings, although they may not contribute to decisions about inspection judgements. By taking part in discussions about evidence collected during the inspection, the nominee can help to ensure that all appropriate evidence is taken into account. Any concerns about evidence should be raised with the lead inspector. The nominee will report to the provider's staff on the progress of the inspection.

107.	Inspectors may hold additional meetings with the provider's staff.

108.	The lead inspector will hold a feedback meeting for the provider and invitees to hear the key messages at the end of the inspection.

Reaching final judgements

109.	Inspectors will discuss emerging findings with the nominee and, where appropriate, with senior staff.

110.	The lead inspector will ensure that the inspection team agrees the judgements for full inspections using the descriptors in part 2 of this handbook.[35] The overall judgements will reflect all of the evidence considered by the inspection team. The evidence base must support the judgements convincingly.

Providing feedback

111.	Before leaving, the lead inspector should ensure that the provider is clear:

- about the grades awarded for each judgement required[36]

- that the grades awarded are provisional and, although unlikely, may be subject to change through moderation and quality assurance[37]
- that the points provided in the feedback, subject to any change, will be generally reflected in the report, although the text of the report may differ slightly from the oral feedback
- about the main findings and areas for improvement
- that inspection findings may be shared with the Further Education Commissioner, ESFA, DfE, Ofqual and/or Office for Students (OfS) before the publication of the report
- about the procedures that will lead to the publication of the report
- about the complaints procedure
- where relevant, about the implications of the provider being judged as requires improvement or inadequate overall[38]
- that, if the overall effectiveness or the leadership and management of a sixth-form college, further education college or designated institution are judged inadequate, this has implications for the college in relation to appointing newly qualified staff in future years.[39]

After the inspection

Arrangements for publishing the report

112.   The lead inspector is responsible for writing the inspection report and submitting the evidence to Ofsted shortly after the inspection ends. The text of the report should reflect the evidence. The findings in the report should be consistent with the feedback given to the provider at the end of the inspection.

113.   Inspection reports will be quality assured before we send a draft copy to the provider. The draft report is restricted and confidential and should not be shared externally or published. The inspection process is not complete until the provider receives the final version of the report. We may share the findings of the inspection with the Further Education Commissioner, ESFA, DfE, Ofqual and OfS as necessary (that might entail sharing the draft report in whole or in part).

114.   We will inform the provider of the timescale for commenting about factual inaccuracies in the draft report. The lead inspector will consider any factual inaccuracies identified by the provider and will make changes as appropriate.

115.   Typically, providers will receive an electronic version of the final report before we publish the report. In most circumstances, we publish the final report on our website within four to six working weeks.

The inspection evidence base

116.   The evidence base for the inspection must be retained for the time specified in our guidance.[40] This is normally six years from the publication of the report. Information must not be disposed of if we still require it.

Quality assurance and complaints

Quality assurance of inspection

117.   All inspectors are responsible for the quality of their work. The lead inspector must ensure that inspections are carried out in accordance with the principles of inspection and the code of conduct (set out in the EIF).

118.   We monitor the quality of inspections through a range of formal processes. Senior HMI or HMI may visit some providers to quality assure inspections. Inspection evidence bases and reports are subject to quality assurance monitoring and moderation within Ofsted. The lead inspector will be responsible for feeding back to the team inspectors about the quality of their work and their conduct.

119.   All providers are invited to take part in a post-inspection evaluation in order to contribute to inspection development.

Handling concerns and complaints

120.   The great majority of Ofsted's work is carried out smoothly and without incident. If concerns arise during an inspection visit, they should be raised with the lead inspector as soon as possible in order to resolve issues before the inspection is completed. The lead inspector should seek advice where necessary. Inspectors should note any concerns raised, and actions taken, in the inspection evidence.

121.   If it is not possible to resolve concerns during the inspection, the provider may wish to lodge a formal complaint. The lead inspector should ensure that the provider is informed of the procedures for making a formal complaint. Information about how to complain is available on our website.[41]

Short inspections

122.   Providers graded good for overall effectiveness at their previous inspection will usually be inspected within five years of the publication of that inspection report. Most will receive a short inspection (see paragraph 11).

123.   A short inspection will determine primarily whether the quality of education/training that learners receive is good. Inspectors will consider the provider's quality of education and/or training and the effectiveness of leadership and management. They will assess whether safeguarding measures are effective and if learners benefit from good-quality careers advice and guidance. Short inspections may also cover any areas particular to a provider that the lead inspector judges necessary.

124.   In order to confirm whether the provider remains good, inspectors will use the criteria set out in part 2 of this handbook. They will not be expected to carry out a full inspection within a reduced timeframe but to arrive at sufficient evidence to demonstrate that the provider remains good overall.

125.   A short inspection report will not give graded judgements for provision types. It will not change the provider's overall effectiveness grade.

126.   Once a provider has received its first short inspection and is confirmed to be good, we will usually carry out a further short inspection within five years of the publication of the

previous report. If risk assessment identifies any decline in performance or if there are any safeguarding or other concerns about the provider, we may carry out a full inspection.[42] Ofsted reserves the right to carry out a full inspection to any provider at any reasonable time.

127.   As with all other inspections under the EIF, the model of short inspections is designed to encourage constructive, challenging professional conversation between inspectors, leaders, managers and governors.

The purpose of a short inspection

128.   The main purpose of short inspections is to evaluate sufficiently whether the provider remains good and in particular:

- whether the provider's quality of education/training is good
- whether safeguarding arrangements are effective
- whether careers education and guidance are of a good quality[43]
- whether leaders, managers and governors have the capacity to make continued improvement and manage change well.

A short inspection will also take into account: any other aspect that the lead inspector considers particularly relevant given the findings of the last inspection report; issues identified at the planning stage; and the particular nature of the provider.

129.   Inspectors will focus primarily on the quality of education during a short inspection. They will not expect to cover the criteria within the quality of education judgement in Part 2 of this handbook to the same extent as on a full inspection. They will focus on a number of key curriculum areas using deep- dive focused curriculum reviews to provide sufficient evidence that the provider remains good. This will follow the same approach as set out in the sections above: 'gathering and recording evidence', 'observations of teaching and training', 'work scrutiny' and 'use of data'.

130.   A short inspection will be carried out by one or more inspectors over one or two days, depending on the size and type of provider.[44]

Outcomes of a short inspection

131.   A short inspection has three possible outcomes.

- Outcome 1 – the provider continues to be a good provider. In these cases, it will receive a short inspection report following the report publication process).
- Outcome 2 – the provider is at least good and there is sufficient evidence of improvement to suggest that the provider may be judged outstanding. In these cases, the short inspection will be extended to a full inspection.
- Outcome 3 – the inspection team has insufficient evidence to satisfy itself that the provider remains good, or there are concerns arising from evidence gathered that the provider may not be good. In these cases, the short inspection will be extended to a full inspection.

132.   Inspectors will always report on whether safeguarding is effective. If safeguarding is not effective, inspectors will extend the short inspection to a full inspection.

Providers that remain good (outcome 1)

133. If inspectors judge that a provider remains good (outcome 1), they will confirm this judgement in the final feedback at the end of the short inspection.

Extending short inspections to full inspections (outcomes 2 and 3)

134. If there is sufficient evidence of improved quality to suggest that the provider may be judged outstanding, the short inspection will be extended to a full inspection (outcome 2).

135. If the lead inspector has insufficient evidence to confirm that the provider remains good **or** if there is evidence that the provider may no longer be good (which may include concerns about safeguarding), the short inspection will be extended to a full inspection (outcome 3).

136. In the cases of outcomes 2 or 3, the lead inspector will inform the provider by the end of the short inspection of the decision to extend the inspection to a full inspection.

137. For outcomes 2 and 3, the short inspection will be extended to a full inspection as soon as possible. This will usually be completed within 15 working days of the short inspection. More inspectors may join the lead inspector on site. This may include HMI and/or OIs. The inspection team will gather and evaluate evidence to make a full set of graded judgements against the EIF. The lead inspector from the short inspection will usually continue the full inspection.

138. A decision to extend the inspection does not predetermine the outcome of the full inspection. At the end of the full inspection, the provider may receive any grade on the four-point grading scale.

139. The lead inspector of the full inspection will contact the nominee and tell them when the full inspection will start. The lead inspector will share the team composition and deployment. The inspector may request further evidence and information for planning before the on-site stage of the inspection begins.

140. Between the end of the short inspection and the beginning of the full inspection following extension, evidence from the short inspection will be shared with the new team. The lead inspector and that team will build on the evidence to complete the full inspection, avoiding repetition or duplication.

141. The full inspection may move straight to evidence gathering, without an initial team meeting.

142. A short inspection report will not be produced when the short inspection converts to a full inspection. Instead, the provider will receive a full inspection report.

Inspectors' planning and preparation

143. The lead inspector will share with the inspection team:
- essential information about the provider and the timings for the inspection
- a short summary of any areas to be focused on, based on a brief analysis of the pre-inspection information
- a brief outline of inspection activity, including planned 'deep dive' curriculum

reviews. This will be finalised on site.

Notification and introduction

144.   We will normally notify the provider up to two working days before the inspection, unless the inspection is unannounced. Ofsted reserves the right to carry out unannounced inspections or visits. We will notify the provider in the morning of the notification day and will email the notification letter. The lead inspector will then contact the provider as soon as possible.

145.   Leaders, managers and governors are not required to prepare documents or other materials for inspection. Inspectors will review documents and other materials that leaders, staff and governors use for normal day-to-day business. Any assessment should be part of the provider's usual evaluation work and not generated solely for inspection purposes. Inspectors will use what the provider has.

146.   During the initial telephone call to a provider selected for short inspection, the lead inspector will:

- establish contact with the provider's nominee
- confirm the date of the inspection
- explain the purpose of the inspection, including the different possible outcomes of the short inspection
- indicate the likely format and timings of the short inspection
- request that the provider alerts learners, employers, parents and carers (where appropriate) and provider staff about the inspection. These groups will be invited to give their views by means of online questionnaires
- make initial arrangements for meeting or interviewing governors, managers, staff, learners, employers and others
- make arrangements to visit employers or subcontractors as necessary.

147.   Inspectors may also request further information during the initial telephone call, by subsequent email or at the first opportunity on site. This information may include:

- information about learners, their types of provision, courses/programmes, subject areas and locations
- timetables for lessons/sessions/workshops or other learning activities
- a list of provider staff and/or a diagram of the organisational structure and key staff contact information
- the current self-assessment report or equivalent and any evaluation of the impact of actions taken to date
- recent data on learners' outcomes, performance, progress and destinations (but note paragraph 97 above about internal progress and attainment data on GCSE and A-level courses where fixed-time terminal examinations comprise the entire assessment of the course)
- lists of employers and subcontractors and their locations.

148.   Requests for a deferral will be handled in accordance with Ofsted's policy.[45]

Feedback at the end of a short inspection

149.   The lead inspector will give oral feedback at the end of the short inspection. The lead inspector is responsible for managing this meeting and agreeing attendance with the nominee.

150.   The lead inspector will:

- state whether the provider continues to be a good provider or
- state that there is evidence that the provider may no longer be good or there is insufficient evidence to conclude that the provider is a good provider; if either is the case, they will explain that the inspection will be extended into a full inspection and the process for this

or

- state that there is sufficient evidence of improved quality to extend the inspection to a full inspection

and

- make clear whether the provider's safeguarding arrangements are judged to be effective and provide feedback on other relevant areas covered in the short inspection (as outlined in paragraph 128).

Reporting on the short inspection

151.   If the quality of provision is good, the provider will receive a short inspection report setting out the inspection findings. These will include statements that the provider is good, a judgement on whether safeguarding arrangements are effective, and a summary of what the provider does well and what it can do better. If the short inspection is extended to become a full inspection, the provider will receive a full inspection report as outlined above and not a short inspection report.

Quality assurance and publication of the short inspection letter

152.   The short inspection report will be published on our website. Quality assurance and publication processes are the same as those for full inspection reports (see paragraphs 112 to 121).

Is the provider a good provider? Is safeguarding effective?

Yes → **Provider remains good**

The provider's quality is good.
It provides a good quality of education/training for learners.
Any weaknesses are known by leaders and are being tackled.

Returns to cycle of inspection

Yes → **Provider may be outstanding**

Is it likely that the provider might be judged outstanding in a full inspection?

Lead may stay on. Ofsted region quickly deploys further inspectors.

Insufficient evidence or concerns about quality/management/safeguarding

Provider informed that insufficient evidence has been gathered or that concerns exist and explains that a full inspection will follow shortly.

Lead may stay on. Ofsted region quickly deploys further inspectors.

236

Part 2. The evaluation schedule: how further education and skills providers will be judged

Background to the evaluation schedule

153.   Inspectors must use the evaluation schedule alongside the guidance set out in part 1 of this handbook and the EIF.

154.   The evaluation schedule is not exhaustive. It does not replace the professional judgement of inspectors. Inspectors must interpret grade descriptors in relation to the type(s) of provision inspected and context of the provider.

155.   In line with the EIF, inspectors will make judgements on the following areas:
- overall effectiveness

and the four key judgements:
- quality of education
- behaviour and attitudes
- personal development
- leadership and management.

156.   We have created the criteria for each of these judgements using inspection experience, areas of consensus in academic research and our own research. You can find a full note of how the judgement criteria relate to the available research in our commentary.[46]

157.   Inspectors use the following four-point scale to make all judgements, including, where applicable, on the effectiveness of the different types of provision offered:
- grade 1: outstanding
- grade 2: good
- grade 3: requires improvement
- grade 4: inadequate.

The evaluation schedule and grade descriptors

Overall effectiveness

158.   Inspectors must use all their evidence to evaluate what it is like to be a learner at the provider. In making their judgements about a provider's overall effectiveness, inspectors will consider whether the quality of provision is good or whether it exceeds good and is therefore outstanding. If it is not good, inspectors will consider whether it requires improvement or is inadequate.

159.   In judging the overall effectiveness, inspectors will take account of:
- the overall effectiveness judgement for each type of provision inspected
- the four key judgements.

160.   Inspectors will first judge the overall effectiveness of each type of provision inspected. To do this, they will apply the grading criteria set out in the EIF. The section 'Evaluating types of provision' in this handbook sets out how inspectors will evaluate the

overall effectiveness of each type of provision. The inspection report will include a numerical grade for each type of provision inspected. Inspectors will then grade the four key judgements. Where there are differences in grades given for a type of provision, inspectors will consider the following when awarding the grade for overall effectiveness:

- the number of learners in/the funding value of the relevant provision
- the impact of the weaker areas on learners' overall experience and quality of education received.

161. Inspectors will always make a written judgement about the effectiveness of the arrangements for safeguarding learners.

162. Before making the final judgement on overall effectiveness, inspectors must evaluate the extent to which the education and training provided meets the needs of all learners. This includes learners with SEND and those who have high needs.

Grade descriptors for overall effectiveness

Outstanding (1)

- **The quality of education is outstanding.**
- **All types of provision offered are likely to be outstanding. In exceptional circumstances, a type of provision may be good, as long as there is convincing evidence that the provider is improving this provision rapidly and securely towards it being outstanding.**
- **All key judgements are likely to be outstanding. In exceptional circumstances, one of the key judgements may be good, as long as there is convincing evidence that the provider is improving this area rapidly and securely towards it being outstanding.**
- **Safeguarding is effective.**

163. To judge whether a provider is **good**, **requires improvement** or is **inadequate**, inspectors will use a 'best fit' approach, relying on the professional judgement of the inspection team.

Good (2)

- **The quality of education is at least good.**
- **All types of provision offered are likely to be good or outstanding. In exceptional circumstances, a type of provision may require improvement, if there is convincing evidence that the provider is improving this provision rapidly and securely towards it being good.**
- **All key judgements are likely to be good or outstanding. In exceptional circumstances, one of the key judgement areas may require improvement, as long as there is convincing evidence that the provider is improving it rapidly and securely towards it being good.**
- **Safeguarding is effective.**

Requires improvement (3)

■ Other than in exceptional circumstances, it is likely that, where the provider requires improvement in any of the key judgements, the provider's overall effectiveness will require improvement.

■ Safeguarding is effective, or, if there are any weaknesses in safeguarding, they are not difficult to rectify, and there are no serious failings that leave learners being harmed or at risk of harm.

Inadequate (4)

■ The judgement on the overall effectiveness is likely to be inadequate when any one of the key judgements is inadequate and/or safeguarding is ineffective.

Evaluating types of provision

164.   The following section outlines what inspectors will look for to demonstrate how the grade descriptors for each key judgement apply to each type of provision.

Education programmes for young people

165.   To achieve comparability with the way in which we inspect and judge 16 to 19 provision in schools and academies under the EIF, the considerations below align with those in the school inspection handbook.

166.   Inspectors will review provision for learners aged 14 to 16 enrolled full time at a college and provision for learners on traineeships aged 16 to 19 as part of this judgement.

■ Inspectors will consider how well leaders and teachers promote high expectations for achievement and progress through the systems they use to monitor and develop the quality of provision for learners, including the most disadvantaged, those with SEND and those with high needs.

■ Inspectors will consider how leaders and teachers develop or take on a purposeful curriculum that provides progression and stretch, as well as mathematics and English for all learners, including those without GCSE legacy grades A* to C (reformed grades 9 to 4), and also, where relevant, work experience or industry placements and non-qualification activities.[47]

■ Inspectors will review how well high-quality impartial careers guidance enables learners to make progress and move on to a higher level of qualification, employment, further training or independent living when they are ready to do so.

■ Inspectors will use observations of teaching and training activities, and discussions with learners, teachers, support staff and, where relevant, employers, to consider how well learners develop personal, social and independent learning skills.

■ Inspectors will judge how well learners achieve high levels of punctuality and attendance, and how well their conduct and attitudes, including in non-qualification or enrichment activities and/or work experience, prepare them for employment or to progress to higher levels of study and/or independence.

- Inspectors will also consider whether arrangements for safeguarding learners are appropriate and effective.

Adult learning programmes

167.   Adult learning comprises a rich variety of learning and training, such as programmes for those with SEND, vocational training, employability training and community learning.

- Inspectors will judge, where appropriate, how well the curriculum, including the wider curriculum, for each strand of a provider's adult learning programme has a clearly defined purpose that is relevant to the education and training needs and interests of learners, and to local employment opportunities, and supports local and national priorities.
- Inspectors will judge how effectively leaders, managers and governors focus public funding on people who are disadvantaged and least likely to participate in education and training, and work with other partners to widen participation and support learners' progression to further learning and/or employment relevant to their personal circumstances.
- Inspectors will assess how well leaders and managers use community learning funding to develop learning programmes and projects that develop stronger communities, where appropriate.
- Inspectors will judge how effectively staff work with learners, employers and other partners such as Jobcentre Plus, to ensure that teaching, learning and assessment enable learners to develop personal, social and employability skills that prepare them well for their intended job role, career aims and/or personal goals.
- Where appropriate, inspectors will judge how well providers record and recognise learners' progress and achievements to inform teaching and support programmes to help learners reach their goals.
- Inspectors will also consider whether arrangements for safeguarding young people and vulnerable learners are appropriate and effective.

Apprenticeships

168.   Inspectors will consider how well leaders and managers ensure that the apprenticeship curriculum meets the principles and requirements of an apprenticeship.

- Evidence will include the extent to which the provider's staff engage with employers to:
  - complete the apprenticeship commitment statement
  - plan the initial assessment, training, assessments, review points and milestones throughout
  - agree any additional qualifications to be included
  - monitor and support apprentices, including those with SEND and those

who have high needs, to progress quickly, gain new knowledge, skills and behaviours and achieve to their full potential.

- Inspectors will judge how well trainers, assessors, coaches and mentors communicate up-to-date vocational and technical subject knowledge that reflects expected industry practice and meets employers' needs.
- Inspectors will determine whether apprentices acquire that knowledge effectively so that they demonstrate the required skills and behaviours that enable them to complete their apprenticeships, contribute to their workplace and fulfil their career aims by progressing to their intended job roles or other sustained employment, promotion or, where appropriate, moving to a higher level of apprenticeship or qualification.
- Inspectors will also consider whether arrangements for safeguarding young people and vulnerable learners are appropriate and effective.

Provision for learners with high needs

169.   Part 3 of the Children and Families Act 2014 explains the current arrangements for young people with learning difficulties and/or disabilities.[48] The Act aims to encourage education, health and social care services to work together. Local authorities must describe the provision available to young people in the area by publicising the 'local offer'. A young person has a learning difficulty or disability if he or she has:

- a significantly greater difficulty in learning than most others of the same age
- a disability that prevents or hinders him or her from using the kind of facilities generally provided for others of the same age in general post-16 institutions.

170.   Inspectors will consider the extent to which leaders, managers and governors use the funding for learners with high needs so that their individual learning programmes challenge learners to: develop their independence; improve their communication skills; make relevant personal choices and decisions; and prepare themselves for adult life.

171.   Inspectors will judge how successfully learners participate in good-quality and individually tailored learning programmes that lead to paid or voluntary employment where appropriate (including to supported internships, traineeships and apprenticeships) and/or to greater independence in their everyday lives.

172.   Inspectors will evaluate how effectively leaders and managers coordinate all specialist support, including speech and language development, behaviour management, occupational therapy and physiotherapy, so that learners develop the skills they need.

173.   Where appropriate, inspectors will determine the extent to which the choice of accreditation helps learners progress towards further learning, vocational training, employment and independent living.

174.   Inspectors will judge whether procedures for recognising and recording learners' progress and achievement are rigorous and purposeful and support the achievement of all learners.

175.   Inspectors will determine whether staff are suitably qualified and/or have

appropriate expertise to support learners or specific groups of learners. They will determine whether learning resources, including assistive technology, are to the required standard and specification and whether they are used effectively to support learners to overcome their barriers to achieving their challenging learning goals.

176. Inspectors will judge how successfully learners develop skills to enhance their employment opportunities and independence in their everyday lives in real-life situations, including meaningful work experience, and how well they take an active part in their local communities.

177. Inspectors will judge how well learners following academic or vocational qualifications make progress and achieve, compared with all learners on the same programme. They will also judge whether learners progress into appropriate paid or voluntary employment, further learning or other activities.

178. Inspectors will also consider whether arrangements for safeguarding learners are appropriate and effective.

Quality of education[49]

179.   Inspectors will take a rounded view of the quality of education that a provider delivers to its learners.

- Inspectors will consider the provider's curriculum, which embodies the decisions the provider has made about the knowledge, skills and behaviours its learners need to acquire to fulfil their aspirations for learning, employment and independence.
- They will also consider the way teachers teach and assess to support learners to build their knowledge and to apply that knowledge as skills.
- Finally, inspectors will consider the outcomes that learners achieve as a result of the education they have received.

Intent

180.   In evaluating the provider's educational intent, inspectors will primarily consider the curriculum leadership provided by senior and subject leaders.

181.   The evaluation focuses on factors that contribute to learners receiving education and training that enables them to achieve highly. These factors are listed below.

- Leaders and managers have selected and developed a curriculum that develops the knowledge, skills and behaviours that learners need in order to take advantage of the opportunities, responsibilities and experiences that prepare them for their next stage in education, training or employment. In this way, it can powerfully address social disadvantage.
- It is clear what the curriculum is preparing learners for. It is also clear what learners will need to be able to know and do at the end of their learning or training programmes.
- Leaders, managers and teachers have planned and sequenced the curriculum so that learners can build on previous teaching and learning and develop the new knowledge and skills they need.
- The curriculum offers learners the knowledge and skills that reflect the needs of the local and regional context.
- The curriculum intent takes into account the needs of learners, employers, and the local, regional and national economy, as necessary.
- The curriculum ensures that all learners benefit from high academic, technical and vocational ambitions. This means that the curriculum should be ambitious for disadvantaged learners or those with SEND, including those who have high needs, and should meet those needs.

The curriculum

182.   The curriculum sets out the aims of a programme of education and training. It also sets out the structure for those aims to be implemented, including the knowledge, skills and behaviours to be gained at each stage. It enables the evaluation of learners' knowledge and understanding against those expectations.

183. We will judge providers taking radically different approaches to the curriculum fairly. We recognise the importance of providers' autonomy to choose their own curriculum approaches. If leaders are able to show that they have thought carefully, that they have built a curriculum with appropriate coverage, content, structure and sequencing, and that it has been implemented effectively, then inspectors will assess a provider's curriculum favourably.

Sources of evidence specific to curriculum intent

184. Inspectors will draw evidence about leaders' intent for the curriculum principally from discussion with senior and subject leaders. Inspectors will explore:

- how leaders have ensured that a subject curriculum includes content that has been identified as most useful and that this content is taught in a logical progression, systematically and explicitly for all learners to acquire the intended knowledge, skills and behaviours
- how leaders ensure that the curriculum supports learners' progression and provides knowledge and/or skills for the future (including non-qualification activity, where relevant)
- how learners see links between different areas of knowledge and skills and recognise that some knowledge and skills are transferable
- how carefully leaders have thought about the sequence of teaching knowledge and skills to build on what learners already know and can do.

Inspectors will also consider any documentary evidence that leaders wish to provide in the format that the provider normally uses. Inspectors will not request materials to be produced or provided in any specific format for inspection.

Implementation

185. In evaluating the implementation of the curriculum, inspectors will focus on how the curriculum is taught at subject, classroom or workshop level.

186. We will focus on the following factors.

- Teachers having expert knowledge of the subjects that they teach. If they do not, they are supported to address gaps so that learners are not disadvantaged by ineffective teaching.
- Teachers enable learners to understand key concepts, presenting information clearly and promoting discussion.
- Teachers check learners' understanding effectively, and identify and correct misunderstandings.
- Teachers ensure that learners embed key concepts in their long-term memory and apply them fluently and consistently.
- Leaders and teachers have designed and they deliver the subject curriculum in a way that allows learners to transfer key knowledge to long- term memory. The curriculum is sequenced so that new knowledge and skills build on what learners know and can do and learners can work towards

defined end points.

- Teachers use assessment to check learners' understanding in order to inform teaching.
- Teachers use assessment to help learners to embed and use knowledge fluently, to develop their understanding, and to gain, extend and improve their skills and not simply memorise disconnected facts.

The use of assessment

187. When used effectively, assessment can help learners to embed and use knowledge fluently and to show that they are competent in applying their skills. The results of effective assessment assist teachers to produce clear and achievable next steps for learners. However, assessment is too often carried out in a way that creates unnecessary burdens for staff and learners. It is therefore important that leaders and teachers understand its limitations and avoid misuse and overuse.

188. Inspectors will evaluate how assessment supports the teaching of the curriculum, while not driving teachers towards excessive individualisation, differentiation or interventions that are almost impossible to deliver without lowering expectations of some learners and/or driving up teachers' workload.

Sources of evidence specific to curriculum implementation

189. The following activities will provide inspectors with evidence about the provider's implementation of its intended curriculum:

- discussions with subject specialists, subject leaders and teachers about:
  - the curriculum that learners follow
  - the intended end points towards which those learners are working
  - their view of how those learners are progressing through the curriculum
- reviews of curriculum plans or other long-term planning (in whatever form teachers and/or subject leaders usually produce and use them)
- visits to classes, workshops and other activities, including observations of teaching and training
- scrutinising work produced by learners
- interviews with learners
- discussions with teachers about how often they are expected to record, upload and review data
- discussions with subject specialists and leaders about the content and pedagogical content knowledge of teachers, and what is done to support them
- discussions with staff, including specialist staff, who support learners in developing their knowledge, skills and behaviours.

190. In order to triangulate evidence effectively, inspectors will ensure that they gather a variety of these types of evidence in relation to the same sample of learners. Inspectors will also ensure that the samples of learners they choose are sufficient to allow them to reach

a valid and sufficiently reliable judgement on the quality of education offered by the provider overall.

Impact

191.   When inspectors evaluate the impact of the education provided by the provider, they will focus on what learners have learned, and the skills they have gained and can apply.

192.   Inspectors will focus on the following factors.

- A well-constructed, well-taught curriculum will lead to good results because those results will reflect what learners have learned. There need be no conflict between teaching a broad, rich curriculum and achieving success in examinations and tests.
- Disadvantaged learners and learners with SEND acquire the knowledge and skills they need to succeed in life.
- End-point assessments and examinations are useful indicators of learners' outcomes, but they only represent a sample of what learners have learned. Inspectors will balance this with their first-hand assessment of learners' work.
- All learning builds towards an end point. Learners are being prepared for their next stage of education, training or employment at each stage of their learning. Inspectors will consider whether learners are ready for their next steps.
- Inspectors will also consider whether learners are ready for the next stage and are going to appropriate, high-quality destinations.

Sources of evidence specific to curriculum impact

193.   Inspectors will gather evidence of the impact of the education offered by the provider from the following sources:

- nationally generated and validated performance information about learners' progress and attainment
- first-hand evidence of the progress learners are making, drawing together the evidence from the interviews, observations, work scrutiny and documentary review, described above (see 'sources of evidence specific to curriculum implementation')
- any information provided by the provider about the destinations to which their learners progress when they leave the provider
- telephone conversations or other similar discussions with a selection of learners about their destinations
- discussions with learners, for instance about what they have remembered about the knowledge and skills they have acquired and how their learning enables them to connect ideas.

194.   Inspectors will evaluate learners' progress in relation to their starting points, based

on their rate of learning, acquisition of knowledge, skills and behaviours and whether they have achieved their individual, challenging targets.

195.   Inspectors will not look at internal progress and attainment data on GCSE and A-level courses where fixed-time terminal examinations comprise the entire assessment of the course. Similarly, inspectors will not normally look at predicted in-year achievement and attainment data more generally.

196.   That does not mean providers cannot use this data if they consider it appropriate. However, inspectors will put more focus on the curriculum and less on providers' generation, analysis and interpretation of performance data. Inspectors will be interested in the conclusions drawn and actions taken from any internal assessment information but they will not examine or verify that information first hand.

Balancing intent, implementation and impact to reach a quality of education judgement

197.   Inspectors will **not** grade intent, implementation and impact separately. Instead, inspectors will reach a single graded judgement for the quality of education and training, drawing on all the evidence they have gathered and using their professional judgement.

Grade descriptors for quality of education

For the quality of education provided to be judged outstanding, it must meet the following criteria.

Outstanding (1)

- **The provider meets all the criteria for a good quality of education securely and consistently.**

- **The quality of education is exceptional.**

In addition, the following apply.

Intent

- **The provider's curriculum intent is strong. Throughout the provider and its subcontractors, teachers have a firm and common understanding of the intended curriculum and what it means for their practice.**

Implementation

- **The provider's implementation of the curriculum is consistently strong. Across all parts of the provider, including in subcontracted provision and for learners with SEND and those with high needs, teaching and training are of a high quality. Training activities contribute well to delivering the curriculum intent.**

- **The work that learners do over time embodies consistently demanding curriculum goals. It matches the aims of the curriculum in being coherently planned and sequenced towards cumulatively sufficient knowledge and skills for future learning and employment.**

Impact

- **The impact of the taught curriculum is strong. Learners acquire and develop high-quality skills and produce work of a consistently high standard.**

- **Learners consistently achieve highly, particularly the most disadvantaged. Learners with SEND achieve the best possible outcomes.**

198. To judge whether the quality of education is **good**, **requires improvement** or is **inadequate**, inspectors will use a 'best fit' approach, relying on the professional judgement of the inspection team.

199. **Note:** Some sections of the criteria appear in [square brackets] below. This is to mark that they are transitional only, because we recognise that not all providers will have had the opportunity to complete the process of taking up or constructing their curriculum fully by September 2019. We will review these bracketed sections before September 2020 to decide whether they should be deleted.

Good (2)

Intent

- **Leaders adopt or construct a curriculum that is ambitious, appropriately relevant to local and regional employment and training priorities and designed to give learners, particularly the most disadvantaged, the knowledge and skills they need to succeed in life. [If this is not yet fully the case, it is clear from leaders' actions that they are in the process of bringing this about.]**

- **The curriculum is coherently planned and sequenced towards cumulatively sufficient knowledge and skills for future learning and employment. [If this is not yet fully the case, it is clear from leaders' actions that they are in the process of bringing this about.]**

- **The provider is ambitious for all its learners, including those with SEND and those who have high needs, and this is reflected in the curriculum. The curriculum remains ambitious and is tailored, where necessary, to meet individual needs. [If this is not yet fully the case, it is clear from leaders' actions that they are in the process of bringing this about.]**

- **Learners study the intended curriculum. Providers ensure this by teaching all components of the full programmes of study.**

Implementation

- **Teachers have expert knowledge of the subject(s) and courses they teach. Leaders provide effective support for those teaching outside their main areas of expertise. Where relevant, teachers have extensive and up-to- date vocational experience.**

- **Teachers present information and/or demonstrate skills clearly, promoting appropriate consideration of the subject matter being taught. They check learners' understanding systematically, identify misconceptions and provide** clear, direct feedback. In doing this, they respond and adapt their teaching as necessary, but without having to use unnecessary, time-consuming, individual approaches to presenting subject matter.

- The work that teachers give to learners is demanding and ensures that learners build knowledge and acquire skills, improving on what they already know and can do.

- Teachers encourage learners to use subject-specific, professional and technical vocabulary well.

- Teachers work effectively with support staff to ensure that all learners achieve as they should.

- Over the course of study, teachers design and use activities to help learners remember long term the content they have been taught, to integrate new knowledge into larger concepts and to apply skills fluently and independently.

- Teachers and leaders use assessment well, for example to help learners embed and use knowledge fluently and flexibly, to evaluate the application of skills, or to check understanding and inform teaching. Leaders understand the limitations of assessment and do not use it in a way that creates unnecessary burdens for staff or learners.

- Teachers create an environment that allows the learner to focus on learning. The resources and materials that teachers and trainers select and produce – in a way that does not create unnecessary workload for staff – reflect the provider's ambitious intentions for the course of study and clearly support the intent of a coherently planned curriculum, sequenced towards cumulatively sufficient knowledge and skills for future learning,

- independent living and employment.

- Impact

  Learners develop detailed knowledge across the curriculum and, as a result, achieve well across all areas of their study. Learners make substantial and sustained progress from their identified and recorded starting points in each of their courses and, where applicable, across the curriculum. Where appropriate, this is reflected in results from national examinations, which meet government expectations, or in the qualifications or apprenticeship standards obtained.

- Learners are ready for the next stage of education, employment or training. They have gained qualifications or have met the standards to go on to destinations that meet their interests and aspirations and the goal of their course of study. Learners with SEND/high needs have greater independence in making decisions about their lives.

Requires improvement (3)

- The quality of education is not yet good.

Inadequate (4)

The quality of education is likely to be inadequate if any one of the following applies:

- The curriculum has little or no structure or coherence, and leaders have not appropriately considered sequencing. Learners experience a jumbled, disconnected series of lessons/training that do not build their knowledge, skills or understanding.
- Learners' experiences in lessons or sessions contribute weakly to their learning of the intended curriculum.
- The curriculum does not prepare learners for the opportunities, responsibilities and experiences of life in modern Britain.
- Weak assessment practice results in teaching that fails to meet learners' needs.
- Learners do not develop or improve the English and mathematical skills they need to succeed in their next stage, whether that is in education, training or employment or in greater independence.
- The attainment and progress of learners are consistently low and show little or no improvement over time, indicating that learners are underachieving considerably.
- Learners with SEND do not benefit from a good-quality education. Staff's expectations of them are low. Staff do not identify learners' needs accurately, and are therefore unable to support learners' development effectively.
- Learners have not attained the qualifications, skills or behaviours appropriate for them to progress to their next stage of education, training or employment.

Behaviour and attitudes

200. This judgement considers how leaders and staff create a safe, disciplined and positive environment within the provider and the impact this has on the behaviour and attitudes of learners.

201. The judgement focuses on the factors that research and inspection evidence indicate contribute most strongly to learners' positive behaviour and attitudes, thereby giving them the greatest possible opportunity to achieve positive outcomes. These factors are:

- A calm and orderly environment in the provider, classroom, workshop and workplace, as this is essential for learners to be able to learn.
- The setting of clear expectations for behaviour across all aspects of provider life, including at work.
- A strong focus on attendance at and punctuality to learning and work settings to minimise disruption, and so that learners gain valuable employability skills.
- Learner motivation and positive attitudes to learning are important predictors of attainment.
- A positive and respectful provider culture in which staff know and care about learners.
- An environment in which learners feel safe because staff and learners do not accept bullying, harassment or discrimination. Staff deal with any issues quickly, consistently and effectively.

Learners with particular needs

202. The provider may be working with learners with particular needs to improve their behaviour or their attendance. When this is the case, 'behaviour and conduct that reflect the provider's high expectations and their consistent, fair implementation' are likely to indicate improvement in the attendance, punctuality and conduct of these learners.

203. Some learners, or groups of learners, who have particular needs may have weak attendance or display challenging behaviour. When this is the case, inspectors will evaluate the impact of the provider's high expectations, the consistent, fair implementation of policies, the support given by the provider to the learners, and the impact on the marked and sustained improvement of the attendance and behaviour of these learners.

Sources of evidence specific to behaviour and attitudes

204. Inspectors will use evidence gathered during the inspection as well as evidence of trends in learners' behaviour and attitudes over time. Inspectors will use first-hand evidence from visits to learning sessions and training workshops, including visits to learners at work or on work placements. Inspectors will also gather evidence from interviews with learners, staff, employers and other partners, for which documents such as attendance registers may also be used.

205. Inspectors' judgements about learners' behaviour and attitudes are concerned with their attitudes to learning and, where appropriate, to work, and the development of the

skills relevant to their learning programme. Inspectors' judgements also take account of learners' ability to demonstrate appropriate behaviour for the learning and the work environments. Inspectors will consider the main purpose of the type of provision when they prioritise the impact that each of the criteria has on learners' behaviour and attitudes.

206.   The learner and staff surveys used in inspection contain questions about safeguarding, how respondents feel about the provider and how well supported and respected they feel in the provider. Inspectors will meet leaders to account for the results of the learner and staff interviews and surveys.

207.   Inspectors will carry out other evidence-gathering activities that include, but are not limited to:

- observing learners' behaviour in a range of different classes/workshops at different times of the day
- observing learners' punctuality in arriving at the provider, to classroom and workshop sessions and to work
- observing learners' courtesy, respect for and good manners towards each other and adults, and pride in themselves and their provider and/or employer
- reviewing documentary evidence about behaviour, including how the provider tackles challenging behaviour
- gathering the views of learners, employers, parents, staff, those with responsibility for governance and other stakeholders
- gathering evidence about the typical behaviour of learners who are not on site during the inspection
- balancing evidence seen during the inspection and evidence of trends over time.

Grade descriptors for behaviour and attitudes

208.   For the behaviour and attitudes of a provider to be judged outstanding, it must meet the following criteria:

Outstanding (1)

- **The provider must meet all the criteria for good behaviour and attitudes, securely and consistently.**
- **Behaviour and attitudes are exceptional.**

In addition, the following apply.

- **Learners have consistently high levels of respect for others. They play a highly positive role in creating an environment that values and nurtures difference. Bullying and harassment are never tolerated.**
- **Learners demonstrate consistently highly positive attitudes and commitment to their education and/or training. They are persistent in the face of difficulties. If learners struggle with this, the provider takes intelligent, swift and highly effective action to support them.**

- There are many examples of commitment beyond the basics, for example high participation in skills competitions or social action projects.

- Learners behave consistently well, demonstrating high levels of self-control and consistently positive attitudes to their education and/or training. If learners struggle with this, the provider takes intelligent, fair and highly effective action to support them to succeed in their programme of learning.

209.   To judge whether behaviour and attitudes are good, requires improvement or are inadequate, inspectors will use a 'best fit' approach, relying on the professional judgement of the inspection team.

Good (2)

- Providers have high expectations of learners' behaviour and conduct and these are applied consistently and fairly. This is reflected in learners' behaviours and conduct.

- Learners' attitudes to their education or training are positive. They improve their attitudes over time. They understand their rights and responsibilities as learners. They are committed to their learning, know how to study effectively, are resilient to setbacks and take pride in their achievements.

- Learners have high attendance and are punctual. This includes participating in any distance-learning activities, such as online learning and virtual learning environments.
Relationships among learners and staff reflect a positive and respectful culture where the principles of equality and diversity are nurtured. Learners feel safe and rarely experience bullying, harassment or discrimination. If incidents occur, learners feel safe and confident to report them, knowing that staff will take swift and appropriate action.

Requires improvement (3)

- Behaviour and attitudes are not yet good.

- Learners feel safe and confident in reporting incidents of bullying, harassment or discrimination, knowing that staff will take swift and appropriate action.

Inadequate (4)

Behaviour and attitudes are likely to be inadequate if any one of the following applies.

- Learners' lack of engagement, motivation or enthusiasm inhibits their progress and development.

- A significant minority of learners show a lack of respect and self-discipline. Learners ignore or rebut requests to moderate their conduct and are not ready for progression or the world of work.

- Attendance is consistently low and shows little sign of sustained improvement.

- Incidents of bullying, harassment or prejudiced and discriminatory behaviour, both direct and indirect, are frequent.

- Learners have little confidence in the provider's ability to tackle bullying, harassment or discrimination successfully.

- Learners are not safe, or do not feel safe, at the provider or at work or subcontractor settings.

Personal development

210. The curriculum should support learners to develop their knowledge and skills beyond the purely academic, technical or vocational. This judgement evaluates the provider's intent to provide for the personal development of learners, and the quality of the way in which it does this.

211. As the provider is working with learners, those learners are also being influenced by other factors in their home environment, their community and elsewhere. Providers can teach and train learners how to build their confidence and resilience, for example, but they cannot determine how well young people and adult learners draw on this. Similarly, providers cannot make their learners active, engaged citizens, but they can help them understand how to engage with society and provide them with plentiful opportunities to do so. Providers can take effective action to prepare learners for many aspects of life, but the impact of this work may not be seen until many years later. In this judgement, therefore, inspectors will seek to evaluate the quality and intent of what a provider offers and will look to see what learners know but will not attempt to measure the impact of the provider's work on the lives of individual learners.

212. The judgement focuses on the most significant dimensions of the personal development of learners that our education system has agreed, either by consensus or statute, are the most significant:

- developing responsible, respectful and active citizens who are able to play their part and know how to become involved in public life
- developing and deepening learners' understanding of the fundamental British values of democracy, individual liberty, the rule of law and mutual respect and tolerance
- promoting equality of opportunity so that all learners can thrive together, understanding that difference is a positive, not a negative, and that individual characteristics make people unique
- promoting an inclusive environment that meets the needs of all learners, irrespective of age, disability, gender reassignment, race, religion or belief, sex or sexual orientation, relationship status or pregnancy
- developing learners' character, which we define as the set of positive personal traits, dispositions and virtues that informs their motivation and guides their conduct so that they reflect wisely, learn eagerly, behave with integrity and cooperate consistently well with others. This gives learners the qualities they need to flourish in our society
- developing learners' confidence, resilience and knowledge so that they can keep themselves mentally healthy
- developing learners' understanding of how to keep physically healthy and maintain an active lifestyle

- developing an age-appropriate understanding of healthy relationships through appropriate relationship and sex education
- providing an effective careers programme that offers advice, experience and contact with employers to encourage learners to aspire, make good choices and understand what they need to do in order to reach and succeed in their chosen career
- supporting readiness for the next phase of education, training or employment so that learners can make the transition to the next stage successfully.

Sources of evidence specific to personal development

213.   To inform this judgement, inspectors will use evidence gathered during the inspection and evidence of trends in learners' personal development over time.

Inspectors will use first-hand evidence from visits to learning sessions and training workshops, including visits to learners at work or on work placements. Inspectors will gather evidence from interviews with learners, staff, employers and other partners. Evidence will also include information provided through learner, employer and parent questionnaires. Inspectors will use a range of evidence to evaluate personal development, including:

- the range, quality and take-up of extra-curricular activities offered
- how well leaders promote British values
- how well leaders develop learners' character through the quality of education that they provide
- where appropriate, the quality of debate and discussions that learners have
- learners' understanding of the protected characteristics and how they can promote equality and diversity, and how they celebrate the things we have in common
- the quality of careers information, education, advice and guidance, and how well these benefit learners in choosing and deciding on their next steps.

Grade descriptors for personal development

214.   For personal development to be judged outstanding, it must meet the following criteria.

Outstanding (1)

- **The provider meets all the criteria for good in personal development securely and consistently.**
- **Personal development is exceptional.**

In addition, the following applies.

- **The provider consistently and extensively promotes the personal development of learners. The provider goes beyond the expected, so that learners have access to a wide, rich set of experiences that teach them why** it is important to contribute actively to society. Opportunities for learners to develop their talents and interests are of exceptional quality.

■ The provider ensures that participation in these activities is very high, particularly among those from disadvantaged backgrounds, and all benefit from these opportunities and experiences.

215. To judge whether personal development is good, requires improvement or is inadequate, inspectors will use a 'best fit' approach, relying on the professional judgement of the inspection team.

Good (2)

■ The curriculum extends beyond the academic/technical/vocational and provides for learners' broader development, enabling them to develop and discover their interests and talents

■ The curriculum and the provider's wider work support learners to develop their character – including their resilience, confidence and independence – and, where relevant, help them know how to keep physically and mentally healthy.

■ The provider prepares learners for future success in education, employment or training by providing: unbiased information to all about potential next steps; high-quality, up-to-date and locally relevant careers guidance; and opportunities for encounters with the world of work.

■ The provider prepares learners for life in modern Britain by: teaching them how to protect themselves from radicalisation and extremist views; helping to equip them to be responsible, respectful, active citizens who contribute positively to society; developing their understanding of fundamental British values; developing their understanding and appreciation of diversity; celebrating what we have in common; and promoting respect for the different protected characteristics as defined in law.

Requires improvement (3)

■ Personal development is not yet good.

Inadequate (4)

Personal development is likely to be inadequate if any one of the following applies.

■ A significant minority of learners do not understand how and why to live healthy, positive lives.

■ Leaders and those responsible for governance, through their words, actions or influence, directly and/or indirectly, undermine or fail to promote equality of opportunity.

■ Leaders and those responsible for governance do not protect learners from radicalisation and extremist views when learners are vulnerable to these.

Policy and practice are poor, which means that learners are at risk.

- The provider does not ensure that learners have access to unbiased information about potential next steps, high-quality careers guidance, and opportunities to experience the world of work.

Leadership and management

216.   Inspectors will look at the work of principals, chief executives, senior leaders, subject leaders and others with leadership and management roles when reaching this judgement.[50]

217.   This judgement is about how leaders, managers and those responsible for governance ensure that the education and training delivered by the provider have a positive impact on all learners, including those with SEND and those who have high needs. It focuses on the areas in which inspection evidence and research show that leaders and managers can have the strongest impact on the quality of education and training provided. Important factors include:

- leaders' high expectations of all learners and the extent to which these are embodied in day-to-day interactions with and support for learners
- the extent to which leaders focus their attention on the education and training they provide, leading to better outcomes for learners and continued and sustainable improvement
- whether continuing professional development for teachers, trainers and other staff is aligned with the curriculum, and the extent to which this develops teachers' subject expertise and pedagogical knowledge over time, so that they deliver high-quality education and training
- the extent to which leaders ensure that learners benefit from effective teaching and high expectations in classrooms, in workshops, at work or with subcontractors
- whether leaders engage with learners, parents, their community and employers to plan and support the education and training that learners get
- the extent to which leaders consider the workload and well-being of their staff, while also developing and strengthening the quality of the workforce
- the extent to which leaders' and managers' high ambitions are for all learners, including those who are difficult to engage
- whether leaders and those responsible for governance understand their respective roles and carry these out to enhance the effectiveness of the provider.

Governance

218.   Inspectors will seek evidence of the impact of those responsible for governance. They will determine whether they provide confident, strategic leadership and create strong accountability for, and oversight and assurance of, educational performance to ensure continuous and sustainable improvement.

219.   Inspectors should consider whether those responsible for governance:

- know the provider and understand its strengths and weaknesses
- support and strengthen the provider's leadership and contribute to shaping its strategic direction

- ensure that the provider meets its statutory responsibilities
- provide challenge and hold senior leaders and managers to account for improving the quality of learning and the effectiveness of performance management systems.

220. Inspectors will satisfy themselves that those responsible for governance understand their responsibilities and are ensuring that these are carried out appropriately within the provider. They are not expected to review a list of duties with inspectors.

College groups and governance arrangements

221. Many providers cooperate as groups, with an overall board and chief executive officer, or similar arrangement. These assume some or all of the responsibilities formerly shouldered by the individual college's/provider's governing body. In these providers, inspectors will seek evidence of the impact of the overall board and its staff as well as the college's/provider's local board, committee or governing body, to which there are relevant delegated responsibilities.

Safeguarding

222. Inspectors will always take into account how well providers help and protect young people and learners so that they are kept safe.[51] Although inspectors will not provide a separate numerical grade for this, they will always make a written judgement in the leadership and management section of the inspection report about whether the arrangements for safeguarding young people and learners are effective.

223. If safeguarding is ineffective, this is likely to lead to a judgement of inadequate leadership and management. Safeguarding is ineffective when:

- learners' behaviour towards each other is unsafe, putting learners at risk of harm
- incidents of bullying or prejudiced and discriminatory behaviour, either direct or indirect, are common
- learners have little confidence that the provider will address concerns about their safety, including concerns about the risk of abuse
- learners or particular groups of learners do not feel safe in the provider, the workplace or in a subcontractor's premises
- leaders and managers do not handle safeguarding allegations about staff members and learners appropriately
- leaders fail to protect learners from the dangers of radicalisation and extremism in accordance with the 'Prevent' duty guidance.[52]

224. However, there may be circumstances when it is appropriate to judge a provider as requires improvement, rather than inadequate, when there are minor weaknesses in safeguarding arrangements that are easy to put right.

225. 'Inspecting safeguarding in early years, education and skills settings'[53] sets out the approach inspectors should take to inspecting safeguarding in all providers covered by the EIF. This should be read alongside the framework and this handbook.

Sources of evidence specific to leadership and management

226.   Inspectors will gather a range of evidence from meetings with leaders, managers and governors and first-hand evidence of their work across the provider, including in subcontracted provision.

227.   Inspectors will use documentary evidence that the provider supplies to evaluate the impact of the work of leaders, managers and governors, both currently and over time. They will use this in conjunction with first-hand evidence. This includes, but is not limited to:

- meetings with leaders and those responsible for governance, to evaluate how well they fulfil their statutory duties, including, for example, the Equality Act 2010, safeguarding and the 'Prevent' duty and the Children and Families Act
- documentary evidence that demonstrates the effectiveness of the provision for all learners and its continuous and sustainable improvement
- interviews with staff and learners to evidence how well leaders have created a positive culture
- first-hand evidence gathered during the inspection
- responses to the staff, learner, employer and parent/carer questionnaires. These will be particularly useful for judging the culture that leaders and managers have established
- any evidence the provider has from regularly surveying the staff and the way in which leaders and managers have responded to concerns raised by staff, parents or employers
- considering the overall aims of bodies giving strategic direction to providers on skills and economic needs, such as mayoral and combined authorities for devolved adult education.

Grade descriptors for leadership and management

228.   For the leadership and management of a provider to be judged outstanding, it must meet the following criteria.

Outstanding (1)

- **The provider meets all the criteria for good leadership and management securely and consistently.**
- **The leadership and management are exceptional.**

In addition, the following apply.

- **Leaders ensure that teachers receive focused and highly effective professional development. Teachers' subject, vocational, technical, pedagogical and pedagogical content knowledge builds and develops consistently over time and improves the quality of education provided to learners.**
- **Leaders' engagement with learners, employers, parents and the local**

community/economy is very effective. They provide clear and direct evidence of the positive impact of how this engagement benefits learners and ensures continuous and sustainable improvement.

■ Leaders ensure that regular, frequent and meaningful engagement takes place with staff at all levels, so that they can be confident that issues will be identified. When issues are identified – in particular about workload – leaders deal with them consistently, appropriately and quickly.

■ Staff consistently report high levels of support for well-being issues.

229. To judge whether leadership and management are good, requires improvement or inadequate, inspectors will use a 'best fit' approach, relying on the professional judgement of the inspection team.

Good (2)

■ Leaders have a clear and ambitious vision for providing high-quality, inclusive education and training to all. This is realised through strong, shared values, policies and practice.

■ Leaders focus on improving teachers' subject and teaching knowledge to enhance the teaching of the curriculum and the appropriate use of assessment. The practice and subject knowledge and up-to-date vocational expertise of staff build and improve over time.

■ Leaders ensure that all learners, including those with SEND and high needs, and disadvantaged learners, get the information, advice, guidance and support to achieve their next steps and progress to positive destinations. Leaders provide the support for staff to make this possible.

■ Leaders engage effectively with their community, including, where relevant, with parents/carers, employers, local services and organisations responsible for local and regional economic planning.

■ Leaders engage with their staff and are aware and take account of the main pressures on them. They are realistic and constructive in the way they manage staff, including their workload

■ Those responsible for governance understand their role and carry this out effectively. They ensure that the provider has a clear vision and strategy and that resources are managed well. They hold leaders to account for the quality of education and training and help to ensure continuous and sustainable improvement.

■ Those responsible for governance ensure that the provider fulfils its legal duties and responsibilities. These include, for example, those under the Equality Act 2010, and those in relation to the 'Prevent' strategy and safeguarding.

- Leaders protect staff from harassment, bullying and discrimination.
- The provider has an effective culture of safeguarding that enables staff to: identify, help and protect learners who may need early help or who are at risk of neglect, abuse, grooming, exploitation, radicalisation or extremism; help learners to reduce their risk of harm by securing the support they need, or referring in a timely way to those who have the expertise to help; and manage safe recruitment and allegations about adults and learners who may be a risk to other learners and vulnerable adults.

Requires improvement (3)

- Leadership and management are not yet good.
- Safeguarding is effective. If any weaknesses in safeguarding exist, these are not difficult to rectify, and there are no serious failings that leave learners being harmed or at risk of harm.

Inadequate (4)

Leadership and management are likely to be inadequate if any one of the following applies:

- Leaders are not doing enough to tackle a poor quality of education or training. This significantly impairs the progress of learners, including the most disadvantaged, learners with SEND and those who have high needs.
- Leaders are not aware of, or do not take effective action to stem, the decline in the quality of provision.
- The curriculum fails to meet the needs of learners, employers, the local community or local and regional economies. This is reflected in the low proportion of learners who progress to destinations relevant to their career or learning aims.
- The curriculum does not equip learners with the skills, knowledge or understanding required to prepare them for life in modern Britain or enable them to progress to their next steps.
- Leaders, managers and those responsible for governance, through their words, actions or influence, directly and/or indirectly undermine or fail to promote equality of opportunity. They do not prevent discriminatory behaviour or prejudiced actions and views.
- Safeguarding is ineffective. The provider's arrangements for safeguarding learners do not meet statutory requirements and do not protect learners, or the provider takes insufficient action to remedy weaknesses following a serious failure of safeguarding arrangements.

- Leaders, managers and governors are not protecting learners from radicalisation and extremist views. Policy and practice are poor, which means that learners are at risk.

FOOTNOTES

1 'Education inspection framework: draft for consultation', Ofsted, January 2019; www.gov.uk/government/publications/education-inspection-framework-draft-for-consultation.

2 Dance and drama colleges are inspected against the principles of the EIF at the request of the DfE. 3 Designated institutions have specially designated educational status under section 28 of the Further and Higher Education Act 1992.

4 Further education and skills: Ofsted privacy notice, www.gov.uk/government/publications/ofsted- privacy-notices/further-education-and-skills-ofsted-privacy-notice. Ofsted will not publish any information that identifies an individual in the report but may name the principal, the chief executive or equivalent.

5 'Methodology note: risk assessment of good and outstanding further education and skills providers', Ofsted, April 2018; www.gov.uk/government/publications/risk-assessment-methodology-for-schools- and-further-education-and-skills-providers.

6 The following types of providerare still subject to routine inspection when they have been judged to be outstanding: higher education institutions offering further education and/or apprenticeship training up to level 5; local authority providers; independent specialist colleges. In these cases, they will normally be inspected again within 6 years from the date of the publication of the report of the previous inspection.

7 When a provider has been graded inadequate for apprenticeship provision and the provider has had its apprenticeship funding terminated/ been removed from the register of apprenticeship training providers, that apprenticeship provision will not normally be covered at the requires improvement monitoring visit.

8 See also ESFA guidance, 'Removal from register of apprenticeship training providers'; www.gov.uk/government/publications/removal-from-register-of-apprenticeship-training-providers.

9 This relates to providers newly and directly funded to deliver apprenticeship provision from or after April 2017 (whether levy or non-levy) and those which are newly funded to deliver education provision from or after August 2017 whether, adult education, 16 to 19 study programme or high needs funded. 10 'Apprenticeship funding: how it works', Department for Education, 2018; www.gov.uk/government/publications/apprenticeship-levy-how-it-will-work/apprenticeship-levy-how- it-will-work.

11 New FE colleges and 16 to 19 academies that began to deliver funded provision from August/ September 2017 will receive their full inspection in their third year, in accordance with pre-existing arrangements. They will not normally receive a monitoring visit.

12 However, new providers that became newly directly funded for apprenticeship provision before April 2017 or other forms of funding before August 2017 and that have not yet received their first full inspection will usually receive a full inspection directly.

13 If the provider's only insufficient progress judgement relates to safeguarding and it then receives a judgement of reasonable or significant progress with respect to safeguarding at the second monitoring visit, the provider will not then have a judgement of insufficient progress. The full inspection will then take place within 24 months of the publication of the first monitoring visit report.

14 This refers to mergers between colleges.

15 This may not apply if the merged college has already received a support and challenge visit or the most recent merger took place before January 2018.

16 See paragraph 8 above for the range of sources that Ofsted draws on for risk assessment.

17 Note the references to insufficient progress judgements with respect to ESFA intervention in this guidance: www.gov.uk/government/publications/removal-from-register-of-apprenticeship-training- providers.

18 If an adult learning provider acquires apprenticeship funding it will then enter the category of a new apprenticeships training provider and the adult learning will be covered under a separate theme which will be the adult learning 'quality of education' theme.

19 www.gov.uk/government/consultations/inspection-visits-to-further-education-and-skills-providers- judged-to-require-improvement.

[20] If a provider judged to require improvement has apprenticeship provision graded inadequate and has been removed from the RoATP, that apprenticeship provision will not normally be covered as part of the monitoring visit.

[21] If a provider judged to be inadequate has apprenticeship provision graded inadequate and has been removed from the RoATP, that apprenticeship provision will not normally be covered as part of the monitoring visit.

[22] Nine combined authorities have been established so far Currently the authorities are: Greater Manchester, Liverpool City Region, Sheffield City Region, West Yorkshire, North of Tyne, Tees Valley, West Midlands, West of England, Cambridgeshire/Peterborough: www.gov.uk/guidance/adult- education-budget-aeb-devolution.

[23] Further education colleges and sixth-form colleges will be inspected at corporation level.

[24] Further and Higher Education Act 1992; www.legislation.gov.uk/ukpga/1992/13/contents.

[25] www.gov.uk/guidance/social-care-common-inspection-framework-sccif-residential-provision-of- further-education-colleges.

[26] www.gov.uk/government/publications/apprenticeship-accountability-statement. Where a higher education institution provides apprenticeship training in one or more apprenticeship standards that includes a mandatory higher education qualification, the Office for Students may provide Ofsted with provider-specific information to inform the inspection judgement relating to the apprenticeship provision.

[27] In the case of monitoring visits, inspectors will use their range of expertise to contribute to the relevant themes.

[28] Inspectors may identify a number of off-site learners and employers to observe and/or interview. The nominee should ensure that they are notified, as well as any other users and partners who inspectors wish to meet.

[29] 'Deferring Ofsted inspections', Ofsted, 2016; www.gov.uk/government/publications/deferring- ofsted-inspections.

[30] This does not apply in the case of monitoring visits.

[31] An Ofsted Inspector is an inspector who is not an HMI but is deployed by Ofsted in a variety of roles, usually as a team inspector on further education and skills inspection.

[32] For other myths relating to inspections, please see 'Ofsted inspection: myths'; www.gov.uk/government/publications/further-education-and-skills-inspection-handbook.

[33] Ofsted will periodically write to all providers to request that they provide a copy of their self- assessment. Providers can send their latest self-assessment to fes.sar@ofsted.gov.uk at any time.

[34] Not all inspectors will necessarily attend this meeting.

[35] For monitoring visits, when grades are referred to, this should be understood to refer to progress judgements.

[36] For monitoring visits, when grades are referred to, this should be understood to refer to progress judgements.

[37] For monitoring visits, when grades are referred to, this should be understood to refer to progress judgements.

[38] Note the references to inadequate judgements on inspections and insufficient progress judgements on monitoring visits with respect to ESFA intervention in this guidance: www.gov.uk/government/publications/removal-from-register-of-apprenticeship-training-providers

[39] See 'Induction for newly qualified teachers (England)', Department for Education, 2018; www.gov.uk/government/publications/induction-for-newly-qualified-teachers-nqts.

[40] 'Retention and disposing of information'. Inspectors can access this through the Ofsted engagement hub (internal only).

[41] 'Raising concerns and making a complaint about Ofsted', Ofsted, 2018; www.gov.uk/government/publications/complaints-about-ofsted.

[42] As at paragraph 11.

[43] Section 41 of the Technical and Further Education Act 2017 requires that Ofsted 'comment[s]' on careers guidance provided to students in further education colleges, sixth-form colleges and designated institutions. The Act defines students for this purpose as those aged 16 to 18 and those up to the age of 25 who have an education, health and care (EHC) plan. While the statutory duty applies only to the inspection of the above institutions, inspectors will inspect and comment in similar fashion on careers advice on short and full inspections of all further education and skills providers as appropriate. If there are no 16- to 19-year olds or those with EHC plans, the inspection may not cover careers guidance.

[44] This is one or two days on site. Additional time is also allocated for the lead inspector to plan the inspection and write the inspection report, some of this work may be completed on site.

[45] 'Deferring Ofsted inspections', Ofsted, 2016; www.gov.uk/government/publications/deferring- ofsted-inspections.

[46] 'Education inspection framework: overview of research', Ofsted, January 2019; www.gov.uk/government/publications/education-inspection-framework-overview-of-research.

[47] Non-qualification activities may include tutorials, work to develop study, leadership teamwork, self-management skills and volunteering.

[48] www.legislation.gov.uk/ukpga/2014/6/part/3/enacted.

[49] This covers the quality of education and training. Where teachers and teaching are referred to, this should be understood to cover trainers and training too.

[50] Research suggests that leadership and management can be highly effective when it is shared by different individuals and distributed across different levels across a provider.

[51] Inspectors should also take into account the provider's safeguarding of any young people below the age of 16 who may be on the premises of a provider, even when the quality of their education is not within the scope of inspection.

[52] www.gov.uk/government/publications/prevent-duty-guidance.

[53] 'Inspecting safeguarding in early years, education and skills settings', Ofsted, August 2015; www.gov.uk/government/publications/inspecting-safeguarding-in-early-years-education-and-skills- from-september-2015.

SECTION F – Inspecting the curriculum

Revising inspection methodology to support the education inspection framework

Inspection methodology for the 'quality of education' judgement

1.   In January 2019, we consulted on proposals for a new inspection framework for education providers. In May 2019, we confirmed our plans for inspection, to begin in September 2019. The most significant change from current arrangements is the introduction of a 'quality of education' judgement. This combines aspects of the previous key judgements of 'teaching, learning and assessment' and 'outcomes' to provide a more holistic view of standards, particularly focusing on the curriculum. We will continue to report on all aspects of a school, as set out in section 5 of the Education Act 2005, but will do so within the new judgement headings.

2.   The feedback we received on this proposal during the consultation was very positive. When respondents had concerns, these centred around implementation, with questions about how evidence would be gathered and assessed to inform the judgement, and about the reliability of discrete inspection methods such as lesson observation and work scrutiny. This document explains how inspectors will assess the quality of education while recognising that each inspection is rightly different and can take differing courses. The document also focuses primarily on inspecting schools. The main principles are applicable across different education remits, but methods will need to be adapted to be appropriate for different settings. We are therefore continuing to gather insight on the best approaches in all settings through piloting and inspection.

An evolution of current practice

3.   The outgoing common inspection framework (CIF, in use until September 2019) asks inspectors to form a view of different aspects of a school's work to deliver high-quality education for children and then to put these together towards the end of an inspection to reach a judgement of 'overall effectiveness'. In order to do this, inspectors take a wide sample of activities across the school (principally teaching, assessment and pupils' work) to reach the 'teaching, learning and assessment' judgement. They discuss pupils' progress and attainment with leaders to form a view of pupils' outcomes and the means by which they achieve these outcomes. Finally, inspectors draw this evidence together with the other evidence they have gathered to reach an 'overall effectiveness' judgement. The final stage of this aggregation takes place at the final team meeting (which is normally observed by school leaders). Throughout the inspection, inspectors will have been sharing and triangulating their evidence and keeping leaders informed of their emerging findings. This evidence- gathering model is appropriately designed to support conclusions under the CIF.

4.   Ofsted's understanding of educational effectiveness[1] has evolved from the CIF, and has informed the development of the new education inspection framework (EIF). Therefore, we require a similar evolution in the way that evidence is gathered and connected.

5.   At the heart of the EIF is the new 'quality of education' judgement, the purpose of which is to put a single conversation about education at the centre of inspection. This conversation draws together curriculum, teaching, assessment and standards. In doing this, we draw heavily on the working definition of the curriculum that Ofsted has used over the last couple of years. This definition uses the concepts of 'intent', 'implementation' and 'impact' to recognise that the curriculum passes through different states: it is conceived, taught and experienced. Leaders and teachers design, structure and sequence a curriculum, which is then implemented through classroom teaching. The end result of a good, well-taught curriculum is that pupils know more and are able to do more. The positive results of pupils' learning can then be seen in the standards they achieve.[2] The EIF starts from the understanding that all of these steps are connected.

6.   The EIF is built around the idea of the connectedness of curriculum, teaching, assessment and standards within the 'quality of education' judgement. It then follows that the inspection methodology for this judgement should be structured so that inspectors are able to gather evidence of how a school's activities to deliver a high-quality education for its pupils link and are coordinated in order to achieve the highest possible standards. The findings and approach set out in this report therefore apply across shorter and fuller types of inspection, for example section 5 and section 8 inspection in schools.[3] This is the process that inspectors will normally follow, but they may, on occasion, choose to operate differently because of circumstances they identify at schools.

Developing an inspection method to assess 'quality of education'

7.   By the time we start to use the EIF on inspection, we will have completed approximately 200 pilot inspections in schools, the largest such programme we have ever carried out. These pilots are helping us to develop and refine a method for evidence-gathering on inspection that reflects the connectedness of the new 'quality of education' judgement.

8.   This method has various elements:

- **Top-level view**: inspectors and leaders start with a top-level view of the school's curriculum, exploring what is on offer, to whom and when, leaders' understanding of curriculum intent and sequencing, and why these choices were made.

- **Deep dive**: then, a 'deep dive', which involves gathering evidence on the curriculum intent, implementation and impact over a sample of subjects, topics or aspects. This is done in collaboration with leaders, teachers and pupils. The intent of the deep dive is to seek to interrogate and establish a coherent evidence base on quality of education.

- **Bringing it together**: inspectors will bring the evidence together to widen coverage and to test whether any issues identified during the deep dives are systemic. This will usually lead to school leaders bringing forward further evidence and inspectors gathering additional evidence.

9. Further evidence-gathering activity will follow in order to test the emerging conclusions from this work. This is likely to include follow-up conversations with leaders, members of staff, those responsible for governance and pupils. It will usually also involve sampling of other areas of education within the school to probe questions that have emerged as a result of the deep-dive work.

10. It is crucial to note that inspectors will not reach judgements on the basis of any single inspection activity; rather, inspection judgements will be reached once inspectors have connected the different types and pieces of evidence in the manner set out above.

11. Our piloting to date has been based on the assumption that, as per the public consultation, most routine inspection types will last two days. At present, short inspections last one day. Our piloting so far tells us that this new methodology can be carried out securely within that timescale, and that the two-day period is useful for both inspectors and school leaders because it gives time for reflection and for schools to bring forward additional evidence on the second day if they feel that the view formed on day 1 could be supplemented or challenged if inspectors were aware of other information.[4] Our piloting has been carried out by the current inspection workforce, and designed on the basis that no additional subject specialism should be required in order to deliver it consistently and reliably.

12. Pilot inspections have tested the full range of judgements and evidence- gathering techniques inspectors will use when they come to inspect against the EIF. The method set out above focuses primarily on the judgement of 'quality of education' but, in parallel with this, inspectors will also be gathering evidence about 'personal development', 'behaviour and attitudes' and 'leadership and management' judgements. These activities are integrated within a single inspection. When inspectors are forming their initial 'top level' view, they will also be gathering evidence about leadership and management. Do leaders have a clear and ambitious vision, for example, for providing high-quality, inclusive education to all pupils?[5] Similarly, when inspectors are gathering evidence first- hand in classrooms, they will be alert to any evidence that helps them understand whether the school has high expectations for pupils' behaviour and conduct, and whether these expectations are applied consistently and fairly. In addition, inspectors will be recording any evidence which helps them to understand whether the curriculum and the school's wider work support pupils to develop character.[6] They will also carry out activities to gather evidence specifically around each of the inspection judgements.

Forming a view of the curriculum offer: taking a 'top level' view

13. We consulted on a proposal to allow inspectors and school leaders to prepare for the inspection at the school on the afternoon before the inspection starts. Following

consultation, we have decided that inspectors will prepare away from the school, as they do now, and arrive at 8am on the first day of inspection.

14.　　However, the extensive piloting we have carried out shows us that there were aspects of the on-site preparation model that inspectors and school leaders valued greatly, in particular the opportunity for extended discussion about the inspection before it started. Inspectors will therefore hold an introductory conversation by telephone with school leaders before the inspection begins. This should include giving school leaders the opportunity to explain their school's specific context and challenges. Inspection experience, including our pilot inspections for this framework, shows that this helps both leaders and inspectors build stronger professional relationships.

15.　　Inspectors will use this conversation to understand:

- the school's context, and the progress the school has made since the previous inspection, including any specific progress made on areas for improvement identified at previous inspections
- the headteacher's assessment of the school's current strengths and weaknesses, particularly in relation to the curriculum, the way teaching supports pupils to learn the curriculum, the standards that pupils achieve, pupils' behaviour and attitudes, and personal development
- the extent to which all pupils have access to the school's full curriculum
- a discussion of specific areas of the school (subjects, year groups, aspects of provision, and so on) that will be a focus of attention during inspection.

16.　　This telephone conversation will last up to 90 minutes. It will help inspectors and school leaders to establish a rapport before inspection and give them a shared understanding of the starting point of the inspection. It will also help inspectors to form an initial understanding of leaders' view of the school's progress and to shape the inspection plan. Our experience from piloting the new framework shows that this is the part of preparation that school leaders and inspectors often find to be the most helpful and constructive.

17.　　Inspectors will then build on the insight from this conversation during the inspection.

Forming a view of the quality of education: carrying out deep dives

18.　　It is essential that the primary focus of inspection is on the education that pupils are actually receiving day-by-day in classes, rather than simply being about the ambitions or intentions of senior leaders. A key mantra used by inspectors is 'let's see that in action together'. This is the core of the deep-dive approach. Its aim is to allow inspectors to gather the evidence necessary to form an accurate evaluation of how education flows from intention to implementation to impact within a school. Without doing this, it would be impossible to form a valid judgement of the quality of the education that a school provides.

19.　　In gathering this deep, rich evidence about the education that a school provides in one subject, topic or aspect, inspectors carrying out the pilot inspections have been careful not to rely on small samples of evidence. One deep dive is insufficient to form a view of the school's provision, but a collection of deep, connected case studies of subjects, topics or aspects can allow inspectors to form a valid and reliable view of the education on offer, provided that it is subject to further evidence-gathering to test the systemic strengths and weaknesses of the curriculum.

20.   In primary schools, inspectors will always carry out a deep dive in reading and deep dives in one or more foundation subjects, always including a foundation subject that is being taught in the school during the time that inspectors are on-site. In addition, inspectors will often carry out a deep dive in mathematics.

The total number of deep dives will vary depending on the size (tariff) of the inspection. In small schools (with less than 150 pupils), the methodology will be adapted to reflect the tariff of inspection.

21.   In secondary schools, the deep dives will typically focus on a sample of four to six subjects, looking at a wide variety of pupils in different year groups across that sample.

22.   The deep dive includes the following elements:

- evaluation of **senior leaders'** intent for the curriculum in this subject or area, and their understanding of its implementation and impact
- evaluation of **curriculum leaders'** long- and medium-term thinking and planning, including the rationale for content choices and curriculum sequencing
- visits to a deliberately and explicitly connected **sample of lessons**
- **work scrutiny** of books or other kinds of work produced by pupils who are part of classes that have also been (or will also be) observed by inspectors
- discussion with **teachers** to understand how the curriculum informs their choices about content and sequencing to support effective learning
- discussions with a group of **pupils** from the lessons observed.

Pre-inspection

Introductory conversation with school leaders
Context
Curriculum

Deep dive

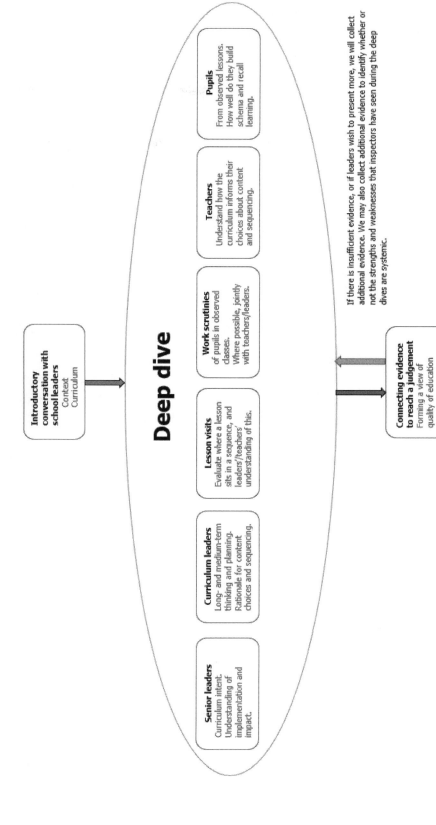

Senior leaders
Curriculum intent.
Understanding of implementation and impact.

Curriculum leaders
Long- and medium-term thinking and planning.
Rationale for content choices and sequencing.

Lesson visits
Evaluate where a lesson sits in a sequence, and leaders'/teachers' understanding of this.

Work scrutinies
of pupils in observed classes.
Where possible, jointly with teachers/leaders.

Teachers
Understand how the curriculum informs their choices about content and sequencing.

Pupils
From observed lessons.
How well do they build schema and recall learning.

If there is insufficient evidence, or if leaders wish to present more, we will collect additional evidence. We may also collect additional evidence to identify whether or not the strengths and weaknesses that inspectors have seen during the deep dives are systemic.

Connecting evidence to reach a judgement
Forming a view of quality of education

Bringing it together

23.   Our research suggests that the following are important considerations for inspectors looking to ensure a robust view of the quality of education:

- **Context matters** – carrying out lesson visits or work scrutiny without context will limit validity. It is important that, in order to make lesson visits and scrutiny more accurate, inspectors know the purpose of the lesson (or the task in a workbook), how it fits into a sequence of lessons over time, and what pupils already knew and understood. Conversations with teachers and subject leads can provide this contextual information.

- **The sequence of lessons, *not* an individual lesson, is the unit of assessment** – inspectors will need to evaluate where a lesson sits in a sequence, and leaders'/teachers' understanding of this. Inspectors will not grade individual lessons or teachers.

- **Work scrutiny will form a part of the evidence we use to judge whether the intended curriculum is being enacted.** Do the pupils' books support other evidence that what the school set out to teach has, indeed, been covered? Work scrutinies can provide part of the evidence to show whether pupils know more, remember more and can do more, but only as one component of the deep dive which includes lesson visits and conversations with leaders, teachers and pupils. Coverage is a prerequisite for learning, but simply having covered a part of the curriculum does not in itself indicate that pupils know or remember more. Work scrutinies cannot be used to demonstrate that an individual pupil is working 'at the expected standard' or similar, and it is not valid to attempt to judge an individual pupil's individual progress by comparing books from that pupil at two points in time.

- **Inspectors can make appropriately secure judgements on curriculum, teaching and behaviour across a particular deep dive when four to six lessons are visited** and inspectors have spoken to the curriculum lead and teachers to understand where each lesson sits in the sequence of lessons. The greater the number of visits, the more inspectors can see the variation in practice across a deep dive. However, there is a point after which additional visits do little to enhance the validity of evidence. Since an inspection evidence base will include multiple deep dives, the total number of lessons visited over the course of the inspection will substantially exceed four to six.

- **Inspectors should review a minimum of six workbooks (or pieces of work) per subject per year group, and scrutinise work from at least two year groups** in order to ensure that evidence is not excessively dependent on a single cohort. Normally, inspectors will repeat this exercise across each of the deep dives, subjects, key stages or year groups in which they carry out lesson visits.

24.   As mentioned above, inspectors may deviate from this process when the

circumstances they identify in the inspected provider require this.

The sequence of evidence-gathering activities

25.   Our experience of the pilot inspections confirms that it is essential to begin the process with the top-level conversations about the intended curriculum offer across the school, and the intended curriculum for the particular subjects, topics or aspects under consideration in the deep dive. This is because, as noted above, inspectors must understand the purpose and context of a particular lesson they visit and the sequence of lessons within which that sits, or of the work that they scrutinise. This is also why inspectors will carry out as many activities as possible jointly with school and curriculum leaders.

26.   Once the inspector is in the midst of carrying out the deep dive, however, it is important that they ensure that they can gather as much rich evidence as possible and make the connections between those pieces of evidence, rather than adhering to any strict or specific sequence. The pilot inspections suggest that the EIF approach allows for much greater depth of evidence to be gathered than the current framework does, and this evidence in turn is more rigorously triangulated. Even when there are challenges on the first day, it is possible to bring all the evidence together and tie up loose ends on the second. Bringing the evidence together and achieving connectedness is an important inspection skill, so this will be a focus area of inspector training. Some concerns exist over the possibility that if one subject which is the focus of the deep dive is a weak subject, then this could give a distorted view of the school, which is why we are proposing to look at four to six subjects in secondary schools and three to five in primary schools, depending on the size of the school and the inspection team. It is also why the follow-on activities to establish whether the issues and strengths identified in deep dives are systemic and replicated elsewhere in the school are so important.

27.   Our piloting has also reinforced our position that intent, implementation and impact are never to be treated as separate, disconnected sub-judgements. Inspectors will always seek to connect and triangulate evidence across the 'quality of education' judgement to form a single view of the quality of education provided.

Bringing the evidence together

28.   At the end of day 1, the inspection team will meet to begin to bring the evidence together. The purpose of this important meeting is to:
-    share the evidence gathered so far to continue to build a picture of the quality of education, identifying which features appear to be systemic and which are isolated to a single aspect
-    allow the lead inspector to quality assure the evidence, and especially its 'connectedness'
-    establish which inspection activities are most appropriate and valid on day 2 to come to conclusions about which features are systemic

    ▢   bring together evidence about personal development, behaviour and attitudes, safeguarding, wider leadership findings, and so on, in order to establish what further inspection activity needs to be done on day 2 to come to the key judgements.

Reaching final judgements

29.   Once evidence gathering has been completed on day 2, the inspection team will meet again. They will discuss the evidence from day 1, consider how the evidence from day 2 develops the picture of the quality of education, and then use the relevant handbook to reach a final judgement.

Implications for inspection

30.   The pilot inspections have shown us that the method described in this report is an effective means of gathering connected evidence towards the new 'quality of education' judgement.

31.   Each handbook has been updated to reflect the understanding set out in this report, to ensure that we are fully transparent about our inspection methodology. This will be reflected in all our training and in ongoing quality assurance of inspections.

32.   The focus of ongoing piloting from May to July will be on further refining the detail of inspection against this model. It is essential that this model is fully tested in all the types of provision that we plan to inspect, and appropriately adapted when needed. To date, we have carried out inspection pilots in nursery schools, pupil referral units (PRUs), special schools, and infant, first, junior, primary, middle and secondary schools, as well as schools with sixth forms.

33.   This piloting in different types of schools has exposed some specific challenges, and these are now a focus for our final phase of EIF piloting during summer term 2019. In small schools, staff capacity is very limited and specific subjects may not be taught during the two days of the inspection or it may be that only a few lessons can actually be observed. In PRUs, there are several sites to visit, and we are working to ensure that our methodology can accommodate this.

34.   This piloting of the methodology in a wide range of provision types will continue, and we will take the findings into account when adapting our methodology.

35.   Since 2017, inspectors have been receiving training on the core elements underpinning the EIF. Our training is now intensifying. From July onwards, all inspectors will undergo training in methodology to prepare them to inspect against the new EIF handbook. The content of that training will reflect the understanding set out in this paper and the further refinements and clarifications emerging from the pilot inspections carried out during the period between now and that time.

36.   Our aim is that all of these elements together will enable us to use an inspection methodology that provides valid and reliable judgements against the new 'quality of education' judgement.

37.   To further ensure this, we carried out research on the validity of lesson visits and work scrutinies, which will be published in June. We will also closely monitor the implementation of the new inspection framework on an ongoing basis.

FOOTNOTES – SECTION 6

[1] 'Education inspection framework: overview of research', Ofsted, January 2019; www.gov.uk/government/publications/education-inspection-framework-overview-of-research [2] 'School inspection update: academic year 2018 to 2019', Ofsted, September 2018; www.gov.uk/government/publications/school-inspection-update-academic-year-2018-to-2019.

[3] As set out later in this note, the methodology will necessarily be different for the very smallest schools and providers. We are continuing to pilot how we will adapt and apply that methodology in those settings.

[4] We have proposed in our consultation approach to carry out shorter (one-day) inspections for the smallest schools and maintained nursery schools, due to the fundamentally different organisation and operation of those schools. We are carrying out further piloting to apply the methodology appropriately in those contexts.

[5] 'Education inspection framework', Ofsted, May 2019; www.gov.uk/government/publications/education- inspection-framework

[6] 'Education inspection framework', Ofsted, May 2019; www.gov.uk/government/publications/education- inspection-framework

SECTION G –Inspecting safeguarding in early years, education and skills settings

Guidance for inspectors carrying out inspections under the education inspection framework from September 2019

Introduction

1.   This guidance sets out the key points inspectors need to consider when inspecting safeguarding in early years, education and skills settings. It needs to be read alongside the education inspection framework (EIF) and the individual remit inspection handbooks.[1]

Safeguarding and inspectors' responsibilities

2.   Everything that Ofsted does should be in the interests of children and young people. This includes ensuring that the providers we regulate and inspect have effective procedures for keeping children [2], learners and vulnerable adults safe from abuse, neglect and exploitation. Inspectors must be familiar with Ofsted's safeguarding policy and guidance on what to do if a safeguarding concern is raised during an inspection.[3]

3.   Early years settings, schools and further education and skills providers should be safe environments where children, learners and vulnerable adults can learn and develop. Inspectors should consider how well leaders and managers in early years settings, schools or further education and skills providers have created a culture of vigilance where children's and learners' welfare are promoted and where timely and appropriate safeguarding action is taken for children or learners who need extra help or who may be suffering or likely to suffer harm.

4.   Inspectors must evaluate how well early years settings, schools, colleges and other further education and skills providers[4] fulfil their statutory and other responsibilities and how well staff exercise their professional judgement in keeping children and learners safe.

5.   It is **essential** that inspectors are familiar with the content of the following documents.

- The Department for Education's (DfE) statutory guidance for schools[5] and colleges,[6] 'Keeping children safe in education' ,[7] which sets out the responsibilities placed on schools and colleges to safeguard and promote the welfare of children.
- The statutory guidance 'Working together to safeguard children',[8] which applies to organisations and professionals who provide services to children.
- 'Prevent duty guidance for England and Wales: guidance for specified authorities in England and Wales on the duty of schools and other providers in the Counter-Terrorism and Security Act 2015 to have due regard to the need to prevent people from being drawn into terrorism', HM Government, 2015, including specific guidance with respect to further education.[9] The DfE has provided additional guidance for schools and childcare providers 'The prevent duty: for schools and childcare providers'.[10] Additional guidance on Prevent for further education and skills providers is available on the Education and Training Foundation's website.[11]

6.   Inspectors of independent schools should be familiar with the content of:

■ the Education (Independent School Standards) Regulations 2014.[12]

7.　Inspectors of schools and early years provision should be familiar with the content of the following key documents:

- ■ 'Statutory framework for the early years foundation stage: setting the standards for learning, development and care for children from birth to five', DfE, 2017[13]
- ■ 'Disqualification under the Childcare Act 2006. Statutory guidance for local authorities, maintained schools, independent schools, academies and free schools', DfE, 2018. The guidance was amended following the 2018 Regulations, under which schools are no longer required to establish whether a member of staff providing, or employed to work in, childcare is disqualified by association. [14]

Definition of safeguarding

8.　In relation to children and young people, safeguarding and promoting their welfare is defined in 'Working together to safeguard children' as:

- ■ protecting children from maltreatment
- ■ preventing impairment of children's health or development
- ■ ensuring that children grow up in circumstances consistent with the provision of safe and effective care
- ■ taking action to enable all children to have the best outcomes.

9.　There is a different legislative and policy base for responding to adults' safeguarding needs. The Care Act 2014 provides a legal framework for how local authorities and other parts of the health and care system should protect adults at risk of abuse or neglect. However, most of the principles and procedures that apply are the same as those for safeguarding children and young people.

10.　Safeguarding action may be needed to protect children and learners from:

- ■ neglect
- ■ physical abuse
- ■ sexual abuse
- ■ emotional abuse
- ■ bullying, including online bullying and prejudice-based bullying
- ■ racist, disability and homophobic or transphobic abuse
- ■ gender-based violence/violence against women and girls
- ■ peer-on-peer abuse, such as sexual violence and harassment
- ■ radicalisation and/or extremist behaviour
- ■ child sexual exploitation and trafficking
- ■ child criminal exploitation, including county lines[15]
- ■ risks linked to using technology and social media, including online bullying; the risks of being groomed online for exploitation or radicalisation; and risks of accessing and generating inappropriate content, for example 'sexting'

- teenage relationship abuse
- substance misuse
- issues that may be specific to a local area or population, for example gang activity and youth violence
- domestic abuse
- female genital mutilation
- forced marriage
- fabricated or induced illness
- poor parenting
- homelessness
- so-called honour-based violence
- other issues not listed here but that pose a risk to children, learners and vulnerable adults.

11.   Safeguarding is not just about protecting children, learners and vulnerable adults from deliberate harm, neglect and failure to act. It relates to broader aspects of care and education, including:

- children's and learners' health and safety and well-being, including their mental health
- meeting the needs of children who have special educational needs and/or disabilities
- the use of reasonable force
- meeting the needs of children and learners with medical conditions
- providing first aid
- educational visits
- intimate care and emotional well-being
- online safety[16] and associated issues
- appropriate arrangements to ensure children's and learners' security, taking into account the local context.

The signs of successful safeguarding arrangements

12.   When inspecting safeguarding, inspectors will need to use their professional judgement about the extent to which arrangements in a setting are having a positive impact on the safety and welfare of children and learners. This list is intended to help inspectors arrive at those judgements.

13.   In settings that have effective safeguarding arrangements, there will be evidence of the following.

- Children and learners are protected and feel safe. Those who are able to communicate know how to complain and understand the process for doing so. There is a strong, robust and proactive response from adults working with children and learners that reduces the risk of harm or actual harm to them. Adults working with them know and understand the indicators that may

284

suggest that a child, young person or vulnerable adult is suffering or is at risk of suffering abuse, neglect or harm[17] and they take the appropriate and necessary action in accordance with local procedures and statutory guidance.

■ Leaders and managers have put in place effective child protection and staff behaviour policies that are well understood by everyone in the setting.

■ All staff and other adults working within the setting are clear about procedures where they are concerned about the safety of a child or learner. There is a named and designated lead who is empowered to play an effective role in pursuing concerns and protecting children and learners.[18]

■ Children and learners can identify a trusted adult with whom they can communicate about any concerns. They report that adults listen to them and take their concerns seriously. Where children or learners have been or are at risk of harm, the trusted adult has been instrumental in helping them to be safe in accordance with agreed local procedures. Children who are unable to share their concerns, for example babies and very young children, form strong attachments to those who care for them through the effective implementation of the key person system.

■ Written records are made in an appropriate and timely way and are held securely where adults working with children or learners are concerned about their safety or welfare. Those records are shared appropriately and, where necessary, with consent.

■ Any child protection and/or safeguarding concerns are shared in a timely way with the relevant local authority. Where the concern is about suspected harm or risk of harm to a child, the referral should be made to the children's social care department of the local authority for the area where the child lives. Where the concern is an allegation about a member of staff in a setting, or another type of safeguarding issue affecting children and young people in a setting, the matter should be referred to the designated officer in the local authority in which the setting is located.

■ A record of that referral is retained and there is evidence that any agreed action following the referral has been taken promptly to protect the child or learner from further harm. There is evidence, where applicable, that staff understand when to make referrals when there are issues concerning peer-on-peer abuse, criminal or sexual exploitation, radicalisation and/or extremism or that they have sought additional advice and support. Children and learners are supported, protected and informed appropriately about the action the adult is taking to share their concerns. Parents and guardians are made aware of concerns and their consent is sought in accordance with local procedures unless doing so would increase the risk of harm to a child.

■ There is a written plan in place that has clear and agreed procedures to protect a child or vulnerable adult. For children who are the subject of a child in need plan or child protection plan or who are looked after, or vulnerable adults that have an Education and Health or Education, Health and Care plan, the plan identifies the help that the child or vulnerable adult should receive and the action to be taken if a professional has further concerns or information to report.

■ Children who go missing from the setting they attend receive well- coordinated responses that reduce the harm or risk of harm to them. Risks are well understood and their impact is minimised. Staff are aware of, and implement in full, local procedures for children who are missing from home and/or from education. Local procedures for notifying the local authority and parents are available, understood and followed. Comprehensive records are held and shared between the relevant agencies to help and protect children.

■ Any risks associated with children and learners offending, misusing drugs or alcohol, self-harming, going missing, being vulnerable to radicalisation or being sexually and/or criminally exploited are known by the adults who care for them and shared with the local authority children's social care service or other relevant agency. There are plans and help in place that are reducing the risk of harm or actual harm and there is evidence that the impact of these risks is being minimised. These risks are kept under regular review and there is regular and effective liaison with other agencies where appropriate.

■ Children and learners are protected and know how to get support if they experience bullying, homophobic behaviour, racism, sexism and other forms of discrimination. Any discriminatory behaviours are challenged and help and support are given to children about how to treat others with respect.

■ Adults understand the risks associated with using technology, including social media, of bullying, grooming, exploiting, radicalising or abusing children or learners. They have well-developed strategies in place to keep children and learners safe and to support them to develop their own understanding of these risks and in learning how to keep themselves and others safe. Leaders oversee the safe use of technology when children and learners are in their care and take action immediately if they are concerned about bullying or children's well-being. Leaders of early years settings implement the required policies with regard to the safe use of mobile phones and cameras in settings.

■ Leaders and staff make clear risk assessments and respond consistently to protect children and learners while enabling them to take age-appropriate and reasonable risks as part of their growth and development.

■ Children and learners feel secure and, where they may present risky behaviours, they experience positive support from all staff. Babies and young children demonstrate their emotional security through the attachments they form with those who look after them and through their physical and emotional well-being. Staff respond with clear boundaries about what is safe and acceptable and they seek to understand the triggers for children's and learners' behaviour. They develop effective responses as a team and review those responses to assess their impact, taking into account the views and experiences of the child or learner.

- Positive behaviour is promoted consistently. Staff use effective de-escalation techniques and creative alternative strategies that are specific to the individual needs of children and learners. Reasonable force, including restraint,[19] is only used in strict accordance with the legislative framework to protect the child or learner and those around them. All incidents are reviewed, recorded and monitored and the views of the child or learner are sought and understood. Monitoring of the management of behaviour is effective and the use of any restraint significantly reduces or ceases over time.[20]

- Adults understand that children's poor behaviour may be a sign that they are suffering harm or that they have been traumatised by abuse.[21]

- In cases of peer-on-peer abuse, staff should consider what support might be needed for the perpetrators as well as the victims.

- Staff and volunteers working with children and learners are carefully selected and vetted according to statutory requirements. Once appointed, consideration is given to their ongoing suitability in order to prevent the opportunity for harm to children or learners or place them at risk.

- There are clear and effective arrangements for staff development and training in respect of the protection and care of children and learners. Staff and other adults receive regular supervision and support if they are working directly and regularly with children and learners whose safety and welfare are at risk.

- The physical environment for babies, children and learners is safe and secure and protects them from harm or the risk of harm.

- All staff and carers have a copy of and understand the written procedures for managing allegations of harm to a child or learner. They know how to make a complaint and understand policies on whistleblowing and how to manage other concerns about the practice of adults in respect of the safety and protection of children and learners.

Evidence to look for when inspecting safeguarding arrangements

14. This section provides guidance on the evidence inspectors should look for when reviewing safeguarding arrangements in a setting. The guidance is not exhaustive and should be read in conjunction with the relevant inspection handbook.

15. Inspectors should look for evidence of the extent to which leaders, governors and managers create a positive culture and ethos where safeguarding is an important part of everyday life in the setting, backed up by training at every level. Inspectors should consider

the content, application and effectiveness of safeguarding policies and procedures and the quality of safeguarding practice, including evidence that staff are aware of the signs that children or learners may be at risk of harm either within the setting or in the family or wider community outside the setting.

16.   Inspectors should consider how far leaders and managers have put in place effective arrangements to:

- **Identify** children and learners who may need early help or are at risk of neglect, abuse, grooming or exploitation
- **Help** prevent abuse by raising awareness among children and learners of safeguarding risks and how and where to get help and support if they need it
- **Help** those children who are at risk of abuse and need early help or statutory social care involvement, keeping accurate records, making timely referrals where necessary and working with other agencies to ensure that children and learners get the help and support they need
- **Manage** allegations about adults who may be a risk, and check the suitability of staff to work with children, learners and vulnerable adults.

Inspecting how effectively leaders and governors create a safeguarding culture in the setting

17.   Inspectors should consider how well leaders and managers in early years settings, schools and further education and skills providers have created a culture of vigilance where children's and learners' welfare is promoted and timely and appropriate safeguarding action is taken for children or learners who need extra help or who may be suffering or likely to suffer harm.

18.   Inspectors should evaluate how well early years settings, schools and further education and skills providers fulfil their statutory responsibilities and how well staff exercise their professional judgement in keeping children and learners safe.

19.   Inspectors should consider evidence that:

- leaders, governors and supervisory bodies (where appropriate) fulfil statutory requirements, such as those for disability, safeguarding, recruitment and health and safety
- child protection/safeguarding and staff behaviour policies and procedures are in place, consistent with government guidance, refer to locally agreed multi-agency safeguarding arrangements and are regularly reviewed[22]
- staff, leaders and managers recognise that children and young people are capable of abusing their peers and this risk is covered adequately in the child protection or safeguarding policy
- the provider has trained staff to understand how to handle reports of sexual violence and harassment between children, both on and outside school premises, in line with the Department for Education's guidance[23]
- the child protection or safeguarding policy reflects the additional barriers that

exist when recognising the signs of abuse and neglect of children who have special educational needs and/or disabilities

- children and learners feel safe
- staff, leaders, governors and supervisory bodies (where appropriate) and volunteers receive appropriate training on safeguarding at induction followed by regular updates. In addition, they receive information (for example, via emails, e-bulletins and newsletters) on safeguarding and child protection at least annually. They demonstrate knowledge of their responsibilities relating to the protection of children, learners and vulnerable adults
- staff are supported to have a good awareness of the signs that a child or learner is being neglected or abused, as described in 'What to do if you're worried a child is being abused'[24]
- staff are confident about what to do if a child reports that they have been sexually abused by another child
- there is a designated senior member of staff in charge of safeguarding arrangements who has been trained to the appropriate level and understands their responsibilities relating to the protection of children, young people and vulnerable adults and the safeguarding of all learners. Designated members of staff in schools and colleges should be a senior member of the school or college leadership team and they should do safeguarding training every two years and their knowledge and skills should be refreshed at regular intervals, but at least annually.[25] Designated safeguarding leads in schools and colleges act as the main point of contact with the local multi-agency safeguarding partner arrangements. During term time, the designated safeguarding lead for a school or college, or an appropriately trained deputy, should be available during opening hours for staff to discuss safeguarding concerns
- staff know who their designated safeguarding lead is, what they are responsible for, and the names of any deputies
- the setting identifies children or learners who may be at risk of abuse or neglect, or who may need support with their mental health
- school and college staff are alert to circumstances when a child may need early help
- the setting has clear policies and procedures for dealing with children and learners who go missing from education, particularly those who go missing on repeat occasions. Leaders, managers and staff are alert to signs that children and learners who are missing might be at risk of abuse, neglect and/or exploitation. Where reasonably possible, a school or college should hold more than one emergency contact number for each pupil or student
- appropriate action is taken when children and learners stop attending the setting or do not attend regularly; for schools, this includes informing the local authority

when a pupil is going to be deleted from the register

- action is taken to ensure that children are taught about safeguarding risks, including online risks

- there is a clear approach to implementing the Prevent duty and keeping children and learners safe from the dangers of radicalisation and extremism

- the setting takes effective action to prevent and tackle discriminatory and derogatory language – this includes language that is derogatory about disabled people and homophobic, sexist and racist language

- as part of the curriculum, children and learners are supported to understand what constitutes a healthy relationship both online and offline, and to recognise risk, for example risks associated with criminal and sexual exploitation, domestic abuse, female genital mutilation, forced marriage, substance misuse, gang activity, radicalisation and extremism, and are aware of the support available to them

- staff, leaders and managers understand the risks posed by adults or young people who use the internet to bully, groom or abuse children, learners and vulnerable adults; there are well-developed strategies in place to keep learners safe and to support them in learning how to recognise when they are at risk and how to get help when they need it

- staff understand the importance of considering wider environmental factors that may be present in a child's life that are a threat to their safety and/or welfare

- teachers understand their mandatory duty to report to police any known case of female genital mutilation on a girl under the age of 18[26]

- staff, leaders and managers oversee the safe use of electronic and social media by staff and learners and take action immediately if they are concerned about bullying or risky behaviours

- appropriate filters and monitoring systems are in place to protect learners from potentially harmful online material

- appropriate arrangements are made with regards to health and safety to protect staff and learners from harm

- staff in schools and colleges are supported to make reasonable judgements about when it may be appropriate to use physical contact with a child to protect them from injury

- the setting's premises provide a safe learning environment with secure access.

Inspecting arrangements for staff recruitment and vetting

20. Ofsted expects early years settings, schools and further education and skills providers to be able to demonstrate that they meet all regulations and duties for the purposes of the safeguarding judgement under leadership and management in the inspection handbook for the appropriate remit.

21.   Inspectors should check the single central record early in inspections of schools and colleges in the expectation that it will be complete and meet statutory requirements. [27] During early years inspections, inspectors will check that the provider is able to produce evidence of suitability of relevant staff and adults.

22.   Inspectors should also check the setting's policy and procedures for ensuring that visitors to the school are suitable and checked and monitored as appropriate, for example external speakers at school assemblies.

23.   Registered early years providers are expected to make all records available at inspection. If evidence of suitability is not kept on site, inspectors can accept this evidence later during the inspection as long as it is provided before final feedback is given.

24.   If there is a **minor** administrative error on a single central record, such as the absence of a date on the record, and this can be easily rectified **before** the final team meeting, the school or college will be given the chance to resolve the issue.

25.   Ofsted has established a definition for 'administrative errors' in relation to the single central record (see below). No allowance will be made, for example, for breaches to the requirements for the Disclosure and Barring Scheme (DBS) disclosures.

26.   Administrative errors may be defined as follows:
   - failure to record one or two dates
   - individual entries that are illegible
   - one or two omissions where it is clear that the information is already held by the school or college but the school or college has failed to transfer over the information in full to the single central record.

27.   For specified early or later years childcare, inspectors are **not** expected to make enquiries as to whether any member of staff is disqualified. However, inspectors should ascertain that the provider knows their legal obligations and has effective systems in place to find out information about whether a person may be disqualified.

28.   To employ a disqualified person knowingly constitutes an offence. Should an inspector become aware that a member of staff is, or may be, disqualified and has not been granted a waiver, this must be considered when making the judgement on the effectiveness of safeguarding.

29.   Where an early years setting, school or college has recruited volunteers who are not checked, inspectors should explore with senior leaders and governors how the registered provider or school has reached this decision – for example how it has assessed the level of supervision provided.

30.   In the case of trainee teachers and students on placement, if they are employed by the setting, school or college, then they should be subject to the same checks under regulations as other members of staff. If trainee teachers are fee-funded, the school or setting should obtain written confirmation from the training provider that these checks have been carried out and that the trainee has been judged by the provider to be suitable to work with children. There is no requirement for a school to record details of fee-funded

trainees on the single central record.

Inspecting the quality of safeguarding practice

31.   Inspectors should look for evidence that the early years setting, school or further education and skills provider is implementing its safeguarding policy and processes effectively and keeping them under review. As well as ensuring that children and learners are safeguarded while on the premises, the setting should be proactive about anticipating and managing risks that children and learners face in the wider community. The setting should adhere to any locally agreed arrangements for safeguarding children. All concerns and the action taken in response should be clearly recorded.

32.   Where a child is currently receiving services or support from children's social care services and/or is subject to a multi-agency plan, or where a child has been referred to services by the setting, inspectors should explore the role, actions and participation of the early years setting, school or further education and skills provider in working in partnership with external agencies with the aim of improving the child's situation.

Inspecting arrangements for handling serious incidents and allegations

33.   On all inspections, the lead inspector **must** check whether there have been any safeguarding incidents or allegations since the last inspection that have either been resolved or that are ongoing. This should be done early in the inspection, if possible. The purpose of this is to establish whether there is any information that could impact on the judgement of the effectiveness of safeguarding or anyother aspect of the inspection that needs to be included in the report. Of particular relevance are the questions as to:

(a)   whether the early years setting, school or further education and skills provider has responded in a timely and appropriate way to concerns or allegations

(b)   how effectively the early years setting, school or further education and skills provider has worked in partnership with external agencies regarding any concerns.

Arriving at judgements about safeguarding arrangements

34.   The impact of safeguarding arrangements will be tested under the EIF judgement on the quality of leadership and management. Inspectors will arrive at a judgement about whether the early years setting, school or further education and skills provider has effective safeguarding arrangements or not. This judgement will contribute towards the overall judgement on the effectiveness of leadership and management.

35.   Judgements must not be made solely based on the evidence that is presented during the inspection. Inspectors must probe further and take into account a range of evidence to evaluate the effectiveness of safeguarding arrangements over time. Inspectors should take into account any comments received by Ofsted from parents of children who attend the setting.

36.   Inspectors will consider the extent to which leaders, managers and those responsible for governance ensure that arrangements to protect children and learners

meet statutory requirements, follow the applicable guidance, and promote their welfare – including the prevention of radicalisation and extremism. The evidence for this will contribute to the inspectors' evaluation of the effectiveness of safeguarding. Evidence gathered in relation to attendance, behaviour – for example bullying – and how well children and learners are supported to keep themselves safe may also contribute, to a greater or lesser degree, to this judgement. In line with statutory guidance, inspectors will gather evidence as to whether staff in all settings are sensitive to signs of possible safeguarding concerns. These include poor or irregular attendance, persistent lateness, or children missing from education. Inspectors will consider during each inspection any inspection survey comments about safeguarding from staff or pupils and any parental comments on Parent View.

37.   Inspectors will evaluate, where applicable, the extent to which the provision is successfully promoting and supporting children's and learners' safety. Inspectors will consider, among other things, children's and learners' understanding of healthy and unhealthy relationships and how they are supported to keep themselves safe from relevant risks such as exploitation and extremism, including when using the internet and social media. Inspectors should include online safety in their discussions with children and learners (covering topics such as online bullying and safe use of the internet and social media). Inspectors should investigate what the school or further education and skills provider does to educate pupils in online safety and how the provider or school deals with issues when they arise.

38.   In relation to early years, inspectors should consider how staff promote young children's understanding of how to keep themselves safe from relevant risks and how this is monitored across the provision.

39.   When judging the effectiveness of safeguarding procedures in independent school inspections, inspectors must take into account whether or not the school meets all the paragraphs in part 2 (spiritual, moral, social and cultural development of pupils), part 3 (welfare, health and safety of pupils), part 4 (suitability of staff, supply staff and proprietors) and part 5 (premises of and accommodation at schools) of the independent school standards.[28]

Inspecting and reporting on safeguarding concerns

40.   Safeguarding concerns about an early years setting, school or further education and skills provider may be identified by inspectors during an inspection, or may be brought to the attention of an inspector or Ofsted before or during an inspection. Safeguarding concerns may include:

- delay or negligence in passing on concerns to the relevant agencies about a child or learner at risk of or suffering significant harm
- the suspension or redeployment of a member of staff and a current safeguarding investigation
- failure to follow statutory requirements, guidance, or locally agreed procedures

for safer recruitment or for dealing with allegations against staff

■ failure to comply with the legal duty to refer to the DBS a member of staff who has harmed, or poses a risk of harm to, a child.

41.   When reporting on these issues, inspectors must take care not to include any information that might lead to identification of an individual child or learner or of a member of staff who is, or may be, under investigation by another agency. Inspectors must be mindful that where a particular matter is under investigation it is not proven. It is also important that the inspection report should not contain information that might raise undue concerns among parents and the wider public that the children and learners in general are unsafe. There are instances when a member of staff may be absent because she or he has been suspended pending a safeguarding investigation. Parents or other staff may not be aware of the suspension and are most unlikely to be aware of any detail.

42.   If a safeguarding issue relating to the provision is already known to Ofsted before an inspection, then the lead inspector (if unsure of what action to take) should seek guidance before the inspection. The lead inspector should record information about the concern known to Ofsted as part of the inspection planning evidence. This is to provide a clear audit trail of the evidence used for the inspection.

43.   Inspectors should ensure that they are aware of any information about safeguarding at the setting that is available to the public, reported in the press or accessible on the internet, including that available on the early years setting, school or further education and skills provider's website, if available. As part of their pre-inspection planning, the lead inspector should run an internet check to see whether there are any safeguarding issues that the inspection team may need to follow up during the inspection. All information that is considered when planning for the inspection should be recorded as evidence.

44.   Inspectors should consider carefully the judgements relating to the effectiveness of safeguarding, when it is known that a member of staff has been convicted of sexual or violent offences.

Reporting on evidence or allegations of child abuse, including serious incidents

45.   If, in the course of an inspection, inspectors come across evidence or allegations of child abuse, the lead inspector should report the concerns using the following wording: 'Concerns raised by [some children or young people or vulnerable adults/a child or young person or vulnerable adult/some parents/one parent] during the inspection are being examined by the appropriate bodies.'

46.   It is not the role of an inspector to investigate a child protection concern or an allegation against a member of staff. Inspectors should, however, satisfy themselves that appropriate referrals have been made in response to any child protection concerns.

47.   In cases where Ofsted has become aware of an investigation by another agency into a serious incident or serious allegations involving a setting, school or provider that

Ofsted is inspecting, it may be appropriate for the inspection report to make a brief reference to the investigation. This should be done in such a way that avoids the risk of prejudicing the outcome of the investigation or identifying individuals who are linked to the investigation. Any references will be confined to the most serious incidents, such as the death of a child or a serious safeguarding failure. Inspectors should avoid making any reference to a serious incident if there is any possibility that doing so would: prejudice an investigation or its outcome; breach confidentiality; or risk identifying individuals subject to, or related to, the investigation. If a reference is to be made, it should be clear that Ofsted has not investigated and is not coming to any determination on the concerns raised.

48.   Inspectors should note that the restrictions in paragraphs 43–45 of this guidance apply to what may be reported in the published inspection report about active, external investigations, not to what may be included as lines of enquiry in the inspection. Inspectors are required and remain free to comment on any matter they believe is relevant to the quality of the safeguarding practice, as long as the comments are based on the inspection evidence.

Sentences to include in inspection reports when an investigation is in progress

49.   Where relevant and appropriate, given the particular circumstances, the lead inspector should consideration carefully, and seek advice about, the insertion of specific text in the 'Information about this setting or school' section of the report template. Before using the sentences below, inspectors must consider whether referring to an incident might cause prejudice to an ongoing investigation or inappropriately identify an individual. If they are in any doubt, inspectors must seek advice on the wording to be used.

A serious incident that involves the setting

'Inspectors were aware during this inspection that a serious incident that occurred at the setting since the previous inspection is under investigation by the appropriate authorities. While Ofsted does not have the power to investigate incidents of this kind, actions taken by the setting/school/provider in response to the incident(s) were considered alongside the other evidence available at the time of the inspection to inform inspectors' judgements.'

An investigation into the death or serious injury of a child at the setting or while in the care of staff

'Inspectors were aware during this inspection that a serious incident that occurred at the setting/while a child was in the care of staff employed by the setting [for example during an educational visit – amend as appropriate] since the previous inspection is under investigation by the appropriate authorities. While Ofsted does not have the power to investigate incidents of this kind, actions taken by the setting/school/provider in response to the incident(s) were considered alongside the other evidence available at the time of the inspection to inform inspectors' judgements.'

50.   In situations where the incident concerns a child who attends or used to attend the early years setting or school, but the incident did not take place in the setting or school, the following form of words could be used: 'Inspectors were aware during this inspection of a

serious incident involving a child who attends/used to attend this setting/school/provision [delete as appropriate] that had occurred since the previous inspection. While Ofsted does not have the power to investigate incidents of this kind, actions taken by the setting/school/provider in response to the incident(s) were considered alongside the other evidence available at the time of the inspection to inform inspectors' judgements.'

An investigation into alleged child protection failings

'Inspectors were aware during this inspection that serious allegations of a child protection nature were being investigated by the appropriate authorities. While Ofsted does not have the power to investigate allegations of this kind, actions taken by the setting/school/provider in response to the allegations(s) were considered alongside the other evidence available at the time of the inspection to inform inspectors' judgements.'

A police investigation into the use of restraint/restriction of liberty at the setting

'Inspectors were aware during this inspection of a police investigation into serious allegations about restriction of liberty at the setting/school/provider. While Ofsted does not have the power to investigate allegations of this kind, actions taken by the setting/school/provider in response to the allegation(s) were considered alongside the other evidence available at the time of the inspection to inform inspectors' judgements.'

Annex 1. Safeguarding requirements for leaders and managers

Governing bodies, boards of trustees, registered providers and proprietors (including management committees) must ensure that they comply with their safeguarding duties under legislation. In the case of academies, free schools and alternative provision academies, references to the proprietor include the academy trust. They must ensure that the policies, procedures and training in their early years settings, schools or colleges are effective and comply with the law at all times.

The responsibilities placed on governing bodies, boards of trustees, registered providers, proprietors and management committees include:

- continuing to contribute to inter-agency working in line with statutory guidance, including 'Working together to safeguard children'
- ensuring that an effective safeguarding/child protection policy is in place, together with a staff behaviour policy, where applicable. For schools and colleges, the child protection policy should include procedures for minimising and dealing with peer-on-peer abuse and the approach to managing reports of sexting
- appointing a designated safeguarding lead and, in schools and colleges, ensuring that they undergo child protection training every two years
- prioritising the welfare of children and learners and creating a culture where staff are confident to challenge senior leaders over any safeguarding concerns
- making sure that children and learners are taught how to recognise risk and know where to go for help when they need it
- putting in place appropriate safeguarding responses to children and learners who go missing from early years and education settings, particularly on repeat occasions
- carrying out reasonable checks, for example for links with extremism, on, and assessing what will be appropriate supervision of, all visitors who are intending to work with children, learners and/or staff or to address assemblies
- if named as a relevant agency, cooperating with the new local multi-agency safeguarding partner arrangements. It is expected that, locally, the three safeguarding partners will name schools and colleges as relevant agencies and ensure that they are fully involved in the new arrangements.

In addition, for schools and colleges:

- having a senior board level (or equivalent) lead to take **leadership** responsibility for the school or college's safeguarding arrangements
- understanding the local criteria for action[29] and the local protocol for assessment[30] and ensuring that these are reflected in the setting's policies and procedures
- having due regard to the need to prevent people from being drawn into terrorism in accordance with the Counter-Terrorism and Security Act 2015

- supporting staff to take a whole establishment approach to preventing sexual violence and sexual harassment between children or learners, and supporting any children who are affected including the alleged victim and perpetrator[31]
- appointing a designated teacher to promote the educational achievement of children who are looked after and who have left care through adoption, special guardianship or child arrangements orders of children who were adopted from state care outside of England and Wales.

In addition, for governing bodies of maintained schools, proprietors of academies and management committees of PRUs:

- meeting their obligations under Section 100 of the Children and Families Act 2014 to make arrangements for supporting pupils at their school with medical conditions.[32]

Safe recruitment

Governing bodies, boards of trustees, registered providers, proprietors and management committees should prevent people who pose a risk of harm from working with children or learners by:

- adhering to statutory responsibilities to carry out checks that enable a decision to be taken on the suitability of staff who work with children and learners
- taking proportionate decisions on whether to ask for checks beyond those that are required
- ensuring that volunteers are appropriately supervised
- making sure that, in relation to maintained schools, at least one person on any appointment panel has had safer recruitment training
- ensuring that there are procedures in place to handle allegations against members of staff and volunteers
- making sure that there are procedures in place to handle allegations against other children or learners.

Governing bodies, boards of trustees, registered providers, proprietors and management committees should ensure that allegations against members of staff and volunteers are referred to the local authority's designated officer(s) who is/are involved in the management and oversight of allegations against people who work with children.[33] There must be procedures in place to make a referral to the Disclosure and Barring Service (DBS) if a person in regulated activity has been dismissed or removed due to safeguarding concerns or would have been removed had they not resigned. This is a legal obligation and failure to do so is a criminal offence. For example, it is a criminal offence for an employer knowingly to take on an individual in a DBS-regulated activity (such as schools or childcare) who has been barred from such an activity.

Governing bodies of maintained schools and boards of trustees of academies must appoint a designated teacher to promote the educational achievement of children who are, or were previously, looked after and ensure that this person has appropriate training. Governing bodies, boards of trustees, registered providers, proprietors and management committees should ensure that staff have the skills, knowledge and understanding necessary to keep looked after children safe.

Early years providers, school leaders and further education and skills providers should create a culture of safe recruitment that includes the adoption of recruitment procedures that help deter, reject or identify people who might abuse children and learners. Governing bodies, boards of trustees, registered providers and proprietors must act reasonably in making decisions about the suitability of prospective employees.

It is the registered provider's, board of trustees', proprietor's or governing body's responsibility to ensure that safe recruitment checks are carried out in line with the statutory requirements, set out in the DfE's Keeping Children Safe in Education guidance. There is no requirement to carry out retrospective checks on current staff

— the necessary checks are those that were in force at the time the appointment was made.

Governing bodies, boards of trustees, registered providers and proprietors must ensure that when an individual is appointed to carry out teaching work, an additional check is carried out to ensure that the individual is not prohibited from teaching. For those who are to be involved in management roles in independent schools (including academies and free schools), an additional check is required to ensure that they are not prohibited from management under Section 128 of the Education and Skills Act 2008.

Schools and colleges **must** keep a single central record. The record must cover the following people:

- all staff (including supply staff and teacher trainees on salaried routes) who work in the school; in colleges, this means those providing education to children
- for independent schools, including academies and free schools, all members of the proprietor body. For academies this means the members and trustees of the academy trust.

The record should also cover all others who work in regular contact with children in the school or college, including volunteers who have been checked.

Registered early years providers must keep the required information above, as set out in paragraphs 3.68–3.73 of the 'Statutory framework for the Early Years Foundation Stage', although they are not required to keep this information as a single central record.

It is the registered provider's or school's responsibility to ensure that all the staff they employ in specified early or later years childcare have had the appropriate checks. This includes ensuring that staff working in early and later years settings are suitable to do so. The 'Statutory framework for the Early Years Foundation Stage' sets out the disqualification requirements that early years providers must meet.

School inspectors should also be aware of the latest version of the statutory guidance 'Disqualification under the Childcare Act 2006' that was issued in July 2018. This statutory guidance applies to governing bodies of maintained schools, including maintained nursery schools, and proprietors of non-maintained and independent schools (including academies) and management committees of pupil referral units.

Governing bodies, boards of trustees, proprietors and management committees must ensure that they are not knowingly employing a person who is disqualified under the School Staffing (England) Regulations 2009 in connection with relevant early years provision. In gathering information to make these decisions, they must ensure that they act proportionately and minimise wherever possible the intrusion into the private lives of their staff and members of their household. Disqualification may also affect individuals providing/working in childcare on domestic premises who are disqualified 'by association'. This means that they are automatically disqualified if they live in the same household as another person who is disqualified or in a household where a disqualified person is employed. The statutory guidance lists the categories of staff covered by the legislation.

A disqualified person may apply to Her Majesty's Chief Inspector for a waiver of disqualification for most grounds of disqualification. Ofsted has published a factsheet setting out how to make a waiver application, which is available from the Ofsted website.[34]

Where a school places a pupil with an alternative provision provider, the school continues to be responsible for safeguarding that pupil and should be satisfied that the provider meets their needs. The school should obtain written confirmation that appropriate checks have been carried out on staff employed by the provider to work with children. The school or commissioner should establish that the provider meets any applicable requirements for registration.[35]

Annex 2. Pre-appointment checks, including Disclosure and Barring Service[36] checks and Secretary of State prohibition orders

Early Years settings, schools and further education and skills providers must check an individual's identity and right to work in the UK.

The level of DBS check required, and whether a prohibition check is required, will depend on the role and duties of an applicant to work in an early years setting, school or further education and skills provider. For most appointments, an enhanced DBS check with barred list information will be appropriate as the majority of staff will be engaging in regulated activity as defined in Schedule 4 to the Safeguarding Vulnerable Groups Act 2006. [37] The scope of regulated activity in relation to children is set out in a factual note published by the Department for Education.[38]

In a school or college, a supervised volunteer who regularly teaches or looks after children is not in regulated activity. The DfE has published separate statutory guidance on supervision and regulated activity that schools and colleges should have regard to when considering which checks should be carried out on volunteers.[39]

When the DBS has completed its check, a DBS certificate is sent to the applicant. The applicant must show the certificate to their potential employer before they take up post or as soon as practicable afterwards. Alternatively, if the applicant has subscribed to it and gives permission, the early years setting, school or college may do an online update check through the DBS Update Service to ensure the information contained within a previously issued certificate remains current. Early Years settings, schools and further education and skills providers should consider any information contained in the certificate and provided by the update service as part of their wider decision on an individual's suitability.

If a school or college allows an individual to start work in regulated activity before the DBS certificate is available, it should ensure that the individual is appropriately supervised and that all other checks are completed to ensure that the individual is not barred by the DBS. If an early years setting allows an individual to start work in a regulated activity before their DBS certificate is available, they should ensure that the person is never left in unsupervised contact with children, and that they are in the process of obtaining a DBS certificate for that individual.

Individuals who have lived or worked outside the UK must undergo the same checks as all other staff in schools or colleges. In addition, schools and colleges must make any further checks they think appropriate so that any relevant events that occurred outside the UK can be considered. These further checks should include a check for information about any teacher sanction or restriction that a European Economic Area professional regulating authority has imposed. Schools and colleges should consider the circumstances that led to the restriction or sanction being imposed when considering a candidate's suitability for employment.

Early years providers should seek additional criminal records checks for anyone who has lived or worked abroad.[40]

Secretary of State prohibition orders prevent a person from carrying out teaching work in schools, sixth form colleges, 16 to 19 academies, relevant youth accommodation and children's homes in England. A person who is prohibited from teaching must not be appointed to work as a teacher in such a setting. Prohibition checks are not normally required when appointing into teaching assistant (TA) positions. This would, however, be necessary if the TA had qualified teacher status and was being appointed to carry out teaching, or if their role changed so that they began teaching work. A section 128 direction prohibits or restricts a person from taking part in the management of an independent school, including academies and free schools.

A check for a teacher prohibition order, section 128 direction, continuing GTCE sanction or restriction, or teacher sanction or restriction imposed by a European Economic Area professional regulating authority can be carried out using the Teacher Services system.[41] An offer of appointment to a successful candidate, including one who has lived or worked abroad, must be conditional on satisfactory completion of pre-employment checks including seeking references. More information about how to conduct these checks is in part 3 of 'Keeping children safe in education'.

Governors and school proprietors are required to have an enhanced criminal records certificate from the DBS and it is the responsibility of the governing body or proprietor to apply for the certificates. A barred list check is not required unless the governor also engages in regulated activity. Also, it is recommended that schools contact the Teaching Regulation Agency (TRA) Teacher Services to check if a person they propose to recruit as a governor is not subject to a section 128 direction.

Annex 3. The single central record

Schools and colleges must keep a single central record of their staff members. Multi-academy trusts (MATs) must maintain the single central record detailing checks carried out in each academy within the MAT. Whilst there is no requirement for the MAT to maintain an individual record for each academy, the information should be recorded in such a way that allows for details for each individual academy to be provided separately, and without delay, to those entitled to view that information, including inspectors.

Generally, the information to be recorded by schools or other providers on individuals is whether or not the following checks have been carried out or certificates obtained and the date on which each check was completed:

- an identity check
- a barred list check
- an enhanced DBS check/certificate
- a prohibition from teaching check
- a check for a section 128 direction (for management positions in independent schools including academies and free schools)
- further checks on people living or working outside the UK
- a check of professional qualifications
- a check to establish the person's right to work in the UK.

For supply staff, schools and other providers should also include whether written confirmation has been received that the employment business supplying the member of supply staff has carried out the relevant checks and obtained the appropriate certificates, whether any enhanced DBS check certificate has been provided in respect of the member of supply staff and the date that confirmation was received.[42]

Where checks are carried out on volunteers, schools should record this on the single central record.

Details of the records that must be kept are contained in:

- for maintained schools: Regulations 12(7) and 24(7) and Schedule 2 to the School Staffing (England) Regulations 2009 and the School Staffing (England) Amendment Regulations 2013 (applied to pupil referral units through the Education (Pupil Referral Units) (Application of Enactments) (England) Regulations 2007)
- for independent schools (including academies and free schools): Part 4 of the Schedule to the Education (Independent School Standards) Regulations 2014
- for colleges: Regulations 20–25 and the Schedule to the Further Education (Providers of Education) (England) Regulations 2006[43]
- for non-maintained special schools: Regulation 3 and Paragraph 6 of Part 1 and Paragraph 18 of Part 2 of the Schedule to the Education (Non- Maintained Special Schools) (England) Regulations 2015.

If a school or college has concerns about an existing staff member's suitability to work with children or learners, it should carry out all relevant checks as if the person were a new member of staff. Similarly, if a person working at the school or college moves from a post that was not regulated activity into work that is regulated activity, the relevant checks for the regulated activity must be carried out. Apart from these circumstances, in respect of existing staff the school or college is not required to request a DBS check or barred list check. The only requirement for those appointed before March 2002 is that they must have been List 99 checked. DBS checks became mandatory for the entire maintained schools workforce from 12 May 2006 (September 2003 for independent schools, including academies).

While registered early years providers are not required to keep a single central record, they are still required to obtain the relevant information to confirm the suitability of those caring for children. The requirements are set out in the 'Statutory framework for the Early Years Foundation Stage' and are referenced earlier in this document.

Annex 4. Safeguarding requirements in further education and skills providers that are not colleges

The following extracts from 'Working together to safeguard children' apply to voluntary organisations and private sector providers in the further education sector.

Chapter 2, paragraphs 57 to 62 include the following:

Voluntary, charity, social enterprise (VCSE) and private sector organisations and agencies play an important role in safeguarding children through the services they deliver. Some of these will work with particular communities, with different races and faith communities and delivering in health, adult social care, housing, prisons and probation services. They may as part of their work provide a wide range of activities for children and have an important role in safeguarding children and supporting families and communities.

Every VCSE, faith-based organisation and private sector organisation or agency should have policies in place to safeguard and protect children from harm. These should be followed and systems should be in place to ensure compliance in this. Individual practitioners, whether paid or volunteer, should be aware of their responsibilities for safeguarding and protecting children from harm, how they should respond to child protection concerns and how to make a referral to local authority children's social care or the police if necessary.

Every VCSE, faith-based organisation and private sector organisation or agency should have in place the arrangements described in this chapter. They should be aware of how they need to work with the safeguarding partners in a local area. Charities (within the meaning of section 1 Charities Act 2011), religious organisations (regulation 34 and schedule 3 to School Admissions) and any person involved in the provision, supervision or oversight of sport or leisure are included within the relevant agency regulations. This means if the safeguarding partners name them as a relevant partner they must cooperate. Other VCSE, faith-based and private sector organisations not on the list of relevant agencies can also be asked to cooperate as part of the local arrangements and should do so.

Chapter 2, paragraph 3 of 'Working together to safeguard children' states that the following organisations:

- local authorities and district councils that provide children's and other types of services, including children's and adult social care services, public health, housing, sport, culture and leisure services, licensing authorities and youth services

- NHS organisations and agencies and the independent sector, including NHS England and clinical commissioning groups, NHS Trusts, NHS Foundation Trusts and GPs

- the police, including police and crime commissioners and the chief officer of each police force in England and the Mayor's Office for Policing and Crime in

London
- the British Transport Police
- the National Probation Service and community rehabilitation companies
- governors/directors of prisons and young offender institutions (YOIs)
- directors of secure training centres (STCs)
- principals of secure colleges
- youth offending teams/services (YOTs)

should have in place arrangements that reflect the importance of safeguarding and promoting the welfare of children, including:

- a clear line of accountability for the commissioning and/or provision of services designed to safeguard and promote the welfare of children
- a senior board level lead with the required knowledge, skills and expertise or sufficiently qualified and experienced to take leadership responsibility for the organisation's/agency's safeguarding arrangements
- a culture of listening to children and taking account of their wishes and feelings, both in individual decisions and the development of services
- clear whistleblowing procedures, which reflect the principles in Sir Robert Francis' Freedom to Speak Up Review and are suitably referenced in staff training and codes of conduct, and a culture that enables issues about safeguarding and promoting the welfare of children to be addressed36
- clear escalation policies for staff to follow when their child safeguarding concerns are not being addressed within their organisation or by other agencies
- arrangements which set out clearly the processes for sharing information, with other practitioners and with safeguarding partners
- a designated practitioner (or, for health commissioning and health provider organisations/agencies, designated and named practitioners) for child safeguarding. Their role is to support other practitioners in their organisations and agencies to recognise the needs of children, including protection from possible abuse or neglect. Designated practitioner roles should always be explicitly defined in job descriptions. Practitioners should be given sufficient time, funding, supervision and support to fulfil their child welfare and safeguarding responsibilities effectively
- safe recruitment practices and ongoing safe working practices for individuals whom the organisation or agency permit to work regularly with children, including policies on when to obtain a criminal record check
- appropriate supervision and support for staff, including undertaking safeguarding training
- creating a culture of safety, equality and protection within the services they

provide.

Employers are responsible for ensuring that their staff are competent to carry out their responsibilities for safeguarding and promoting the welfare of children and creating an environment where staff feel able to raise concerns and feel supported in their safeguarding role.

Staff should be given a mandatory induction, which includes familiarisation with child protection responsibilities and the procedures to be followed if anyone has any concerns about a child's safety or welfare.

All practitioners should have regular reviews of their own practice to ensure they have knowledge, skills and expertise that improve over time

Organisations should have clear policies for dealing with allegations against people who work with children. An allegation may relate to a person who works with children who has:

- behaved in a way that has harmed a child, or may have harmed a child
- possibly committed a criminal offence against or related to a child; or behaved towards a child or children in a way that indicates they may pose a risk of harm to children.

Any allegation against people who work with children should be reported immediately to a senior manager within the organisation or agency. The designated officer, or team of officers, should also be informed within one working day of all allegations that come to an employer's attention or that are made directly to the police.

Providers with funding contracts or direct grants from the Education and Skill Funding Agency Skills Funding Agency for the provision of education and/or training or contracts with employers for the delivery of levy-funded apprenticeships have a range of contractual obligations and funding conditions with respect to the safeguarding and protection of learners.

Some providers only train their own employees. Employers are not required to undertake DBS checks on staff who are supervising employed trainees under the age of 18.

However, if any staff are employed principally to carry out teaching, training, assessing, mentoring or coaching of learners under 16 years old on a frequent or intensive basis, they are engaged in regulated activity and the employer should undertake a DBS check on those staff.

Annex 5. Inspection and health and safety, particularly in further education and skills providers

Ofsted often receives questions about inspectors' approach to inspecting health and safety. Providers want to find out whether Ofsted expects to see rigorous health and safety checks on inspection; the extent to which inspectors check health and safety documentation for learners on work placements; and whether Ofsted conducts a health and safety audit.

Ofsted is not a health and safety authority and it is not responsible for auditing health and safety standards within the learning environment. However, inspectors have a duty to take prompt and proportionate action and to report any significant health and safety risks affecting learners that are identified during the course of an inspection.

Inspection visits to vocational workshops or learners' workplaces are primarily to observe a teaching or training session or an assessment and to evaluate learners' standards of work. However, during the course of an inspection, inspectors may also identify good or poor health and safety practices as they affect learners and their areas of work. For example, inspectors will check whether the correct personal protective equipment is being worn on a construction site, or whether learners are using correct procedures for storing knives in a catering kitchen.

Subject specialist inspectors should have a working knowledge of the relevant guidance from the Health and Safety Executive. However, inspectors are not health and safety experts and are not expected to have the detailed knowledge that appropriately qualified specialists in this field possess.

Any learning environment or work placement must be fit for purpose and properly planned and evaluated to ensure that it meets appropriate standards and learners' needs. Nevertheless, inspections should not be regarded as health and safety audits, although inspectors will adopt a proportionate approach to checking that the employer has appropriate health and safety systems in place and will identify significant health and safety issues affecting learners where they arise.

The responsibilities of the provider and the employer with respect to health and safety in the context of work experience[44]

Inspectors will have regard to guidance from the Health and Safety Executive about the relative responsibilities of the training provider and the employer, which emphasises the following:

- the employer has primary responsibility for the health and safety of the learner and should be managing any risks
- the training provider should take reasonable steps to satisfy itself that the employer is managing the risks and understands the specific factors relevant to employing young people
- the training provider should keep checks in proportion to the level of risk,

which will vary in relation to the type of working environment involved

■ the provider should avoid seeking paperwork for assurance purposes, using an exchange of emails or correspondence to provide an audit trail if this is needed.

Annex 6. Assessment of risk in settings that children attend because individuals reside on the premises or have access to children and young people

This annex sets out details of how Ofsted inspectors check that early years providers ensure that any risks arising from individuals, other than staff or users, living on or accessing the premises (both those employed by the setting and those who do not work for the organisation), are determined, assessed and acted on.[45]

During an inspection or registration visit, inspectors must explore whether anyone lives on the setting premises[46] or whether anyone other than staff and users of the service has access to the premises. This requirement applies to the inspection of any setting that children attend and/or where they are resident.

Inspectors need to be vigilant when assessing how the provider mitigates all risks, including those arising from any individuals living on the premises. They must avoid making assumptions about who has access to the premises. Inspectors must not allow more immediate concerns to overshadow their assessment of arrangements where an individual, not employed by the provider, lives on or has access to the premises; this is a key safeguarding issue. Access to the premises by other individuals must be assessed even where there may appear to be less risk. For example, because the fact that those who have access are council staff does not, in itself, mitigate possible risk to children and young people. The assessment of access needs to take account of the age and vulnerability of the children or young people who attend, or who are resident at, the premises.

Where individuals other than members of staff reside on or in the vicinity of the premises, the provider must demonstrate that they have fully assessed any risks they may pose to children. In the case of a regulated setting, this is a regulatory requirement.[47] Inspectors should always establish whether residential accommodation exists in, or in close proximity to, the premises irrespective of whether anyone is actually living in that accommodation at the time of the inspection (or registration visit). Inspectors should also establish who makes the decision about letting the accommodation (be that for rent or not) and what vetting of prospective tenants is carried out before arranging any letting.

Inspectors should take account of the availability of access to the premises through any linked residential accommodation. If, for example, the residential area where the individual or individuals live constitutes a fire escape route (which would be unacceptable in settings where children reside), inspectors should take account of whether access into the setting is also possible by the individual living there and whether children could gain access to the accommodation other than in the case of fire.

In evaluating the risks posed because of close residential accommodation for third parties, the inspector should take account of the provider's track record in responding appropriately to previous actions/requirements or recommendations.

Where actions/requirements or recommendations have been made previously, these must be followed up.

Where residential premises are occupied by an individual who is not directly connected with the provision, inspectors should take account of:

- the views of children and, where appropriate, young people, parents and carers
- the behaviour of that individual and any impact that their presence in the vicinity has on the experiences and safety of children and young people.

Inspectors should test how well staff would deal with a safeguarding concern relating to a third-party resident should it arise and how they monitor the situation and implement safeguarding procedures.

If an inspector is concerned about the arrangements in a provision or setting and is unclear what to do, they should consult a more senior officer within Ofsted or their regional duty desk.

All aspects of the assessment of risk posed by any individual living on the premises or having access to children and young people must be fully recorded on the relevant electronic recording system (for example, EEG or Cygnum). When actions need to be taken, this should be in line with the relevant compliance handbook in regulated settings and, for non-regulated settings, in line with Ofsted's safeguarding policy and guidance. Recording must be sufficiently robust to form an audit trail for scrutiny later. The records should show clearly the discussion with the provider about how the risks of either current or future residents were or will be conducted, but such records should not name any individual.

In summary, inspectors should:

- ensure that a thorough review of the premises is conducted at the inspection or registration visit and that the evidence of the review is clearly recorded; particular attention should be paid to:
  - the layout and location of the premises
  - use of the outdoor space, who has access to the premises and whether there are residential facilities on or in close proximity to the premises
  - scrutiny of how effectively the provider has identified and taken steps to minimise any potential risks arising
- raise awareness at each visit of the importance of checking the premises, who has access to the premises and whether anyone lives on or is in close proximity to the premises and, if so, whether they have any opportunity of access to the provision or to the children attending
- consider whether the provider has fully assessed the risks posed by residence or access and is able to explain how children are safeguarded.

FOOTNOTES

[1] Education inspection framework, Ofsted, September 2019.

[2] 'Children' includes everyone under the age of 18.

[3] Ofsted's safeguarding policy, Ofsted, 2018; www.gov.uk/government/publications/ofsted- safeguarding-policy.

[4] Institutions in the further education sector (Section 91(3) of the Further and Higher Education Act 1992). For expectations on further education and skills providers that are not colleges, see Annex 5.

[5] The guidance applies to all schools (whether maintained, non-maintained or independent), including academies, free schools, pupil referral units and maintained nursery schools.

[6] The guidance applies to further education colleges, sixth form colleges and institutions designated as being within the further education sector and relates to young people under the age of 18, but excludes 16 to 19 academies and free schools (which are required to comply with relevant safeguarding legislation by virtue of their funding agreement).

[7] 'Keeping children safe in education', Department for Education, 2018; www.gov.uk/government/publications/keeping-children-safe-in-education--2.

[8] www.gov.uk/government/publications/working-together-to-safeguard-children--2.

[9] www.gov.uk/government/publications/prevent-duty-guidance.

[10] www.gov.uk/government/publications/protecting-children-from-radicalisation-the-prevent-duty.

[11] www.preventforfeandtraining.org.uk.

[12] www.legislation.gov.uk/uksi/2014/3283/contents/made.

[13] www.gov.uk/government/publications/early-years-foundation-stage-framework--2.

[14] www.gov.uk/government/publications/disq ualification-under-the-childcare-act-2006.

[15] We use the term 'county lines' to describe situations where children may be trafficked within England for the purpose of criminal exploitation by urban gangs that supply drugs to suburban areas, market or coastal towns and/ or other urban areas. You can read more about this in our report: www.gov.uk/government/news/criminal-exploitation-and-county-lines-learn-from-past-mistakes- report-finds.

[16] The term 'online safety' reflects a widening range of issues associated with technology and a user's access to content, contact with others and behavioural issues.

[17] This includes the risk of abuse and neglect in the home as well as risks outside the home such as sexual and/or criminal exploitation, radicalisation, bullying and children going missing.

[18] 'Keeping children safe in education', paragraphs 59-65 and Annex B, sets out who the designated safeguarding lead should be in schools and colleges and what they should do; www.gov.uk/government/publications/keeping-children-safe-in-education--2. The 'Early years foundation stage framework' states that a practitioner must be designated to take lead responsibility for safeguarding children in every early years setting. Childminders must take the lead responsibility themselves: www.gov.uk/government/publications/early-years-foundation-stage-framework--2.

[19] 'Use of reasonable force in schools', Department for Education, July 2013; www.gov.uk/government/publications/use-of-reasonable-force-in-schools.

[20] Further guidance on inspecting the use of restraint and restrictions of liberty is in 'Positive environments where children can flourish', Ofsted, March 2018; www.gov.uk/government/publications/positive-environments-where-children-can-flourish.

[21] For more information, see 'Growing up neglected', Ofsted 2018; www.gov.uk/government/publications/growing-up-neglected-a-multi-agency-response-to-older- children.

[22] The term in statutory guidance for schools and colleges is 'child protection policy', whereas the framework for early years refers to a 'safeguarding policy'.

[23] 'Sexual violence and sexual harassment between children in schools and colleges', Department for Education, 2017; www.gov.uk/government/publications/sexual-violence-and-sexual-harassment- between-children-in-schools-and-colleges.

[24] 'What to do if you're worried a child is being abused: advice for practitioners', Department for Education, March 2015; www.gov.uk/government/publications/what-to-do-if-youre-worried-a-child-is- being-abused--2.

[25] 'Keeping children safe in education', paragraphs 52–58 and Annex B; www.gov.uk/government/publications/keeping-children-safe-in-education--2.

[26] Mandatory reporting of female genital mutilation: procedural information, Home Office and DfE, 2015; www.gov.uk/government/publications/mandatory-reporting-of-female-genital-mutilation- procedural-information.

[27] In the case of further education and skills providers, the requirement to have a single central record applies only to colleges (see footnote 4

[28] The Education (Independent School Standards) Regulations 2014; www.legislation.gov.uk/uksi/2014/3283/contents/made.

and annex 5).

[29] Each local authority will have multi-agency safeguarding partner arrangements in place by September 2019 to replace Local Safeguarding Children Boards.The safeguarding partners are responsible for publishing a document that sets out the local criteria for action in a way that is transparent, accessible and easily understood. This should include: the process for the early help assessment and the type and level of early help services to be provided; the criteria, including level of need, for when a case should be referred to local authority children's social care for assessment and for statutory services under section 17, 20, 31 and 47 of the Children Act 1989; and clear procedures and processes for cases relating to the exploitation of children, children managed within the youth secure estate and disabled children.

[30] The local authority, with their partners, is responsible for publishing local protocols for assessment. Protocols should set out clear arrangements for how cases will be managed once a referral is made to children's social care.

[31] See the DfE advice in: Sexual violence and sexual harassment between children in schools and colleges

[32] See the statutory guidance: Supporting pupils at school with medical conditions.

[33] This person was and may still be known as the local authority designated officer (LADO).

[34] 'Applying to waive disqualification: early years and childcare provision', Ofsted, September 2014, www.gov.uk/government/publications/applying-to-waive-disqualification-early-years-and-childcare- providers.

[35] A provider must be registered if it provides full-time education for five or more pupils of compulsory school age; or one or more pupils of compulsory school age who has an education, health and care (EHC) plan or statement of special educational needs; or one or more pupils of compulsory school age who are looked after by a local council.

[36] For more information see the DBS website: www.gov.uk/government/organisations/disclosure-and-barring- service. [37] www.legislation.gov.uk/ukpga/2006/47/schedule/4.

[38] 'Regulated activity in relation to children: scope', DfE, 2012; www.gov.uk/government/publications/keeping- children-safe-in-education--2.

[39] See Annex F of 'Keeping children safe in education'; www.gov.uk/government/publications/keeping- children-safe-in-education--2.

[40] For more information, please see: Criminal records checks for overseas applicants, Home Office 2017.

[41] The Teacher Services system is accessed via the DfE's secure access portal; https://teacherservices.education.gov.uk.

[42] Independent schools and non-maintained special schools should also include the date on which any certificate was obtained.

[43] 16 to 19 academies and free schools are covered through their funding agreements.

[44] The Health and Safety Executive guidance is available at: www.hse.gov.uk/youngpeople/workexperience/index.htm.

[45] In the case of childminders who operate on domestic premises, household members who live in and have access to the premises (but do not work for the organisation) are routinely checked by Ofsted.

[46] For the purposes of this guidance, 'premises' is not restricted to the definition as set out in regulation (i.e. only those areas where the early years' service is provided); rather, it includes accommodation within the same main building, a completely self-contained apartment, with a separate entrance, that is part of that

building or a residence in the grounds.

[47] In an early years setting, this is a requirement where it pertains to the regulatory definition of 'the premises' (only those areas where the early years service is provided).

Printed in Great Britain
by Amazon